READING THE OLD TESTAMENT

READING THE OLD TESTAMENT

Method in Biblical Study

REVISED AND ENLARGED

JOHN BARTON

Westminster John Knox Press
Louisville, Kentucky

Cover design by Alec Bartsch
Cover illustration: Baruch, *James J. Tissot, 1836–1902. French.*
Jewish Museum, New York City. Courtesy of SuperStock.

First published in Great Britain 1984,
second edition 1996, by Darton, Longman & Todd Ltd.

First American edition published 1984 by The Westminster Press;
revised and enlarged edition published 1996
by Westminster John Knox Press,
Louisville, Kentucky

This book is printed on acid-free paper that meets the
American National Standards Institute Z39.48 standard ∞

PRINTED IN THE UNITED STATES OF AMERICA
97 98 99 00 01 02 03 04 05 06 — 10 9 8 7 6 5 4 3 2 1

Library of Congress Cataloging-in-Publication Data

Barton, John, date.
    Reading the Old Testament : method in biblical study /
John Barton. — Rev. and enlarged.
        p.   cm.
    Includes bibliographical references and indexes.
    ISBN 0-664-25724-0 (alk. paper)
    1. Bible. O.T.—Criticism, interpretation, etc.   2. Bible.
O.T.—Hermeneutics.   I. Title.
BS1171.2.B33   1997
221.6′01—dc21   96-48556

FOR MARY

CONTENTS

vii

FOREWORD
TO THE SECOND EDITION

Since *Reading the Old Testament* was published in 1984 there have been significant changes in the style of both biblical and literary studies. I have added two chapters (13 and 14) to introduce the reader to some of these newer movements, and to comment critically on them in the same way as I did on older methods in the first edition. There are some consequential changes to the Introduction and Conclusion.

I have tried to take account of some criticisms made by reviewers. Several people pointed out that I had exaggerated the extent to which mainstream biblical scholarship has ever represented itself as 'scientific' (as opposed to *wissenschaftlich*, i.e., properly academic), and although I think there have been such claims, I accept that they have not been so common as to bear the weight I put on them.

James Barr, reviewing the book in the *Journal of Theological Studies*, showed that my treatment of the Biblical Theology Movement was badly flawed, and that I had not recognized how deeply anti-critical it often was; I have dealt with this mainly by removing the Appendix. There is no other radical surgery in this new edition, however. I hope its life will be prolonged a bit by the changes I have carried out.

Oriel College, Oxford
June 1996

xi

FOREWORD

This book began life as a series of lectures in the Oxford Theology Faculty, first delivered in 1979 and repeated, with continual modification, every year since then. Apart from the obvious aim of helping students to understand what lies behind the often puzzling 'methods' used by Old Testament scholars, I was also looking for an opportunity to develop a long-standing interest in the relation of biblical studies to literary criticism. As an undergraduate I studied the New Testament with Austin Farrer and learned from him that the Bible cannot very well be understood if it is treated in detachment from all other literature: it may be *more* than literature, it certainly is not less. Like many of Farrer's pupils I am conscious of owing him a debt that cannot be repaid, not least because in widening our intellectual horizons he never imposed his own system of ideas so as to produce a 'school'. More recently, my more specific interest in recent literary theories such as structuralism owes a great deal to conversations with John Rogerson, whose own writings have done a great deal to make these matters accessible to students of the Bible.

Two scholars whose books and articles have been crucial for me are James Barr, my debt to whom will be apparent in practically every chapter; and Frank Kermode, whose use of 'structural' insights but detachment from the ideological side of structuralism I have tried to imitate.

I have discussed many of the ideas presented here with colleagues, pupils and friends too numerous to list, but must mention especially Andrew Louth, who has helped me to see more clearly on a number of points concerning the relation of biblical studies to theology, and of theology to the humanities in general. I am also particularly grateful to two friends whose kindness has involved them in prolonged exposure to the book over the two years and more that it has taken to write. Nicola Mitra read extensive sections of the first draft and made invaluable suggestions for improvements in style and presentation as well as listening patiently to many of the arguments of other sections in a more or less incoherent form. Ernest Nicholson encouraged me to publish the original lectures and took a detailed interest in the progress of the work, finally reading the entire typescript and spending a great deal of time in suggesting improvements and clarifications. The defects that remain are of course all my own work. I must also thank John Todd and Lesley Riddle, of Darton, Longman and Todd, who originally asked me to write another book altogether, but who allowed me to divert myself into this different channel and then waited uncomplainingly for a longer time than was reasonable for me to complete my work.

My wife has had to live with the ideas in this book for some years: it is a great pleasure, even though it is no more than justice, to dedicate it to her.

St Cross College, Oxford
March 1983

ACKNOWLEDGEMENT

Thanks are due to Constable Publishers for permission to reproduce four lines from a poem by Boethius translated by Helen Waddell in *Medieval Latin Lyrics*, and to the Society of Authors as the literary representative of the A. E. Housman Estate and Jonathan Cape Ltd, publishers of A. E. Housman's *Collected Poems*, for permission to quote eight lines from 'More Poems'.

ABBREVIATIONS

AcOr(L)	Acta Orientalia (Leiden)
BHTh	Beiträge zur historischen Theologie
BJRL	*Bulletin of the John Rylands Library*
BK	Biblischer Kommentar
BWANT	Beiträge zur Wissenschaft vom Alten und Neuen Testament
BZAW	Beihefte zur *Zeitschrift für die alttestamentlichen Wissenschaft*
CBQ	*Catholic Biblical Quarterly*
EvTh	*Evangelische Theologie*
EvThBeih	Beihefte zu *Evangelische Theologie*
HAT	Handbuch zum Alten Testament
HKAT	Handkommentar zum Alten Testament
JLA	Jewish Law Annual
JR	*Journal of Religion*
JSOT	*Journal for the Study of the Old Testament*
JSOTS	*Journal for the Study of the Old Testament*, Supplement Series
JSS	*Journal of Semitic Studies*
NEB	The New English Bible
OS	*Oudtestamentische Studiën*
OTL	Old Testament Library
PMLA	*Proceedings of the Modern Languages Association*
RB	*Revue biblique*
SBTh	Studies in Biblical Theology
SNVAO	Skrifter utgitt av Det Norske Videnskaps Akademi i Oslo
ThR	*Theologischer Rundschau*
TLS	*Times Literary Supplement*
VT	*Vetus Testamentum*
VTS	*Vetus Testamentum*, Supplement series

WMANT Wissenschaftliche Monographien zum Alten und
Neuen Testament

ZAW *Zeitschrift für die alttestamentliche Wissenschaft*

INTRODUCTION

Methods of Old Testament Study

This book has a dual purpose: to introduce students of the Old Testament to certain critical methods and certain debated questions about those methods; and to argue for certain convictions about the place of method in general in the study of the Old Testament. As a whole it is an introductory book, which presupposes only as much familiarity with the Old Testament as readers who have completed a year of a university or college course in biblical studies or theology might have. But it is *not* an 'Introduction to the Old Testament'; what it presupposes really is presupposed, not repeated. My aim has been to fill several gaps in the literature about biblical study, not just to provide my own version of what is already available.

(1) There are, I believe, enough books that tell students how the now traditional methods of source (or literary) criticism, form criticism and redaction criticism work, when they are applied to the Old Testament – just as there are many books on the history of ancient Israel, or the religious ideas of the Old Testament. But there are few books that raise, at a level accessible to students whose knowledge of the text is not yet exhaustive, questions about the *purpose* of practising these methods. Students often say, 'I can see how you *do* source criticism of the Pentateuch; but what good does it do you?' With these familiar methods, then, there is room for a study that tries to explain their purpose against a rather broader background than is possible in any book that is simply describing how they work. Another factor here is that books introducing the various methods are almost bound to have a slightly evangelistic flavour, winning the reader over to an exciting technique; while the only criticism of these methods is likely to be found in fundamentalist works, attacking them root and branch and trying to convince

1

readers that they can damage their spiritual health. I thought it might be useful to approach the accepted methods in a critical frame of mind but without any doctrinaire commitment, and this can be done best if enough knowledge is presupposed to avoid having to give an exhaustive description first. In these early chapters, and indeed throughout the book, the familiarity with the various methods the reader is expected to have can be gauged from the list of 'Preliminary Reading' at the beginning of each chapter. This is not an (obviously futile) attempt to legislate for how the book is to be read; it is meant to tell the reader, 'If you have already read this much, or something similar, then anything you find incomprehensible in the chapter is the writer's fault. If you haven't, well, you have been warned.'

(2) In addition to the methods that all courses on the Bible nowadays cover, the last thirty years have seen a wholly new movement in biblical studies. This is the development of what is often called 'text-immanent' exegesis, which looks for the meaning of biblical texts as we now meet them in our Bibles instead of trying to get back behind the finished form of the text to earlier stages (as in the three kinds of 'historical' criticism just mentioned). I do not believe there is as yet an accessible study of this for the student. Such studies as there are tend to be highly technical; and where they are not, they are usually even more wildly partisan than books on the historical methods. Furthermore, there are two quite distinct types of 'text-immanent' approach. One goes by the name of 'structural' or 'structuralist' exegesis; its ancestry is French, though it is widely practised in North America and Great Britain. The other is the 'canonical method' associated with Professor B. S. Childs of Yale, whose antecedents are purely Anglo-Saxon, and in which theological factors are much more important. So far as I know, no one has tried to present the two approaches together, and certainly not with students in mind. The reason may be that proponents of each approach tend to have no time for the other, and scholars who subscribe to neither tend to regard both as beneath discussion. I believe it is worth getting to know about both kinds of 'text-immanent' exegesis *and* tracing the connections and differences between them. But here it is naturally necessary to describe, as well as evaluate, the methods involved, since as yet they are not likely to be familiar to many people outside specialist departments.

2

(3) One of the problems most students of the Bible experience is that the various methods they have to learn to practise seem to follow one another in steady succession, and yet not to be at all clearly interrelated. Redaction criticism, we learn, comes 'after' form criticism: but in what sense 'after'? The first four chapters try to answer this question, while chapters 6–9 analyse 'canon' and 'structural' criticism with the same aim in view: to trace logical connections and to draw a map of biblical criticism on which the methods can all be located. My intention is to show that these methods are not just a random collection of techniques but hang together, make up a family, cover the range of possible questions people can ask about texts. This is quite an ambitious aim, but even if the reader does not find it completely convincing, it may at least help to make the methods, and the differences between them, easier to remember, since they are all being measured against a common standard.

However, in trying to find this standard I have come to the conclusion that it is essential to widen one's horizons beyond those usually found in books on biblical criticism. To make coherent sense of the methods of Old Testament study, they must be set against the background of literary criticism in general, in the world of English literature and of the study of modern languages and literature. This is self-evidently true for structuralist criticism, which deliberately applies methods from the wider literary world to the Bible, but it seems to me that it is also true for the other methods. A third issue, therefore, which I discuss here is the relation of biblical criticism to 'secular' literary criticism. Sometimes my argument is that there is interdependence, often of a stronger kind than many scholars would support; but at other times I argue, less controversially, that an understanding of secular literary criticism can at least be a great help to us in drawing our map of biblical methods. Wherever possible, I draw out parallels between discussions in biblical scholarship and in literary criticism – sometimes to press the case for one's dependence on the other, but more often simply to show that biblical and 'secular' critics live in much the same world, and that their investigations can be mutually illuminating.

For my discussions of literary criticism it is certain that I owe apologies to experts in the field, who will at once be aware how far it is from being my own. I have tried to avoid mere blunders, but I am aware how dangerous an understanding this has been. Perhaps it should be stressed, however, that I have not even tried to be comprehensive in this area. The aim is to tell the student of the Bible enough to make it clear how Old Testament studies are related to literary criticism; perhaps also to encourage the student with a 'literary' background to believe that biblical studies are not as alien as they may look. The literary discussions, especially those in chapters 10–14, have no purpose beyond that and are certainly not meant to provide any guide to the state of modern literary criticism in its own right. For the same reason, the examples selected and the authors referred to are chosen purely for their accessibility to theologians and students of the Bible. The discussion will look out of focus to a literary critic – much as the history of Israel looks out of focus to the ancient historian. Mistakes, however, no doubt remain, for which I am sorry.

In an attempt to anchor what is sometimes a highly abstract discussion, I have related all the methods to one particular text, the book of Ecclesiastes; this has a chapter to itself (chapter 5), where it is analysed from the point of view of the three 'historical' methods, but the later chapters keep returning to it, so that the more modern methods, too, are given a chance to show what they can do on a text which should by then be an old friend to the reader. By the time all the threads of the discussion have been worked into Ecclesiastes, it has turned into a small sampler of Old Testament critical methods, and may be (metaphorically) cut out and framed as an aid to memory.

Method in Old Testament Study

These are the themes of the book; but it also has a thesis. The thesis concerns the place and proper understanding of *method* in a discipline like Old Testament studies. On one level, I am writing to help students to understand familiar methods, to introduce new methods and to place Old Testament criticism against the background of literary studies in modern culture. But on another level, I am trying through this discussion to introduce what I call a 'metacritical' issue, namely, 'What is the role of method in understanding and reading the Old Testament?' This again, to be handled

4

properly, would need a book to itself, and a wealth of philosophical discussions would have to be drawn in. This undertaking lies beyond my competence. What I have tried to do is to show how questions of this kind arise for the thoughtful student of the Old Testament, even one who is not familiar with the way they have been discussed elsewhere. And I suggest some answers that might help us to avoid some of the tight corners in which we often find ourselves in Old Testament criticism.

The primary thesis is that much harm has been done in biblical studies by insisting that there is, somewhere, a 'correct' method which, if only we could find it, would unlock the mysteries of the text. From the quest for this method flow many evils: for example, the tendency of each newly-discovered method to excommunicate its predecessors (never clearer than with the latest, canon criticism), and the tendency to denigrate the 'ordinary' reader as 'non-critical'. I try to argue – not in any one place, but wherever the issue arises – that all of the methods being examined have something in them, but none of them is the 'correct' method which scholars are seeking. This can be done at a simple level, by showing how each in turn falls short of perfection; but my argument goes further than this. I believe that the quest for a correct method is, not just in practice but inherently, incapable of succeeding. The pursuit of method assimilates reading a text to the procedures of technology: it tries to process the text, rather than to read it. Instead, I propose that we should see each of our 'methods' as a codification of intuitions about the text which may occur to intelligent readers. Such intuitions can well arrive at truth; but it will not be the kind of truth familiar in the natural sciences. Reading the Old Testament, with whatever aim in view, belongs to the humanities and cannot operate with an idea of watertight, correct method.

One of the ways in which critical reading of the text differs from an objective 'method' is brought out in almost every chapter. I try to show how each method, however modestly it is applied, always brings in its wake some kind of circularity in argument. Reading turns out never to be a linear process, in which a method is used on a piece of text which initially is not understood at all. On the contrary, no method can be used until there is some prior understanding of the text, even though this prior understanding is corrected as the methodical reading proceeds, I suggest that reading a text depends crucially on decisions about *genre*, about what a text is to be read *as*, and that this can only partly be brought under the control of any method. On the other hand, this does not mean that reading texts is a totally subjective matter, and that we can read the biblical books in any way we like. The circle is not necessarily a vicious circle. Critics will recognize here, of course, the principle of the so-called 'hermeneutic circle'. My intention in this book is merely to make readers of the Old Testament aware of it, and to argue that it undermines some of the exaggerated claims of biblical critics to have discovered watertight methods for elucidating the Old Testament text. Conversely, it means that 'unscientific' should not be used as a pejorative term when discussing other people's approaches. Biblical criticism is *non*-scientific and needs to be evaluated with the tools proper to the humanities, not the sciences.

In short, my thesis is that criticism is a descriptive pursuit, analysing, explaining and codifying the questions that perceptive readers put to the text; not a prescriptive discipline laying down rules about how the text ought to be read. This means that my discussion can afford to be well-disposed towards all the methods in question so far as their achievements are concerned, but on the other hand that it tends to be highly critical of each of them in respect of its claims to supremacy. To offend no one is perhaps to offend everyone, but I have certainly tried to be as even-handed as possible.

Using This Book

The 'Preliminary Reading' lists have already been mentioned. At the end of each chapter there are suggestions for further reading which would enable the reader to go more deeply into topics handled in the chapter, and to find full bibliographies that take the subject further still. But the chapter that follows never presupposes any of this additional reading. I have stressed above that this book does *not* provide a general introduction to the historical-critical methods ('literary', form, and redaction criticism), and I have therefore given references to works that do. I am not trying to replace any of the standard introductory material that students read at the beginning of courses in Old Testament studies, but to provide something that reflects on the experience of successfully completing such courses and helps with the question, 'What next?'

I have provided relatively full notes, which serve two purposes. First, they provide the normal kind of academic documentation that will be expected by colleagues and that is necessary to anchor the discussion firmly in the relevant scholarly literature: though I have made no attempt to be exhaustive. But second, they are meant to help readers who are seriously interested in the subject to explore further, both by referring them to more obscure material that does not even appear in the further reading lists, and sometimes also by developing subsidiary arguments at some length. The book can therefore be read quite satisfactorily without referring to the notes, but some of its contentions – especially those that belong to what I have called its thesis, rather than its themes – surface more explicitly in the notes. With the notes, it is an essay on method in Old Testament criticism, illustrated from the individual methods in current use; without the notes, it is a guide to current methods, with some analysis of theoretical issues. The reader who is ignoring the notes could also omit chapters 10–14 on a first reading.

Books and articles are cited by their full title on their first appearance and thereafter by a self-explanatory short title – unless the first appearance was so long before that a full title needs to be repeated. All bibliographical details are provided in the bibliography and are not duplicated in the footnotes.

'LITERARY COMPETENCE' AND GENRE-RECOGNITION

There is a narrow sense of understanding a language in which one may be said to understand a language when he knows the grammar, the literal meanings of all the terms, and even the meaning of idioms. Such understanding does not suffice for the understanding of the metaphors of the language. In addition one must know something of the linguistic conventions . . . and even minor facets of the general culture, such as what characteristics of bears are uppermost in people's minds.

Language, Thought and Culture, ed. P. Henle
(Ann Arbor, Michigan 1965), pp. 185–6

Preliminary Reading

Proverbs 1–9; 31
Daniel 7
R. J. Coggins, *Introducing the Old Testament* (Oxford 1990), pp. 116–29

What are Critical Methods for?

How should we read the Old Testament? What methods should we use, and what sorts of result can we expect from them? Anyone beginning a course in biblical studies will find plenty of text-books that give quite straightforward answers to these questions.[1] They describe the methods that biblical scholars have developed over the last century or so – methods that go by such names as source criticism, form criticism, redaction criticism, and traditio-historical criticism; and they show the student how to apply them to various sorts of text. They also generally recommend the methods as being 'correct' or 'valid': in other words, they are methods which, if applied properly, yield reliable results that give us accurate and objectively true information about the Bible. So at a certain level there seems to be no problem in answering our questions.

But from another point of view a good many people, when they begin to study the Bible, find these answers less satisfying than they expected. Text-books tell the student how the various traditional methods 'work'. For example, any handbook on source criticism will show how the Pentateuch can be divided up into four originally separate sources which have been woven together to form the work we now have. But anyone who is not yet used to such methods is likely to ask the rather more fundamental question: even if we can do this sort of thing with the Pentateuch, why should we want to? When we know that this is how the Pentateuch came into being, how are we better off? How does this really help us to understand it? And again, even if we agree that methods like source criticism *do* achieve the results they set out to achieve, is it really right to claim that they are 'valid' in a way that other ways of reading the text (for example, reading it in a devotional way, or 'as literature') are not valid? The description of any kind of literary study as 'scientific', found occasionally in biblical scholarship, is specially puzzling to most people, because it seems so obviously different from the study of the natural sciences that it is difficult to see quite what can be meant. Sometimes we may begin to suspect that 'scientific' is a rather loaded word, a way of making methods of biblical study sound more respectable. But if that suspicion is right, it means that the claim of text-books on method to tell us the *right* way to read the Old Testament is more fragile than it looks at first sight.

So beyond the question of how the Old Testament generally *is* studied in modern academic courses, which it is fairly easy to discover from a wide range of books, more fundamental questions remain which are less easily dealt with. How *ought* the Old Testament to be studied? When we have learned to apply all the methods biblical critics have devised, what have we really achieved? And is it true that there *are* correct methods that have a privileged position, or is it really impossible to prescribe rules for reading texts like these? Such questions are very large, but in one form or another people do ask them, and it is important that anyone studying the Old Testament should face up to them and not get lost too soon in the mass of detail that biblical study necessary involves.

A *Literary Approach*

In asking about the *aims* of the various methods under discussion here we need first to be clear how long a view we are taking. Most study-guides to biblical methods concern themselves with the very immediate aims of each method – and, indeed, it is otherwise impossible to show how each method differs from the others, which is the first thing the student needs to learn. Our interest is wider than this just because we are looking for aims common to several methods. But on the other hand it would broaden the discussion beyond what is manageable, and also lose a great deal in precision, if we tried to examine not only the understanding of the biblical texts which biblical methods are supposed to yield, but also the uses to which the texts, so understood, can then be put.

Two such uses that come immediately to mind are the theological and the historical. There can be no doubt that one motivation for engaging in critical study of the Bible is to gain insight into the history of Judaeo-Christian theology, or even (if we believe that Scripture is inspired by God) into theological truth; but it would be odd to say that the aim of the *methods* themselves was to yield such insight. Rather, the methods are meant to aid us in understanding the texts; the rest is a matter of the (personal) aims of the critic who uses them. Again, by studying the Old Testament critically we can come to a number of conclusions about the ancient history of Israel and its neighbours, and it may be in order to do this that particular scholars engage in critical study; but the methods they use have as their *primary* aim the elucidation of the Old Testament texts, not the reconstruction of ancient history. It is for this reason that I have not included here any consideration of the so-called traditio-historical approach, which is really a way of using the conclusions attainable through source and form criticism in the interests of reconstructing history: either the political history of Israel or the history of its theological traditions. Although the uses to which the information provided by biblical methods can be put will be touched on at times, our chief concern is with the

10

literary aspects of biblical study: with what may be called the 'internal' aims of biblical criticism. We shall be asking, in fact, how each of the methods familiar in modern study of the Bible is intended to help us in understanding the text, and we shall not spend any time on the uses that can be made of that understanding in writing about the theology of the Old Testament or the history of Israel.

'Literary Competence'

But to describe the aim of biblical criticism as 'understanding the text' may sound utterly banal. How does this extremely general description help us to grasp what is going on in biblical study? I believe that the point can be made with much more precision if we borrow some terms from the most recent addition to the repertoire of the biblical scholar, the movement known as literary structuralism. In a later chapter I shall examine this movement in its own right and shall express a good many reservations about it. But in mapping out their own programmes for literary study structuralists have succeeded, I believe, in formulating some quite helpful descriptions of what happens in *all* study of literature: here, as so often, (and this is a theme to which we shall return)[2] what purports to be a newly discovered prescription for correctness of method turns out, less excitingly but perhaps more usefully, to be a serviceable description of what was happening all the time.

The structuralist term that may help us most is 'literary competence'. Instead of saying simply that methods of biblical study aim to assist understanding of the text, we may say that they aim to make the student *competent in reading* biblical material. Again, at the level of ordinary usage this may seem obvious: any course of study aims to make one competent at the subject. But 'competence' in structuralist writing has a more pregnant sense than this, and it will be worth spending a little space on a preliminary sketch of the background to this important term. Later we shall have to consider it in more detail and try to define it more exactly.

'Competence', like many other terms favoured by structuralists, derives from the vocabulary of modern linguistics, and especially from the linguistic movement that took its rise from the work of Ferdinand de Saussure (1857–1913).[3] 'Linguistic competence' does

11

not mean 'being *good at* English/French/German etc', but 'being in command of the conventions governing the use of English/French/German'. One could easily illustrate the difference from another sphere, say chess. A *good* chess player is one who plays well, has a good grasp of chess strategy, and so on, but a *competent* chess player, in this technical sense of the term, would be one who (irrespective of how well or badly he plays) knows what sorts of move are permitted by the rules of the game, who does not try, for example, to move pawns backwards or to castle with his bishop. In the case of language, competence can be assessed by the speaker's ability to recognize the meaning of sentences he has never heard before and to produce new sentences himself without infringing the rules of what are traditionally called grammar and syntax. For example, most of the sentences on this page have never been used before, but the reader who is competent in English can understand them because his mental structures include (mostly subconsciously) the recipes for reading English sentences, the ground-rules by which sentences in English are enabled to have meaning. Of course, one can easily make up a sentence so bizarre that it's difficult to see what it would 'mean' – e.g., 'The Eiffel Tower always reminds me of the Trans-Siberian railway' – but the native speaker of English has no difficulty in grasping that this (though puzzling) is a possible English sentence, as compared with 'Day what gives this talks bang orange' which not only has no meaning but *could not have* any meaning within the system of the English language. We may say that the second sentence is literally meaningless, whereas the first is meaningful but silly.

Again, the competent English speaker recognizes, without having to work it out, that a sentence such as 'I like moving pictures' is multiply ambiguous. It may mean that I like furniture-removing; or that I like paintings that stir my emotions; or that I like watching films (though this would be an old-fashioned usage). It is very hard to discover how speakers of a language *acquire* the implicit awareness of the conventions that make such understanding possible – how, for instance, a child faced with a verb it has never heard before will coin a past tense in -ed and will soon come to recognize that there is something 'funny' about verbs with differently formed past tenses (e.g., 'went'). But it is quite clearly a fact that we *do* recognize and assess sentences we've never heard before. And it is this ability to

12

produce ('generate' in technical jargon) new forms and sentences, and to distinguish between meaningful and meaningless or impossible ('ill-formed') new utterances, that linguists describe as linguistic competence.

Now structuralism has raised the question whether this notion of competence may usefully be applied to linguistic units larger than the sentence: to whole works of literature, entire conversations, complete books. At one level this is obviously reasonable. If one can understand any given sentence, as one can if one is linguistically competent, then there is no problem in principle about understanding any number of sentences in sequence. But more is meant than this, as may be seen from the following example.

Suppose one morning I am confronted with the following 'text':

Dear Sir,

Account No 23579D

Since this account continues to show a debit of £559.67, I have no alternative but to inform you that unless it is cleared within seven days from the above date we shall be obliged to take steps to recover the sum in question.

Yours faithfully,
A. Clerk

Now my linguistic competence enables me to construe and make sense of each phrase and sentence here, and therefore at a certain level to understand what is being said. However, it must be something more than merely *linguistic* competence that leads me to go and consult my bank manager when I receive a letter like this. This can easily be shown. Suppose I were a Martian who had learned the English language but had no knowledge of English life, customs or social conventions. My linguistic competence would then enable me to understand the 'meaning' of the text that dropped through the letter-box; but I would have no idea at all how to interpret it; it would not 'mean' anything to me. For example, it could easily be some kind of lyric poem, shown to be so by the short paired opening and closing lines, which have an aesthetically pleasing effect. You may say that no one writes lyric poems on this subject,

13

but a Martian wouldn't know that, and in any case it is very doubtful whether it is true.

But even if I knew that it was a letter, I still would not know how to take it, unless I also knew some quite specific details of English letter-writing conventions. Perhaps this is the conventionally polite way of notifying a customer that a debt has been incurred, with the talk of 'taking steps' merely an empty form? The fact that the letter begins with an expression of endearment and ends with a respectful reference to the writer's faithfulness, might suggest that the veiled threat in the body of the text is to be understood as a joke between friends. We could go on indefinitely. The reason why the native English speaker goes to see his bank manager when he receives a letter of this sort is not just that he has the *linguistic* competence to understand the sentences of which it is composed, but that he has what may be called *textual* or *literary* competence. Just as he knows the rules for making English sentences, so he knows the rules for writing English letters. He knows (he does not need to think about it) that in such letters it is 'Dear Sir' and 'Yours faithfully' that are the empty forms and the phrase 'obliged to take steps' that is the serious matter being communicated, and not the other way about. He knows that a document in this form *is* a letter, not something else. He knows, in fact, some of the literary *conventions* that enable letters to be written, that enable one to distinguish between, and respond appropriately to, different types of modern English writing.

Structuralists maintain that there is an *exact* parallel between literary and linguistic competence, a claim which to the uncommitted will seem exaggerated. Nevertheless, without pushing the case to its logical conclusion, we may say that the notion of literary competence is an obviously fruitful one, if we may be allowed to use it fairly loosely. Just as there are rules (though they are difficult to formulate, and operate, from a psychological point of view, at a subconscious level) which enable us to produce correct English sentences, so there are rules or conventions which enable us to produce 'correct' (or acceptable) English letters, poems and novels. It is simply the same principle at a higher level. Indeed, without a set of conventions about what constitutes a letter it would be impossible to write one: that is, it would be possible to set down the words that in our culture would constitute a letter, but they could not be read as meaning anything at this level. The text above would be just as 'meaningless' (at a literary level) in a literary culture that did not use letters as it would be empty of content in a culture that did not use money; and this irrespective of the fact that it would still have *linguistic* meaning. It is because we have literary competence within our own system that we are able at once to recognize the example above as a business letter and react to it appropriately.

In the same way, we are able to recognize when a piece of writing is not sufficiently marked with signs of the category it belongs to for us to assign it with confidence to one type rather than another, and so to 'read' it with understanding. This phenomenon is what corresponds, at the literary level, to ambiguity at the purely linguistic level. Take, for example, the following snippet of text: 'Sir Christopher Wren said, "I am going to dine with some men." ' We do not have enough to go on to know how to react to it, even though there is no obscurity at all at the linguistic level. It could be an excerpt from a biography, a historical novel, a poem, a speech, almost anything. And the appropriate response would be different in each case.[4]

We can often remove linguistic ambiguity by providing more information – by adding some more words. Thus the ambiguity in 'I like moving pictures' can be resolved if we continue the sentence 'but I prefer moving potted plants'. Similarly in the literary case, we can remove the ambiguity by continuing,

> If anyone calls
> Say I'm designing St Paul's

– which reveals the original line to be the first couplet of the verse form known as a clerihew. Our literary competence at once springs to life, dockets the text under 'verse: comic', and renders inappropriate and even ridiculous very many questions we might have wanted to ask if the text had revealed itself as belonging to some other genre (e.g., What is the evidence for Sir Christopher Wren's dining habits? What is the date of the occasion in question? Where did they go?). And though it would be going too far to say that a text in which clerihews mingled indiscriminately with sober historian's prose could not exist, we should be deeply suspicious, if we encountered such a work, that something had gone wrong, either

15

with the printer's schedules or with the author's brain. Such a work would be, to borrow the linguistic term again, 'ill-formed', not a 'correct' piece of historiography.

Structuralists sometimes seem to forget that we are speaking of an *analogy* between language and literature, not a precise parallel. Nevertheless we have now arrived, with the help of the linguistic model, at an idea of literary competence which makes it possible to define it principally as *the ability to recognize genre*.[5] By 'genre' is meant any recognizable and distinguishable type of writing or speech – whether 'literary' in the complimentary sense of that word or merely utilitarian, like a business letter – which operates within certain conventions that are in principle (not necessarily in practice) stateable. This may seem an obvious and rather meagre conclusion to have been arrived at by such a circuitous and, for the biblical student, unfamiliar route. But I think that it is of fundamental importance, and very easily lost sight of in the way that biblical studies are often taught, with its emphasis on breaking the text up into its component parts before work can begin. It is not too much to say that it is impossible to understand any text without at least an implicit recognition of the genre to which it belongs. All texts must be texts of some kind or type: no one can, or ever could, sit down to write simply 'a text'. This is far from implying that all texts are 'conventional' in the evaluative sense of that word. Indeed, it is 'unconventional' texts that bring most forcibly to our attention how important genre is when we try to read a new work. An unconventional novel can only be so if it is a novel; and 'free' verse could not exist, if our literary culture did not have conventions about metre and rhyme.[6]

'Genre' in Old Testament Study

If we turn to look at biblical, especially Old Testament, study with this discussion in mind, we can see at once that much of what biblical study has achieved is the discovery of the conventions governing certain types of literature in the Old Testament: the genres into which they can be classified, the *kinds* of meanings they are capable of having. In this way modern critical study has made it possible to read with understanding texts which previously had to a greater or lesser extent been misread, because they were seen as something they were not. A good example would be 'wisdom' literature. Most biblical students soon feel that they have acquired the 'competence' to know whether or not a particular book is to be assigned to the genre described by modern scholars as 'wisdom'. This is a genre of which many examples are extant, both from ancient Israel and from surrounding cultures. We learn to recognize 'wisdom' partly by formal characteristics – for example, the prevalence of parallel proverbs in a metrical form ('He who forgives an offence seeks love; but he who repeats a matter alienates a friend', Prov. 17:9) – and partly on the grounds of the topics dealt with (mostly relating to human social life).[7]

Again, in spite of intense scholarly debate as to whether 'apocalyptic' should be accepted as the name of a literary genre, no one can study the Old Testament for long without forming a reasonably clear idea of what constitutes an 'apocalypse' and developing some sense of *what sorts of questions it makes sense to ask* of such a work. When we encounter mysterious animals in such works we know that they are very likely to have a symbolic meaning: we should be misreading the book of Daniel if we went to it for information about zoology,[8] and it would be a genre-mistake to look for the fourth beast of chapter 7 in the Natural History Museum. Because of our competence, our 'feel' for apocalyptic, we know that a text which began, 'The stars will fall from heaven, and the sun will cease its shining; the moon will be turned to blood, and fire mingled with hail will fall from the heavens' would not be likely to continue, 'The rest of the country will have sunny intervals and scattered showers.'[9]

Similarly, when we read a wisdom book, we know from our competence in the genre that a lot of illustrations will be drawn from the natural world. But we also know that these are likely to be meant not primarily as useful guidance to the natural world, but rather as generalizable truths providing insights into the human world. Until you have seen this, you cannot be said to be 'competent' in wisdom literature; you do not know what are the appropriate questions to put to a wisdom book. Thus 'He that touches pitch will be defiled' (Ecclus. 13:1) is not chiefly meant to give us information about the adhesive properties of pitch – as it might be if it stood in some sort of scientific treatise – but to remind us of what we *already* know about pitch in order to suggest that there are parallels in the sphere of human relationships. Indeed, the verse

17

continues, 'and whoever associates with a proud man will become like him'. It is, as a matter of fact, a disputed question whether this is universally true of wisdom literature. Some scholars believe that some of these observations about nature were originally recorded for their own sake.[10] But at least it should be clear that this question is itself a question about genre, about whether we have correctly stated the conventions with which wisdom literature operates. If the question cannot be resolved, then we must admit that we are to that extent not competent in wisdom literature. But – and this is crucially important – it cannot be resolved by simple exegesis, by improving our competence at the linguistic level; for there is no dispute at this level. The statement in Ecclesiasticus 13:1a undoubtedly means that pitch is sticky. The question is at the level of *literary* competence: when it says that, what kind of information is it seeking to give us? This is a question about the genre to which Ecclesiasticus belongs, and the kinds of meanings it is appropriate to seek in this genre. We cannot say, *First* you must establish the 'meaning' of the passage, and then you can ask about the genre to which it belongs; for the meaning depends on the genre. Yet, on the other hand, there is no way of establishing the genre to which the text belongs except by reading it, and that must involve decisions about meaning.

Already, therefore, we have stumbled against a certain circularity in understanding texts, and the reader should be warned that there is a great deal more of it in store; but at least at this stage it should be fairly plain that it is by no means necessarily a vicious circularity, since we are never in practice dealing with just one verse, but always with collections of material which have a cumulative effect. Our initial judgement about genre and our initial attempt at exegesis play back and forth on each other and are mutually corrective.[11] On the whole the claim that biblical scholars are now 'competent' in wisdom and apocalyptic literature is a well-founded one, and in both cases modern scholarship can safely congratulate itself on a significant advance. Wisdom and apocalyptic are now 'readable' for us, where once they were obscure and incoherent.

'LITERARY COMPETENCE' AND GENRE-RECOGNITION

A Perspective for Understanding Old Testament Methods

My purpose in the next few chapters is to outline what I see as
the achievements (and also the shortcomings) of modern biblical
criticism, using the models of 'literary competence' and 'genre-
recognition' developed in this chapter as points of reference. I shall
try to show that the really significant way in which biblical studies
have advanced is through increasingly sophisticated techniques for
recognizing genres, and that by applying these techniques they have
extracted a great deal of information about the biblical text, and
understood it better, than earlier ('pre-critical') approaches. In
short, I shall argue that biblical criticism has been concerned with
enabling the reader to acquire the competence necessary to read
the various types of literature that make up the Bible. It will become
clear as we proceed that the critics in question have by no means
always seen their work in these terms, and that they have claimed
both greater and other objectives for their methods. I hope to
suggest that the approach adopted here encourages a sober assessment of biblical methods which neither carps at the critics for failing
in aims they did not have in any case, nor regards modern biblical
studies as having said the last word about the Bible.

Further Reading

K. Koch, *The Growth of the Biblical Tradition*. London 1969
D. S. Russell, *The Method and Message of Jewish Apocalyptic* (London
    1964), pp. 104–39
G. von Rad, *Wisdom in Israel* (London 1972), pp. 24–60, 74–96
J. Culler, *Structuralist Poetics* (London 1975), pp. 113–30
J. L. Crenshaw, *Old Testament Wisdom: An Introduction* (Atlanta 1981),
    pp. 11–25

19

'LITERARY' CRITICISM

What is it that enables an editor to detect the presence of 'obvious blunders and misprints'? The fact that blunders and misprints don't make sense!

F. W. Bateson, 'Textual Criticism and Its Problems', *Essays in Criticism* 17 (1967), p. 387

Preliminary Reading

Genesis 1—2, 6—9

E. B. Mellor, *The Making of the Old Testament* (Cambridge Bible Commentary on the *New English Bible*. Cambridge 1972), pp. 46–74

Source Analysis

People who come to biblical studies after a training in the study of modern literature are usually puzzled by the sense in which biblical scholars use the term 'literary criticism'. For them, 'literary' criticism is simply the study of literature, especially from the point of view of what in French is called *explication de texte*: the attempt to read the text in such a way as to bring out its inner coherence, the techniques of style and composition used by the author, all that makes it a piece of literary art. In biblical studies the term is used in a much narrower sense.[1] 'Literary' criticism for the biblical scholar is a method used in handling texts that have been produced by amalgamating other, older texts. A good many biblical books, it is thought, were produced in this way; and 'literary' criticism is the attempt to divide them up into their component parts, and then to assess the relative ages of these parts, rather as archaeologists date the various strata of a site.

This approach is rarely called for in dealing with modern texts, where laws against plagiarism and the convention that authors identify themselves by name militate against the production of composite texts. But one can sometimes find examples at the non-artistic end of 'literature': for example, committee-produced documents where the sensitive reader will suspect (from abrupt changes in style, punctuation or tone) that more than one author has had a hand in producing the final version, or that earlier drafts have been incorporated without all the necessary consequential alterations. The 'literary' critic (also known in older books as the 'higher' critic)[2] looks for such tell-tale signs of multiple authorship in biblical texts and tries to trace the development of the text through however many stages seem to him to have been involved. Sometimes it seems to scholars that many different sections of a lengthy work such as the Pentateuch have passed through much the same stages of growth, and so they have been led to argue that quite long earlier 'sources' can be identified as running through the entire work. This is rather as though, in many documents produced by a committee, we kept noticing sections with distinctive features of style, such as to suggest that one person had submitted drafts for all of them and that these drafts had been worked into each final document. By this means the hypothesis that the Pentateuch derives, not from a multiplicity of fragments, but from four major sources, each of which was originally a more or less finished work in its own right, was established and has so far weathered most attacks.[3]

We shall make most progress in understanding the interests that gave rise to 'literary' or 'source' criticism if we consider for a moment the most fundamental of these attacks, the one that from the very beginnings of the method has been directed against biblical critics by those of what we may call a fundamentalist persuasion. In conservative polemic against 'the higher criticism' it has been customary for many years to speak as though biblical critics approached the text with a *presupposition* or prejudice, deriving from no rational source, that the biblical books are collections of fragments which have been artificially stuck together – rather than being the unified works, each deriving from one author (in the case of the Pentateuch, Moses), which they have been treated as by Jewish and Christian tradition.[4] If you start by looking for sources, so the taunt goes, you will end by finding them, but the process is wholly circular; the conclusion is built into the premisses. Biblical critics have, as it were, a vested interest in there being inconsistencies of style, tone and content within the Pentateuch – inconsistencies that can be attributed to the presence of different sources – where an unprejudiced, open-minded reader would see nothing but a smooth and satisfactory whole.

Now this attack both seriously misunderstands source criticism and yet, in a curious way, points to some important truths about it. The attack misunderstands source criticism because it quite fails to see that there was really no pressure on early biblical critics to detect the existence of sources in the Pentateuch – however much there may be pressure on their academic descendants to maintain what have now become respectable scholarly traditions. Pentateuchal criticism did not arise because a number of ill-natured or blasphemous scholars said, 'Here is a beautifully unified and coherent work; how can we chop it up into little pieces?' It arose because *observable discrepancies* within the Pentateuchal narrative, very many of which had been noticed for hundreds of years before, bore in upon scholars that it was very difficult to see what kind of literature such a rambling and inconsistent work could possibly be. To put the matter in the terms developed in the previous chapter, we may say that once scholars raised the question what *kind* or *genre* of writing the Pentateuch was, they were forced to see that it was, from a literary point of view, 'ambiguous'.[5] A work which consists of narrative mixed with poems and hymns and laws, which contains two or even three versions of the same story set down with no apparent awareness that they are the same, and which changes style so drastically from paragraph to paragraph and from verse to verse, cannot in a certain sense be read at all: you simply don't know where you are with it. To write such a work would be like writing our hypothetical history in which sober prose mingled with comic verse – inconceivable except for some specialized purpose such as a textbook on literary genre. It was therefore suggested that the Pentateuch was not one work at all, but an amalgamation of several smaller works; and it was found (or at least it seemed so at the time) that it was possible to extract these works from it; and when they had been extracted, they proved to be internally coherent and capable of being read, because it was possible to see what kind of thing they were.

This seems to me to vindicate source critics against the fundamentalist kind of attack. But I am not sure that it is a way of formulating the line of defence that all such critics would welcome because, as I have already suggested, it does in fact allow a certain truth in the attack to come in by the back door. We can see how this is so if we look briefly at a quite different attack on traditional source analysis that has come from the important German writer on biblical methodology, Wolfgang Richter.[6] According to him, much that passes for sound 'literary' criticism of the Bible is in reality methodologically faulty, because it asks questions about the genre (or form or *Gattung*) of biblical passages *before* a rigorous analysis of a 'literary' or source-critical kind has been undertaken. Thus, he says accusingly, Old Testament scholars very often make up their minds that a text must be composite because it contains different *kinds* of material (say, narrative and law in a chapter such as Exodus 20); whereas they ought first to separate out the originally independent sections of which the chapter is composed (on the basis of linguistic differences, inconsistencies of phraseology or names of characters, stylistic tricks and so on), and only then go on to assign the 'sources' thus established to literary types or genres.

Now my impression is that many biblical critics will reply to such a criticism, not by saying that Richter is wrong about the methods that ought to be followed, but by saying simply that they are not in fact guilty of the charge brought against them. They will agree that we ought not to put the cart before the horse in the way Richter disapproves of, but will claim that they never do anyway. Obviously we would need to examine a lot of works of biblical criticism to decide the rights and wrongs of such a disagreement. But my point at the moment is this. If the way of describing 'literary' criticism of the Bible I have set out is correct, then Richter may well be mistaken in any case when he says there is only one correct order for applying various methods to the text. Like Richter, handbooks on source criticism very often do suggest that we must *first* do our source analysis and only *then* go on to ask questions about the literary genre or type of the text we are studying. But I have been trying to suggest that these two approaches are necessarily simultaneous. 'Literary' criticism is not a technique which we practise mechanically, as it were blindfold, before we go on to try to understand and read the text intelligently. On the contrary, 'literary' criticism begins with the attempt to understand and make sense of the text; and its conclusions about the composite character of many texts arise from noticing that the text actually cannot *be* understood as it stands, because it is full of inconsistencies, inexplicable dislocations of theme, form, style and so on, which make it impossible to know what to read it *as*. And as we saw in chapter 1, unless we can read a text *as* something – unless we can assign it to some genre, however ill-defined and in need of subsequent refinement – we cannot really read it at all; we can only construe it sentence by sentence, like an 'unseen' translation in a foreign-language examination.

The impulse towards source criticism of the Pentateuch arises, then, from an attempt to classify in order to understand. As we have seen, there is a sense in which all intelligent reading of texts begins from the same impulse. But in the case of the Bible the conscious asking of the sorts of questions that eventually led to the four-document hypothesis associated with the names of Graf and Wellhausen had been for long inhibited by a prior conviction on the part of readers of the Bible that they *already knew* how biblical texts should be classified: namely, as some form (no doubt a very sophisticated form) of divine speech to men. The European Enlightenment made it possible to see the biblical books as primarily just 'texts from the past', leaving on one side the question of inspiration. And then, as part of the attempt to read these texts intelligently, people were bound to ask what *kind* of texts they were. Before long it was clear that the Pentateuch in particular, considered as a single text or even as a corpus of five books, simply defied classification. No thinkable type of writing could possibly contain the inconsistencies, doublings back, apparently aimless changes of style, of titles for God, of narrative tone, that these books encompass. For one man to write such a text, he would have to be mentally incoherent or disturbed, or – and here source criticism really begins – he would need to be using a lot of already existing material which, for whatever reason, he was unable to change, and setting it down in all its inconsistency.

The biblical critic's task, on this view, was to reconstruct the raw materials, on the understanding that each of the underlying documents when reconstructed would exhibit an internal consistency such that it could be read as a text of some determinable kind. And just as we saw that someone who is 'competent' linguistically in a given language is able to tell, say, where one sentence ends and the next begins in a stream of conversation; so a critic who claims to be competent in the conventions of literature will be able to tell where one source ends and the next begins. He will know, for example, where a collection of early legendary material ends and a post-exilic genealogy begins. Of course early source critics did not use this sort of terminology. Nevertheless, I believe that the process in practice worked much as I have described it, and that questions of source analysis and questions of genre-recognition were from the beginning bound up together.[7]

At this point we can perhaps begin to see why there is some truth (though not at all the kind of truth that its proponents intend) in the fundamentalist jibe that source criticism is an essentially circular method, capable of finding only what it is looking for, creating the evidence that it claims to interpret and explain. As we have seen, at the most obvious level this is false. Biblical critics did not begin by *deciding* that the Pentateuch must be composed from several sources; the conclusion forced itself upon them, in some cases much against their will. But on the other hand it is a little over-simple to say that they 'discovered' that the Pentateuch had this character, as as astronomer might discover a new star or planet. It was a hypothesis which began to suggest itself as more and more data seemed difficult to understand on the assumption that the Pentateuch was a single, unified work; a hypothesis which seemed to be confirmed as more and more passages were read with it in mind and found to be amenable to such a reading. In this it somewhat resembles a scientific hypothesis: a hunch suggested by an imaginative guess by an informed mind already at work in the appropriate area of inquiry, which is found to illuminate new data and to find confirmation in experimental trials. We do not begin by knowing what the conventions of the literature we are studying are, but nor do we simply stumble upon them; we keep trying to formulate them more precisely as we go along, constantly correcting our ideas of them, sometimes retracing our steps and trying a different approach, until we think we have found a stable understanding of the text. This manner of encounter with the text is repeated at every level of the critical enterprise; and it provides, perhaps, the only true sense in which criticism can be called 'scientific'.

If 'literary' critics of the Old Testament tried to establish that their approach was scientific in a much stronger sense, or one at any rate that claimed not just analogy but direct relation to the methods of the natural sciences,[8] they would be ignoring the fact that source analysis did not really begin with the application of a 'scientific' technique to the text of the Pentateuch, but with an intuition about the text, springing from an attempt to read it with understanding, to grasp it as a coherent whole. And in ignoring this, they would be open to attack on two fronts. The fundamentalist for his part would quite rightly say that there is nothing scientific about applying a technique unless you know that it is appropriate to the material you are applying it to, and that that is here the very point at issue. How can you know that you have a correct method for dividing a book into sources, unless you already know that the book is composite? Scholars such as Richter, on the other hand, would point out that no one ever has applied the method with proper scientific rigour anyway. Critics have always allowed their intuitions about what a given source is 'likely' to have contained, or which particular literary genres could be 'expected' to occur in a given section of text, to colour and influence their judgement about the extent of material from this source or that to be found in a particular part of the Pentateuch.

Too much can be claimed for literary-critical method – that it is fully objective, completely scientific, entirely open-minded; or the wrong thing can be claimed for it – that it is a pure technique, not a hypothesis or theory. This gives its opponents all too easy a time, for it is not at all difficult to show that, as it has actually been practised, it is none of these things. But these claims should not have been made in the first place, and they were generally *not* made by the founders of the literary criticism of the Bible; and when they have been refuted, literary criticism has not been deprived of any of its real value.

Whose Conventions?

There is, indeed, one objection to traditional 'literary' criticisms of the Old Testament which is much harder to meet. Suppose we accept the suggestion that such criticism arises from the desire to understand to become competent in reading, Old Testament literature. Suppose we also accept that scholars came to see the Pentateuch as composed of pre-existing fragments (or, more probably, extensive literary sources) because they found it impossible to make sense of it as a single work. It may then still be argued that biblical studies set off much too soon on the quest for genres within the Pentateuch that could be made sense of. The critics, it may be said, had too hard-and-fast an idea of what sorts of literary genre existed or were capable of existing in the ancient world.[9] For example, whatever may be the case in modern Western or even classical literature, is it necessarily true that a text containing two somewhat incompatible versions of essentially the same story could not occur within the conventions of ancient Israelite literature? And if a work so multi-layered and complex as the Pentateuch really cannot be taken seriously as a single piece of writing, but must be seen as an amalgamation of originally separate texts from different periods, why was this not felt to be far more of a difficulty by the Jewish community in the days when this same work was first coming to be recognized as 'the Law', the foundation document of the Jewish faith? Presumably there was *some* period in the life of ancient Israel when this strange compendium of narrative, law, poetry and exhortation was felt to be a coherent whole – to be, in our terminology, 'readable'. Of course it may still be the case that it had actually *arisen* by the combination of earlier source-materials, in much the way that literary critics suggest. But it would not be true that such a work was unthinkable in its finished form, and so a certain amount of the initial thrust towards a source-critical approach to the work would necessarily be weakened.

An exclusive acquaintance with the literary genres available within our own culture can all too easily lead us to regard as impossible or composite works which are in fact entirely unproblematical within a different literary system. For example, someone brought up to think that classical French tragedy represented the only conceivable way of writing tragedies would be likely to ridicule the tragedies of Shakespeare – as indeed French critics in the seventeenth and eighteenth centuries did ridicule them – for being crude and barbaric in conception; or even (which is the point here) to refuse to believe they were properly finished works at all. Such a reader might point to the bizarre mixing of prose and verse, and of elevated and familiar styles, and to the constant changes of scene, as tell-tale indications that these plays were imperfectly edited collections of rough drafts, or even conflations of alternative versions – quite failing to grasp that these features of style and construction actually contribute to an overall unity within the genre of *English* tragedy. Surely then, where such gaps in culture and experience are involved as separate the modern critic from the writers of the Old Testament, it would not be surprising if misunderstandings like this were very frequent; and it is no doubt partly a sense of the dangers here that leads modern practitioners of 'literary' criticism of the Old Testament to be much more cautious than some of their predecessors.

Again, however, it would be foolish to lapse into complete scepticism about the possibility of carrying out fruitful work along literary-critical lines. No one, to my way of thinking, has yet shown that the flood narrative of Genesis 6—9 forms a coherent unit, according to any literary conventions that can plausibly be reconstructed even if one is looking for them.[10] It seems to me that the hypothesis that this narrative is a conflation of two versions of the story, each of which had an inner coherence and independent currency before the conflation was effected, remains by far the most convincing explanation of its many inconsistencies and repetitions. Much the same may be said of the source hypothesis which most students encounter first in their Old Testament studies, that which concerns Genesis 1 and 2. The case which argues that Genesis 1:1—2:4a and 2:4b–25 formed originally separate accounts of the creation is an exceedingly difficult one to refute or even to weaken.

Now it is true that in both these cases the argument for the now traditional hypothesis must inevitably take the form, 'No author could possibly write an account as inconsistent/incoherent as that'; and it is always open to an objector to reply, 'How can you possibly know what an author in such a remote and ancient culture could or could not have done?' But this is such a blanket objection, it hardly sweeps away the hypothesis in these very well-tried cases, although it will certainly make the thoughtful student of the Bible wary of accepting what biblical critics tell him simply on authority – a result much to be welcomed. After all, we cannot *know* that the scribes who produced the Old Testament thought in ways that have any affinities whatever with ourselves, if 'know' is to be understood in a sense akin to its sense in mathematics or even in the natural sciences. But no work in literature, or in the humanities in general, can proceed on such an austerely limited view of what it is to know. All literary study must assume that even quite remote cultures have *some* affinities with our own. We must think that we can form some idea of what writers in other cultures, working with their conventions, could or could not have done. Objections like the one just mentioned warn us to be on our guard, as biblical critics have sometimes failed to be, against thinking we know more than we do about the literary conventions of ancient Israel; but they should not be allowed to drive us into a kind of critical nihilism according to which texts from the past are simply inscrutable.[11]

Form Criticism: Oral Genres

The earliest successor to 'literary' criticism in Old Testament studies, at any rate, was not worried by the anxiety that nothing could be known about ancient literature; on the contrary, it was convinced that a great deal more could be known than the source critics had allowed for. Source criticism had worked with too restricted and narrowly 'academic' a view of this ancient society, as if its members were all scholars not unlike the higher critics themselves, bent over desks from morning till night. But the true path to understanding the literature of the Old Testament lay in recognizing that it was the literature of a whole culture, a people like other peoples past and present. Ancient Israel used the various genres which can be detected in the pages of the Old Testament not just in 'literature' – written texts – but also in *oral* communication, in telling stories, worshipping God, going to law, administering affairs of state and teaching its children. So there was a shift in emphasis from written to oral genres, from the literary pre-history of the Old Testament text to the oral pre-history of even the earliest discernible literary strata; and one effect of this was that the very idea of genre, type, or form, came to be much more consciously articulated and defined. Thus we arrive at form criticism.

Further Reading

N. C. Habel, *Literary Criticism of the Old Testament*. Philadelphia 1971
R. E. Clements, *A Century of Old Testament Study* (Guildford and London 1976), pp. 7–30

3

FORM CRITICISM

Forms may be regarded as institutional imperatives.

> N. H. Pearson in *Literary Forms and Types*,
> ed. R. Kirk (New York 1940), p. 70

Preliminary Reading

Deuteronomy
Psalms 15, 20, 24, 93—100, 118
K. Koch, *The Growth of the Biblical Tradition* (London 1969), pp. 3–16

The Idea of Genre in Speech

Source criticism, as we have seen, began with the impulse to understand the Bible, especially the books of the Pentateuch; but by the time that it reached its classic expression in the Graf–Wellhausen hypothesis, its main *use* in Old Testament studies had come to be the light it shed on the history of ancient Israel's religious institutions. Wellhausen's epoch-making insight that 'P' was the latest, rather than (as had formerly been thought) the earliest, of the four Pentateuchal sources[1] was to have the effect of revolutionizing every critical Bible reader's understanding of the relation of post-exilic Judaism to the pre-exilic faith expressed in J, E and D. Pre-exilic 'Yahwism' now for the first time stood out clearly as something distinct from the later Jewish religion. But this is certainly a secondary consequence of applying 'literary' criticism to the Pentateuch, not in any sense its original guiding purpose; indeed, Wellhausen's work presupposed a good century or so of serious attempts at documentary analysis as such.

With form criticism things are rather different. From the beginning this was understood not only as affording insight into the biblical text by isolating pre-literary stages in its growth, but also as a tool in reconstructing the social life and institutions (both sacred and secular) of ancient Israel. In accordance with the general aim of this book I shall not say very much about the wider uses to which the knowledge gained through form criticism has been put in studies of Israelite history and sociology, but such questions are bound to play a greater role here than in any of the other methods, so there will be occasional digressions.

As I pointed out in the last chapter, it was with form criticism that the idea of genre moved to the conscious centre of interest in Old Testament studies. Form criticism developed in a German context, and all its technical terms are German, no really successful attempt ever having been made to provide satisfactory English equivalents; but the central concept of the method, variously *Form* or *Gattung* in German,[2] is probably better captured by 'genre' than by any other term current in normal English. Perhaps there is one drawback in using this term, which may explain why many English-speaking scholars have preferred to adopt *Gattung* untranslated for their form-critical work. This is that 'genre' in English usage tends to imply a *literary* type, often of a rather large-scale sort: thus one may speak of tragedy, comedy, epic, novels and lyric verse as genres in English literature. It may be slightly less common to describe smaller forms such as sonnets, limericks, ballads or epigrams as 'genres', though the usage is perfectly permissible; and we do not usually use the term in referring to the component parts of larger works (such as scenes, couplets, conversations or *dénouements*) for all of which the German *Gattung* is acceptable. But it is very unusual indeed to speak of 'genres' in referring to oral forms of communication. There is no obvious reason why: we might just as well speak of the genre 'political speech', 'sermon' or 'summing-up', as of the genre 'epic' or 'tragedy', since in all these cases one is dealing with the casting of words into a particular set of conventions for use in a context in which such conventions apply. It simply happens that we do not use 'genre' in this way, whereas German writers do use *Gattung*.

Whatever term we use, however, this discussion gives us as good a working definition as any of what *Gattung* regularly means for the form critic. A *Gattung* or genre is *a conventional pattern, recognizable by certain formal criteria* (style, shape, tone, particular syntactic or even grammatical structures, recurring formulaic patterns), which is *used in a particular society in social contexts which are governed by certain formal conventions*. With this definition we are equipped to move on a little further.

'Sitz im Leben'

There is no difficulty in finding oral *Gattungen* in modern English society. The ability to recognize genre in speech as well as in literature is one of the basic skills of life in society, and one may be fully in command of it without having any conscious awareness of being so. Very many such genres are instantly recognizable by their opening formulas: 'Ladies and gentlemen . . .', 'May it please your Lordship . . .', 'Mr Speaker . . .' or 'Good morning, campers!' All these formulas at once imply that the speaker is taking part in a specific social activity for which the conventions are very closely defined and for which certain styles of speech, mannerisms and even subject-matter are held to be appropriate in our society. It is precisely because we are so sensitive to genre-conventions in speech that we can derive so much amusement, as in an old-fashioned game of 'Consequences', from supplying inappropriate continuations to opening formulas such as these. It must be remembered that an oral genre can be extremely short: the following, for example, are all examples of complete *Gattungen*, and even if (as often happens with the *Gattungen* that occur in the Old Testament) they appeared within a piece of continuous text without any indication of where they began and ended we should still have no difficulty at all in lifting them out and classifying them:

> I name this ship *Prince of Denmark*. May God bless her and all who sail in her.

> With this ring I thee wed, with my body I thee worship, and with all my worldly goods I thee endow.

> Not guilty.

> Fire!

The technical term for the social context or situation within which

32

a given *Gattung* is appropriate is *Sitz im Leben* – a term which has suffered badly at the hands of both its users (who sometimes treat it as if it meant 'historical period') and its translators. We shall leave it untranslated, since English has no natural equivalent: 'social context' is vaguer, and 'setting-in-life' conveys nothing unless one has already learned the meaning of the German, in which case it is unnecessary.[3]

Form criticism, especially as practised by Hermann Gunkel,[4] sharpened biblical critics' awareness that, even in practising the 'literary' criticism described in the previous chapter, they were involved in what we have called 'genre-recognition'. They were dividing the biblical text into portions in order to reassemble these into 'sources' which were conceivable as the work of single authors, because they could be read as having internal coherence – in other words as being texts of some definite *sort* or genre. But a much more important change that resulted from form criticism was that interest shifted from the written to the pre-literary, oral level of many biblical texts. This came about because form critics discovered that there were *Gattungen* embedded within the written form of the text that must originally have had a *Sitz im Leben* in which they would have been *spoken*. And the form critics' contention was that we could not understand such portions of text properly if we tried to read them within *literary* conventions; for the conventions within which they were able to have meaning were essentially the conventions of the social life of ancient Israel, with its great variety of *speech-forms* appropriate to different public occasions, both formal and informal.

To put all this in the terms we have been using so far: the form critics maintained, in effect, that there were great (and hitherto unsuspected) gaps in the competence of biblical scholars. Though they had acquired the competence to read certain *literary* genres – some narratives in their finished form, genealogical lists, some sorts of law-collections – they had not even seen the need to acquire competence in the *oral* genres that were found outside, and even in some cases embedded within, the Pentateuch.[5] Indeed, it was not long before it began to be suspected that virtually the whole Pentateuch, including laws and narratives, rested on oral prototypes. In that case, the conventions within which it was written were not really literary at all, since it was little more than the fixing in

33

writing of material whose ground-rules were wholly those of oral communication.

What social context, then, can have served as the *Sitz im Leben* for handing on (by word of mouth) the traditions of the nation's history that the Pentateuch preserves? Most scholars tended to think of this context as a 'cultic' one: the setting of public worship. It was in its public, liturgical life that Israel transmitted the oral forms that were eventually to be collected into the Pentateuch. Of course it is easy for such a shift of emphasis to make one wonder whether the great guiding question of source criticism – 'Could one man possibly have written such a confused/inconsistent/repetitious text as this?' – does not lose a great deal of its validity. The sorts of consistency it is reasonable to look for in a written text may be very different from what can be expected of a collection of speeches, narrations or sermons, uttered in the context of worship. Different genres demand different sorts of consistency. With this conclusion, which was drawn with special clarity by some Scandinavian scholars,[6] form criticism turned on source analysis and began to bite the hand that fed it. But within mainstream German scholarship form critics continued to build on the work of the 'literary' scholars, and the work of such men as Martin Noth[7] and Gerhard von Rad[8] represents a combination of the two approaches or at any rate a fairly stable truce between them.

Form Criticism and the Psalms: Historical Retrospect

However, these more ambiguous developments belong to a secondary stage in form criticism's understanding of its own role. Let me try to show, with the aid of one particular example, how a form-critical approach is able to provide new possibilities for understanding the biblical text, and how it can extend the reader's competence in knowing what kinds of meanings to look for. Some of the most interesting form-critical work in Old Testament study has been done on the Psalms. In the literary-critical phase of Old Testament study it was assumed that the Psalms were essentially poems written by an individual 'author' or 'poet' expressing his thoughts, desires, praises, etc. Though it was known that Jews and Christians had for many centuries used the Psalms in public, corporate worship, and though the books of Chronicles showed that such a use was already current in the post-exilic age, this was taken to be a secondary development – analogous to the congregational use of some Christian lyric poems as hymns in the modern Church. The Psalms had begun their life as lyric expressions of various personal religious sentiments, although they had been turned by the later Jewish community into 'the hymn-book of the Second Temple'.[9] A correct reading of them, therefore, would be one that attempted to understand them as the personal outpouring of thanksgiving, penitence, grief or whatever other sentiment was to be found in them, by an individual at prayer: not of course David, as pre-critical exegetes had assumed, but still a particular 'poet' rather than a group or a community.

Gunkel, the founder of biblical form criticism, fully shared this view of the biblical psalms. He pointed out, however, that the forms in which they were cast were very highly stereotyped and could be classified under quite a small number of headings. And he went on to argue that many of these psalm-types were only explicable on the supposition that they had originally been developed for use (whether by individuals or by the whole congregation makes no difference) *within the context of public worship*.[10] To take an analogy: given that the political speech is an established *Gattung* in our society, it is possible to produce purely literary imitations of such speeches, never intended for delivery, and no one will be able to tell that such speeches are not 'genuine' unless there is some extraneous evidence; but it would be impossible for 'literary' speeches to exist in a society which had no institution of real speeches and *never had had one*. Just so, the Psalms we have in our Bible might well be purely 'poetic' lyrics: Gunkel thought there were good reasons for holding that they were. But innumerable features in their formal structure show that in that case they must be imitations of, or developments from, *genuinely* public and usable hymns, prayers, laments, thanksgivings and so on. The *prototypes* of those biblical Psalms that are cast in the first person plural, and where God is implored to deliver his people from oppression by their enemies (e.g. Psalms 44, 74, 79) must have developed for use in a *Sitz im Leben* in public worship – for occasions when the congregation of Israelites came together to pray for help in some national crisis. Once such a type of psalm was established, there is no difficulty in believing that individuals took it over as a vehicle to express their private griefs, and to pray for personal relief and salvation; but the form cannot have *originated* in such a use.

One of the most convincing arguments in favour of such an approach was its power to explain features in the Psalms that had been puzzling on the older hypothesis. Readers of the Psalms soon notice that in a good many of these texts there are quite abrupt transitions from petititons for divine aid to expressions of confidence that the prayer has been heard, or even to thanksgiving for benefits received; see, for example, the change of tone at verse 22 in Psalm 22, or at verse 4 in Psalm 54. Again, there is often a curious shift in the imagined speaker in many Psalms, where some verses seem to be spoken by the psalmist himself, others by God, and yet others by some dimly outlined third party. Note, for instance, Psalm 55:22, where a mysterious voice comforts the main speaker in his anguish; or Psalm 91:14–16, where God himself seems to enter to endorse the reassuring remarks of the psalmist, who in any case is not praying but offering advice to some unspecified listener.

All this is very odd and seems to require some explanation beyond the conventional suggestion that the poet is communing with his own (personified) soul or – in the case of the change from prayer to praise – that the very vehemence of his petitions convinces him that God is bound to hear them. The form-critical insight here is that we do not need to read such Psalms as expressive of deep psychological states in order to make sense of them. Once the Psalms are restored to a setting in the public worship of the community, such hypotheses become as unnecessary as they are implausible. The change of speaker can be explained far more simply by suggesting that the speaker actually did change: in other words, that the Psalms in question are the text of a service for which the rubrics are missing, and that in their actual performance different religious functionaries would have uttered different parts of the Psalm. Some portions of the Psalms are cast in the language appropriate to lay worshippers, others to priests, others to – perhaps – 'cultic prophets'; and to read them with understanding we must see that, so far from being inventories of private religious emotions, they are conventionalized liturgical formulas, expressing more or less 'official' religious attitudes and viewpoints and designed for use in the performance of the official cult. Indeed, the very conventional and stylized language of the Psalms has always been a problem for interpretations in terms of the psalmist's personal psychology or spirituality; and the form-critical approach gives a far more satisfying explanation of this.[11]

Two developments which followed closely on these insights of Gunkel's may be briefly mentioned. First, if the *Sitz im Leben* of the Psalms in the Israelite cult throws light on the meaning of the Psalms – or rather on the *kinds* of meaning it makes sense to look for in them – then equally the Psalms themselves become some of our most important evidence for what sorts of activity went on in the Israelite cult. The text and its *Sitz im Leben* are mutually illuminating. We understand the Psalm better if we see that parts of it must have been spoken by a priest; and conversely, if we can see that part of the Psalm must have been spoken by a priest, then we know that priests must have spoken words like these in the course of worship. The force of 'must have' here is debatable and might cause discomfort to a logician: the risk of circularity is undoubtedly very high. However that may be, Gunkel's initial idea was certainly taken up with great enthusiasm by historians of Israelite religion. They saw in it an exciting new tool for extracting from the biblical text vastly more information about the liturgical life of ancient Israel than had ever previously been thought possible; the Bible contains, after all, very little explicit description of the conduct of worship. For the first time, scholars could try to reconstruct the worship at the great festivals in Israel; and this task was undertaken with enormous gusto by Sigmund Mowinckel, a disciple of Gunkel.[12] These reconstructions lie outside the scope of this book; but (however plausible or implausible they are judged to be) they provide ample confirmation of the claims of form criticism to have opened up new avenues in Old Testament study. It was not long before scholars began to reconstruct other occasions in the life of the Israelites, such as the operation of their lawcourts, their commercial practices and their political gatherings, by practising a similar kind of form criticism on *Gattungen* discovered within the historical and prophetic books.[13]

Secondly, and again through the work of Mowinckel, it came to be thought that Gunkel had been somewhat half-hearted in his own application of form-critical techniques to the Psalter. It seemed almost as if he had seen the true answer to the riddles the Psalms presented and then drawn back at the last minute, unable to break decisively enough with the prevailing scholarly tradition. If his method had shown – as it surely had – that the psalm-types to which the biblical Psalms belonged had their origins in actual cultic use, what justification could there be for continuing to hold that all genuine cultic psalms had perished, and that those extant in the Psalter were only late imitations of them? Why could not the Psalms we still have actually *be* the original cultic texts?[14] Once the question is put in that way, it is hard to see why they should not be; and most students of the Psalms up to the present have been persuaded by Mowinckel and his followers that the biblical Psalms are indeed the very same texts that the Israelites used in their public worship.

Speculative and unprovable though it undoubtedly is, it has to be conceded that Mowinckel's hypothesis is an attractive one. Above all it has the merit of not postulating old texts, very like the present Psalms, which have disappeared without trace; in other words, it is a simpler hypothesis than Gunkel's. One effect of Mowinckel's work has been a much earlier dating for many Psalms previously thought post-exilic or even Maccabean (i.e. second century B.C.), and it is now academically 'respectable' to suggest a date in the age of Solomon or even of David for some of the Psalms, especially those such as the 'Psalms of Zion' (46, 48, etc.) which seem to reflect ideas about the Temple and its site that must have been important from its very first construction. That this is not simply a return to a pre-critical reading of the Psalter as the work of David himself should, however, be obvious enough.

Form Criticism and the Psalms: Implications

So much, then, for the wider consequences of the form-critical approach to the Psalms as it affects the social history of ancient Israel, especially the history of its religious institutions, and the dating of certain Old Testament texts. What does form criticism contribute to our understanding of the Psalms themselves? I have already suggested that it makes good sense to see it as offering us a much more developed 'competence', in the pregnant sense of that term developed in chapter 1, in reading these poetic texts. Form criticism is very much a matter of genre-recognition, not just in the sense that it involves a deliberate attempt to describe and define the various genres into which the category 'psalm' may be subdiv-

ided, but in a much more far-reaching sense. By calling attention
to the originally oral and *usable* character of the Psalms it makes us
aware that they must have had a quite concrete *Sitz im Leben*: some
context or set of occasions in the life of the people when they were
recited or sung as part of the public worship of God. Now this
means that, instead of reading them with an eye to the conventions
that we would use in reading modern (or ancient) lyric verse, we
have to read them as liturgical texts; and liturgical texts are essentially impersonal, stylized, multi-purpose texts, reusable on many
similar or even regularly recurring occasions.

How far-reaching the effects of this shift can be may be seen if
we ask what we may mean by the *theology* of the Psalms. On the
pre-form-critical view, this would mean the religious convictions
held by the individuals who wrote the Psalms: their personal faith
with all its emotional colouring and individualistic fervour. Once
we take the vantage-point of a form critic, all that vanishes. It is
not just that the Psalms do not *in fact* express the religious feelings
of particular poets, but rather that they are not the kind of texts
that *could* do so, even in principle. To a form critic, they are public,
official and anonymous examples of a genre that can be paralleled
in many nations in the ancient world. Of course such texts can
become the vehicles of intensely personal prayer and faith, as subsequent Jewish and Christian use abundantly testifies; but in studying
that, we should be studying the meanings worshippers have poured
into them, as part of the history of biblical interpretation, rather
than studying the Psalms themselves.

Now in fact the question what kind of 'meaning' an anonymous,
official text is capable of having is a very complex as well as a very
interesting one, far more complex than many form critics allow for;
indeed, in the work of structuralist critics it comes to dominate
literary study. Early form critics were not yet in a position to see
the shape of the spirit they had summoned up in replacing the
'author' with the 'community' as the creator of the biblical Psalms.
Furthermore, an anxiety to 'use' the results of their work in reconstructing Israel's social and cultic history deflected attention from
its literary potential. But what they had achieved was greatly to
extend the range of biblical scholars' competence. They now had
techniques for recognizing not only literary but also oral genres.
They also had the ability to see what sorts of questions about

meaning and significance it was reasonable to put to passages that bore unmistakable traces of having once belonged to such genres. These passages had been incorporated into written documents, and this had led people in the past to misread them as 'learned' or 'scribal' works: now they could be seen in their true colours again.

Form Criticism and Deuteronomy

A particularly clear illustration of the light that can be shed by a form-critical approach may be seen in recent work on the book of Deuteronomy. There was a time when Deuteronomy could be regarded as the fixed point in Old Testament study. Whatever else might shift, Deuteronomy was the 'book of the law' found in the Temple in the days of Josiah, and its ideas and theology, being thus fixed in the seventh century B.C., could be used to date other Old Testament books and to account for influences and developments between them. Now one way in which this rather simple picture has been modified in recent Old Testament study is through the realization that, whatever the date of the finished form of Deuteronomy, it probably contains much older material and is likely to be the result of a lengthy process of accretion and compilation; and that it has also undergone glossing and expansion in a period later than that of Josiah. In other words, 'literary' or source-critical studies of the book have blurred the clear outlines of the traditional theory.[15] But a far more fundamental change in perspective has resulted from posing what are generally described as form-critical questions. What is the *Sitz im Leben*, the social context and the formal occasion, of a work so variegated as Deuteronomy? How are we to account for the mixing of genres within it: historical surveys, moral exhortation, ceremonial laws, curses, poems and descriptions of solemn rituals? What *kind* of book is it that can contain all these diverse elements and yet have some overall unity and coherence?[16]

Various answers have been proposed to these questions. Probably the most influential, in recent years, has been the suggestion that the formal shape of Deuteronomy is reminiscent of the well-attested ancient genre known as the 'vassal' or 'suzerainty' treaty. This also tends to contain historical narratives (setting out what the overlord has done for his vassal), regulations (enjoining the vassal to behave in certain ways), and curses (outlining the consequences of disloyalty), all within the same document – and, incidentally, certain treaties even exhibit stylistic similarities with some sections of Deuteronomy.[17] If this is correct, then we will need to postulate some context in ancient Israel in which the relationship between God and Israel was presented as analogous to the relationship between the ruler of a great power and his client states, and in which this was done by means of solemn proclamation of the terms of the 'treaty' ('covenant') in the manner of Moses addressing the Israelites.

Many scholars have concluded that some sort of liturgical setting is the only context adequate to explain all this. They have produced reconstructions, varying in detail, of a regularly recurring 'covenant renewal festival' in Israel which would provide a convincing *Sitz im Leben* for Deuteronomy by enabling us to imagine how the various elements in the book were used in the public proclamation and 'preaching' of the covenant between God and his people.[18] Similar explanations are available for the Ten Commandments – which in their present form exhibit something like the same structure, in miniature, as Deuteronomy – and even for other law collections in the Pentateuch.[19] It is clear, however, that if what was proclaimed in such ceremonies and is enshrined in Deuteronomy is still to be described as 'law', this term will have to be understood very differently from its usual English sense. To read 'law-books' in the Old Testament (Exodus, Leviticus, Deuteronomy) will plainly entail acquiring a rather different set of conventions than would be needed to read, say, an English Act of Parliament.

Whether or not Deuteronomy was Josiah's 'law-book', such approaches as these are bound to give a fresh meaning to what a 'law-book' is, and to result in differences even in the exegesis of specific passages. To take only one example: one of the most characteristic ideas of Deuteronomy is that the Israelites should 'love' God with all their 'heart, soul, and might' (Deut. 6:4); and we naturally tend to read this as an injunction to show fervent and intimate devotion to a very 'personal' God. But a number of comparative studies have suggested that 'love' is often a technical term of ancient vassal-treaties, in which the vassal is urged to 'love', i.e. be entirely loyal, politically, to his overlord, and not enter into intrigues with opposing powers; and in such contexts (so it is said) it has no emotional overtones. If Deuteronomy is indeed a text intended for reading at a public ceremony modelled on the ceremonies at which political treaties were solemnly ratified, then its injunctions to 'love' God may well be understood as using the technical vocabulary of the vassal-treaty to stress the central concern of the covenant: namely, Israel's obligation to worship Yahweh alone and to eschew all other gods.[20] But it is misread if deep emotional undertones are detected in it. Such a conclusion would have far-reaching consequences for our understanding of the 'message' of Deuteronomy (I do not say that I think it correct, but simply cite it as an illustration of what form criticism can achieve); and it is clear that it results from the form-critical insight that Deuteronomy is to be assigned to a particular genre or *Gattung*, with a particular social setting within which only some sorts of meaning are possible – those in fact which are permitted by the conventions of the genre. It must be said, in conclusion, that by no means all scholars share the view just presented of the genre of Deuteronomy. Some prefer to see it as much closer to a 'wisdom' book, and hence as having its *Sitz im Leben* in the classroom or the family.[21] In those contexts the 'hortatory' material takes on far less the tone of public 'proclamation' and is read as having a quieter, more domestic flavour of persuasion and advice; and the exhortation to 'love' God once more regains its personal and emotional appeal!

This exposition of possible form-critical approaches to Deuteronomy may well make the reader feel that the ground is shifting under his feet. We do not know how to read Deuteronomy until we know which genre to assign it to; yet there seems no unambiguous way of deciding on its genre. To some extent this certainly does mean that form criticism can never be an exact method. But that, as we have seen, is not necessarily to say that it is suspect: all decisions about genre rest on informed intuition, rather than on knock-down proof, but some are more plausible than others. But it is clear that a good part of the problem, in the case of Deuteronomy, is simply that we do not know enough about the genres available in ancient Israel. However hard we may want to argue the case for Deuteronomy as a (metaphorical) vassal-treaty, or for Deuteronomy as a 'wisdom book', we must admit, if we are candid, that it is not *obviously* very close to being either. There is nothing else quite like it in the Old Testament or elsewhere. This being so, we are faced with the problem that always confronts us when we try to read books of no known genre, that our understanding is bound to be more or less imperfect however hard we try. In the end we have to try and reconstruct the conventions of the genre from the only extant example, and this is obviously going to be a hazardous undertaking. We can imagine the dangers by thinking for a moment of the definition of a symphony we might reconstruct if the only evidence were Schubert's *Unfinished*, without that title to serve as a warning. Deuteronomy, for all we know, may be a very atypical 'law-book'.

But if form criticism achieves nothing else, at least it helps us to see the limits of our knowledge and to define more closely the sorts of things we would need to know if we were to make any further progress. By bringing the question of genre-recognition more clearly to the forefront of our attention, it helps us to map out the limits of our competence and perhaps to extend them a little.

Redaction Criticism

The two methods we have examined so far, 'literary' and form criticism, arose from the observation that the Old Testament text is puzzling in various ways. Both ask, 'How could one author possibly have written this text?' Source criticism then proceeds by breaking the text up into sections that one author *could* have written; form criticism detects elements embedded within the text, or aspects of the finished text, which suggest that it was not *written* so much as used in particular settings whose conventions account for features inexplicable in literary terms. Both methods tend, and are often criticized for tending, to fragment the text, to cut it up into pieces that can be more readily understood. But we have seen that, so far from stemming from a sort of disrespect for the text, this is essentially the product of an overwhelming desire to understand, to perceive the text as intelligible – a desire which is frustrated unless the text *is* cut into pieces.

However, the fact remains that the finished text of a work as complex, 'incomprehensible', genre-less as the Pentateuch does now exist and must presumably have been assembled by *someone*: it is not a natural phenomenon. And the person who assembled it (like the people who collected the Psalms or edited the books of the prophets) no doubt intended to produce a comprehensible work, and had some notion of its genre. As we saw, no one can produce 'just' a text. So even when we have divided Old Testament books up into sections or fragments, the question remains how we should read the longer complexes into which they have subsequently been arranged. With that question we reach the next method we must review: redaction criticism.

Further Reading

G. M Tucker, *Form Criticism of the Old Testament.* Philadelphia 1971

S. Mowinckel, *The Psalms in Israel's Worship.* Oxford 1962

J. H. Hayes (ed.), *Old Testament Form Criticism.* San Antonio, Texas, 1974

A. Alt, 'The Origins of Israelite Law' in his *Essays on Old Testament History and Religion* (Oxford 1966), pp. 79–132

4

REDACTION CRITICISM

It is not very grateful to consider how little the succession of editors
has added to this author's power of pleasing. He was read, admired,
studied, and imitated, while he was yet deformed with all the impropri-
eties which ignorance and neglect could accumulate upon him.

Samuel Johnson, *Preface to Shakespeare*, 1765 in *Works*
(Yale edn. vol. vi. New Haven and London 1968) p. 111

Preliminary Reading

Judges
Isaiah 1—12
G. von Rad, *Genesis* (London 1961), pp. 13–42

Rediscovering the Redactor

In discovering 'sources' in such works as the Pentateuch, literary
critics simultaneously discovered 'redactors', the Israelite scribes,
archivists or collectors who must have been responsible for combining the sources into the finished works we now encounter in the
Old Testament. But throughout the formative period of source
analysis, no one took much interest in these shadowy figures. For
one thing, the excitement of reconstructing the earlier stages in the
text's growth deflected interest from its final form; for another, it
was probably felt that the redactors could hardly have been people
of much originality or even intelligence, or they would have made
a better job of their work, and not left the tell-tale traces of inconsistency and meandering narrative thread that has enabled modern
scholarship to reconstruct the raw materials with which they plied
their tedious trade. The only active contribution the redactors of

the Pentateuch could be credited with was to be seen in little 'link' passages papering over the more palpable gaps between two sources; or in the occasional phrase which was designed to persuade the reader that the text was a smooth, continuous whole, but which was so ineptly obtruded into the narrative that it actually made matters worse.[1] A classic (or notorious) example would be Genesis 26:1. This chapter tells a story about Isaac and Rebekah which already occurs twice in Genesis as a story about Abraham and Sarah (12:10–20 and 20:1–18). Thinking no doubt that the reader will hardly believe his eyes if yet a third version of the story is presented without comment, the redactor resolves on disarming criticism, like speakers who begin, 'I make no apology for using a cliché . . .'. His source began, 'Now there was a famine in the land'; and the alert reader is bound to remember that this was just the problem that led to all the trouble in Genesis 12. So he adds, nervously, 'besides the former famine, that was in the days of Abraham'.[2] If that is the sort of thing redactors do once they leave the safety of their source material, it is not surprising that they were of small interest to literary critics.

But in both Old and New Testament study (for some reason it is in the latter that the *term* 'redaction criticism' is more often used)[3] the very success of literary and form criticism meant that these maligned figures were bound eventually to become the object of more interest. Once critics had established with a fair degree of confidence what the contents of books like the Pentateuch originally looked like, and how very different they had once been from what they are now, it was only a matter of time before someone would think it worth asking how, then, they came to be changed and combined in such puzzling ways, and what interests and objectives were at work in the process. In a way, the odder the redactors' work appeared to be, the more it deserved investigation in its own right. Besides, there were also the *historical* achievements of source and form criticism to be borne in mind. If a study of the raw materials of the Pentateuch could tell us so much about the history of Israelite religion, and an analysis of its pre-literary forms about Israel's social institutions, then presumably one might learn at least as much about the later stages of both by investigating the intentions and assumptions of those who put the raw materials together. So for various reasons biblical scholars began to study the collectors and editors of the biblical books, and came to see them much less as mere technicians and far more as writers with their own beliefs, theological concerns and literary skills. The tendency can be summed up in the suggestion made by the great Jewish scholar, Franz Rosenzweig, that 'R' (the conventional symbol for 'redactor') should be regarded as standing for *rabbenu*, 'our Master', since it is from the redactors' hands that we receive the Scriptures, and we cannot shrug them off.

This remark is cited in Gerhard von Rad's classic *Genesis* commentary[4]; and though he rejects it as it stands, it is through his work above all that the redaction-critical approach has really established itself in Old Testament studies. Von Rad is always anxious to move beyond the mere reconstruction of earlier stages in the growth of the biblical text and to begin to listen to the redactor, to ask how *he* meant us to read his finished text, and what he was trying to tell us. Besides his work on Genesis, von Rad wrote extensively on the theology of the 'Yahwist' (the redactor of the 'J' strand in the Pentateuch as a whole).[5] Others have written on the compiler of the 'Deuteronomistic History' (Joshua—2 Kings),[6] on the theology of the 'Chronicler' (responsible for 1 and 2 Chronicles and perhaps for Ezra-Nehemiah),[7] and on the intentions of those who edited the various prophetic books.[8] In New Testament studies redaction criticism is a particularly flourishing industry.[9]

Genealogies

One curious resemblance between redaction criticism and the methods already considered is its tendency to be most fruitful in handling the aspects or portions of the biblical text that are least attractive to the general reader. Source critics like nothing better than a narrative that is repetitious, inconsistent and rambling; form critics thrive on incoherent collections of unrelated sayings, like some of the chapters of Isaiah, and delight in stereotyped formulas and conventional phrases. With redaction criticism we find that even the genealogies, stock-in-trade of bad jokes about the unedifying quality of the Old Testament, have become interesting and theologically significant.[10] While it would be too much to say that a redaction critic reads 1 Chronicles with mounting excitement, there can be no doubt that he often sees much of great significance in such traditionally despised works.

Among genealogical lists in the Old Testament, one that has attracted particular interest among redaction critics is the one in Genesis 10, the so-called 'Table of Nations', which is generally assigned to the priestly source ('P') of the Pentateuch, though it may contain excerpts from other sources as well. On the face of it, this is unpromising material in which to look for the 'theology' of the priestly source. Older commentators were interested in it chiefly as typical of the sort of material favoured by 'P' – archival lists or catalogues, likely to have been preserved at sanctuaries: the very material, in fact, that would interest a religious official, and so justify us in using 'priestly' as a convenient shorthand description for such a source. But the theological significance of the Table of Nations turns out to be very great indeed, once we attend not just to its contents but to the place it occupies within the whole corpus of 'P' material. The function of Genesis 10 is to link the history of Abraham and his descendants, the chosen people of God, with the so-called 'primeval history' of the preceding chapters, and so to present the history of Israel as the climax and chief purpose of the history of the whole world.

There are two theological ideas being expressed here, both of which would be regarded by many scholars as typical of the outlook of 'P'. First, it is often said that 'creation' in the ancient Near East generally, and in Israel in early times, was thought of as belonging to a timeless, 'mythical' realm, unconnected with the time-scale in terms of which human history is registered. If this is true, then the priestly writer's purpose in linking it with the history of Abraham by means of the Table of Nations represents a very far-reaching innovation.[11] The creation now becomes what it has remained for the Judaeo-Christian tradition ever since, an 'event': the first event in world history, it may be called. And this has important consequences for the character of God as understood in the religious tradition of Israel, since it means that one and the same God is responsible *both* for creating the world *and* for directing its subsequent history – which in many religions is not the case; and also that he has a purpose which is already implicit from the moment the world is formed, a purpose which works itself out over an immensely long span of time but which is never frustrated or lost

48

in the intricate currents of history. The movement of God's plan towards the establishment of Abraham's descendants in Palestine does not begin when he intervenes in a history that is already under way – as we might suppose, if the Genesis account began (as 'J' may have done) in Genesis 12. It goes back without a break to the moment of creation itself. Furthermore, although Abraham is specially chosen, all the nations of the world are within this God's control, and he has something in mind for them all, since all are included in the account provided by Genesis 10. (All mankind, of course, is descended from the three sons of Noah, and the Table of Nations covers all the known world.)

But secondly, and conversely, the very insistence in this chapter that God does control the destinies of *all* the nations makes the choice of Abraham and his offspring alone as the bearers of God's ultimate plan that much more striking. No one can misunderstand the stories that follow as tales of a merely local or tribal god, bound by necessity to his own people, once it has been made clear that he directs the courses of all the peoples of the earth and could, in principle, choose any one of them as his own special possession. Here is a whole theology expressed, not in the overt meanings of a text considered on its own – for no doubt the Table of Nations existed before it was placed at Genesis 10[12] – but in *the arrangement of source-material in a significant way*. The interest lies not in the genealogy itself, but in what the redactor has done with it.

Another, related example may help to show the versatility and interest of a redaction-critical approach, and also some of its hazards. It comes from the work of B. S. Childs and lies on the borderline between redaction criticism proper and what he calls 'the canonical method', which will be discussed in chapter 6.[13] In traditional source analysis of the Pentateuch, one of the best known of all hypotheses is that Genesis 1 belongs to the 'P' source and Genesis 2, or most of it, to 'J', which is generally considered the older of the two creation accounts. There has, however, never been complete unanimity about the exact point of division.[14] As a rule, the 'J' version is said to begin in Genesis 2:4b – 'In the day that the LORD God made the earth and the heavens' – which is formally very close to other ancient Near Eastern creation stories: thus the Babylonian text *enuma elish* begins, 'When on high the heaven had not been named, and below the earth had not been given a name'.[15]

On the other hand the 'P' account appears to end with Genesis 2:3, 'So God blessed the seventh day, and hallowed it, because on it God rested from all his work which he had done in creation.' The half-verse, 2:4a, floats loosely between the two narratives. It is no doubt to be regarded as a 'redactional' note, either by the compiler of the 'P' source or by the redactor of the final form of Genesis; and it is generally taken as a *concluding* formula, analogous to 'Here endeth the second lesson': 'What you have just read is an account of how heaven and earth came into being.' If it is read in this way, then the fact that what follows is an alternative account of the same events becomes very plain.

But Childs points out that the expression 'These are the generations of . . .' is elsewhere in Genesis never used as a conclusion, but always as an *introductory* formula. It always leads into a genealogical list, in which the history is carried forward a further stage, and events to be narrated in detail are linked with earlier narratives. Examples are Genesis 5:1, 10:1 and 11:10; compare also Numbers 3:1. In such genealogies the Pentateuchal narrative pauses, while the reader is given a sort of map with which he can orientate himself in the history to date, and so grasp what the events about to be described imply about relations between various groups within Israel or between the different nations of the world. Childs's suggestion is that the redactional device in Genesis 2:4a functions in a similar way. It is not the conclusion of the 'P' account, but a heading or title for the 'J' account that follows; and its function is precisely to mitigate the problem caused by the fact (which is so obvious to a trained source critic) that the two accounts are in origin not consecutive but alternative. Its purpose is to *constrain the reader* to understand Genesis 2:4bff. (J) not as an account of what happened *next* – which would inevitably lead him to detect the artificiality of the arrangement – but as a more explicit statement of the detailed course of some of the events touched only lightly in the 'P' version: specifically, the creation of man and woman, mentioned in Genesis 1:26–27. Instead of taking 2:4b as the beginning of an independent creation story, referring to the creation of the world in a subordinate temporal clause because that was the conventional ancient Near Eastern way of referring to it, we are forced by the insertion of 2:4a to understand it as an oblique reference back to the account in Genesis 1: 'When all the events just

50

mentioned were taking place, things had reached the stage of the earth being watered by a mist by the time God created man; and when he did so, it happened like this – he planted a garden . . .'

The formula 'These are the generations of the heavens and the earth . . .' thus means something like 'Here is a circumstantial account of the events that followed the creation of heaven and earth' (lit. the 'descendants' of heaven and earth). This ensures that the 'J' narrative will be read (as in fact it was read by most readers before the rise of source criticism, and as it is no doubt still read by many) as simply a detailed exposition of the part of Genesis 1 that most nearly concerns mankind, the account of its own origins. The redactor who achieved this aim was clearly no mere collector, pasting various creation stories into an album; he was a creative writer, with important theological purposes of his own, blending disparate and partly inconsistent materials into a coherent whole.

'Trivial' Details Rehabilitated

A redaction-critical approach has many advantages in helping us to read the Old Testament with understanding. It takes the compilers of the various books seriously and tries to get inside their minds, to see what they were about when they combined source materials in ways that are superficially so puzzling. It has the great merit of refusing to treat externally unattractive or bizarre features of the text as necessarily a barrier to the modern reader's penetrating its meaning, or on the other hand as merely trivial and culture-bound incidentals that can safely be ignored when we are looking for the 'message' of the biblical writers. Thus although the redaction critic is interested in what may be called the 'ideas' of biblical authors rather than in minute historical details of the growth of the text, no method could be further than redaction criticism from that cavalier indifference to the actual form of the text that is sometimes found in more superficial attempts at stating the 'theology' of the Bible. For example, biblical critics have often countered a fundamentalist insistence on the exact details of the events of creation in Genesis 1 by maintaining that none of these details matters, since the chapter is 'really about' the *fact* that God is creator, not the *process* of creation.[16] But this kind of casual indifference to the verbal form of the text finds no echo in the painstaking work of redaction critics, who are as concerned with every minute verbal nuance as is the most committed proponent of verbal inspiration.

It is, indeed, with redaction criticism that we come closest to what the student trained in other literatures would mean by 'literary criticism': the attempt to give what is sometimes called a 'close reading' of the text, analysing how the author/editor achieves his effects, why he arranges his material as he does, and above all what devices he uses to give unity and coherence to his work.[17] In fact, if we wish to relate the achievements of redaction criticism to our theme of literary competence – the attempt to discover what kinds of literature the Old Testament consists of, and so how it should appropriately be read – we may say that redaction critics see far more Old Testament books as works of something like conscious art than did source and form critics.

The latter, though deeply concerned with reading and understanding the text for its own sake, are nearly always looking beyond or behind the text to the historical events or social institutions that produced it and can therefore be reconstructed from it; and this tends to produce a certain insensitivity to what may (non-technically) be called 'literary' questions: questions of style, structure and aesthetic skill. Redaction critics, by contrast, are interested in the possibility of reading Old Testament documents as the works of creative writers – writers whose creativity may be seen in the great difference between their comparatively crude and fragmentary raw materials and the polished works of art that they have produced from them, rich in allusion, structural subtlety and thematic unity.[18]

Trivial Details Exaggerated?

Once the matter is put in this way, however, it is hard not to feel a certain unease about whether the difference between the conventions of modern literature and those of the biblical writers is being fully appreciated.[19] May there not be some danger of anachronism in attributing so much conscious art to these writers? It is, indeed, very difficult to decide this issue without in some measure begging the question. An opponent of redaction criticism will tend to argue that there is no external evidence (i.e. evidence outside the text in question itself) to show that the 'compiler' of the Pentateuch was anything more than just that. He will suggest that many of the deep meanings critics detect in this compiler's work – such as in the two examples we have examined – are being read into the text because it is being approached with modern literary presuppositions about what constitutes consistency, unity, 'richness' and so forth. The committed redaction critic will reply that he is not *forcing* the evidence of the text or even deliberately looking for evidence of literary art. He is simply clearing his mind of the prejudice (for it is no more) that ancient authors did not operate within conventions analogous to those of modern literature. Once the text is approached with an open mind, evidence of literary patterning, of skilful manipulation of theme and imagery, of dovetailing of disparate sources simply springs from the page.

A detached observer may soon detect a familiar circularity on both sides of this disagreement. Redaction critics can often make out a good case for their interpretations; but these interpretations are seldom so completely convincing that they can be said to *prove* a skilful redactor has been at work. If there were good external evidence to show that the arrangement of the text was simply an accident, we should be unlikely to reject that evidence simply because a redaction critic could give us a plausible account of what the text might have meant, if the arrangement had been deliberate! What I have in mind is this. The interpretations of Genesis 2:4a and Genesis 10 given above certainly seem possible and meaningful; we do not *immediately* want to say, 'No ancient author could possibly have meant that.' But on the other hand, if someone produced some evidence that seemed to show Genesis 2:4a was a mere marginal gloss that had somehow crept into the text by mistake, or that Genesis 10 had originally stood in quite a different part of Genesis, that would probably be enough to talk us out of the redaction-critical interpretations. We should probably not think that the interpretations were so convincing that they would make us want to challenge the external evidence: we shouldn't suggest, for example, that Genesis 2:4a could not really be simply a gloss, despite the evidence for this, because the redaction-critical interpretation was so obviously correct. To put it another way: when we *know* that we are definitely dealing with a redactor who was deliberately altering his raw materials, we tend to accept redaction critics' explanations of what he was setting out to do with them; hence the willingness of all biblical scholars to accept redaction-critical interpretations of

1 and 2 Chronicles, which are unquestionably a fresh redaction of the materials in Samuel and Kings. But when we do not know how much freedom our redactor had with his material, we take rather more convincing that the critics have understood him, for many of the 'deliberate effects' that they analyse could so easily be happy accidents. And we are specially likely to be hard to convince if the redaction critic's reading seems to imply that the redactor must have worked with literary conventions that seem more at home in modern than in ancient literature – though we will need to be fully aware that our ideas of what an ancient redactor 'could have' meant are just as open to question as a redaction critic's.

An example of what I mean can be found in Martin Noth's discussion of Deuteronomy 2:16—3:11.[20] This passage records how in consecutive campaigns the Israelites overcame the kings Sihon of Heshbon and Og of Bashan; but a glance at a map of biblical Palestine will show that this is geographically unlikely, in view of the fact that Bashan is a great distance from Heshbon, and anyway not on the Israelites' route into the promised land. According to Noth, the reason why both campaigns 'had to be' placed in the period before the crossing of the Jordan, although this was historically implausible, is that the Deuteronomistic History is structured in such a way that all the Israelites' wars in Transjordan are fought in the lifetime of Moses, and all those in Palestine west of the Jordan under Joshua and the judges. What we have here is theological history and theological geography; the redaction of the sources of Joshua-Kings involved sorting material into certain pigeon-holes, and Sihon and Og turned out to be in the same pigeon-hole when the material came to be written up.

This is an interesting suggestion (reminiscent of some of Hans Conzelmann's suggestions about Lucan geography[21]); but it is surely rather vulnerable to attack. Suppose, for example, that we *knew* (not that we ever shall) that Sihon and Og were already linked in tradition long before the deuteronomistic redactor came along; or suppose that we discovered the whole work had been compiled in Babylonia, and that the author had no idea where Heshbon was anyway. Surely in that case we should say that Noth's hypothesis, attractive though it is, must be given up: he would be seeing significance where there was no significance at all. Now the problem is that we know, in reality, so little about the compilers of Old Testament books that we can *hardly ever* be sure that what we are interpreting is an arrangement they intended, rather than a mere accident. In particular, we do not know that the types of writing available in ancient Israel included genres for which the conventions of deep internal coherence, studied allusiveness and precisely nuanced phrasing – the conventions with which redaction critics mostly work – were appropriate. There may indeed be much more order in apparently rambling collections such as the Pentateuch than earlier scholars supposed. It may have been wrong to dismiss these works as unclassifiable, genre-less, mere accidental anthologies. On the other hand there may be less order in them than redaction critics suppose; and the deep internal coherence now being detected in them may owe more to the modern reader than to the ancient writer.[22]

Yet on the other hand, there are places where the unprejudiced reader is likely to feel that there really are signs of careful and deliberate redaction. In case the above remarks are felt to do scant justice to Noth's monumental work, it may be said that the evidence he uncovers of deliberate patterning in Judges,[23] above all, is likely to convince the most sceptical opponent of redaction criticism. One cannot read Judges without noticing the scheme, frequently repeated, of rebellion, oppression, penitence, deliverance through the success of a 'judge', and 'rest' – lasting twenty, forty or eighty years. However much the individual stories which serve to fill out this theme may be traditional and unaffected by any touching-up on the historian's part, it seems hard to resist the suggestion that he has woven them together and given them a unity, as part of the history of 'Israel' (understood as a single people) within the purposes of a just but patient and forbearing God. We misread these stories unless we take account of the framework in which they are set. The framework is part of the meaning; and the recovery and proper understanding of this framework is accomplished by redaction criticism, which thereby clearly delineates the character of a particular literary genre – the theological history-work – whose conventions and setting were not previously appreciated. So there is much in the claim that redaction criticism adds to our competence in reading the Old Testament, however much its practitioners may at times overplay their hand.

The Disappearing Redactor

I drew attention in the last chapter to one rather unexpected feature of the form-critical approach: that, although it arose out of a full acceptance of the results of source analysis and a desire to build on them, it tended at times to suggest that source criticism rested on a mistake about the true character of the biblical material, and thus could be seen as partly undermining its own foundations. However, form criticism could exist even if there were no source criticism; its character would be affected by the demise of the earlier method, but it would probably survive. With redaction criticism a similar but far more serious danger lies half-hidden beneath its impressive surface; and we ought to give it some consideration now, since from it we shall be better able to understand one of the strands of motivation that lead into more recent approaches such as structuralism and 'canon criticism'. The danger may best be illustrated by describing the technique for performing a biblical critic's conjuring trick, which we may call 'The Disappearing Redactor'.[24]

Let us first look closely at the Pentateuch. We shall see at once (if we are familiar with the work of literary criticism) that it contains innumerable inconsistencies and incoherences, which are difficult to understand on the hypothesis that it is a single, unified work by one author. (This author, since he obviously does not exist, may safely be called Moses). We can see that there are clearly two different versions of the creation story, that the Flood narrative is rambling and contains incompatible details (how long did the Flood last? How many animals went into the ark?), that the style swings incomprehensibly from lively narrative to ponderous catalogues, and so on; hence we can readily deduce the existence of several sources of varying ages and characters. We are alerted to the presence of these sources, in fact, because we can see that the text reads *awkwardly* rather than smoothly. Once we are quite clear about this, we can ask a redaction critic to go to work on the text, and he will be able to show us how the final redactor has gone about dealing with the inconsistencies and awkwardnesses we have seen. The redactor, it will appear, has moulded the different sources together with great skill and has succeeded, out of very unpromising material, in producing a harmonious and unified text. Thus – to revert to an earlier example – the redactor of Genesis has so cleverly integrated the two accounts of creation, 'J' and 'P', by inserting Genesis 2:4a, that they no longer read roughly and awkwardly, and so he has achieved (what one could barely have believed possible) a text which the reader is deceived into thinking both smooth and consistent. We must watch redaction critics working through many texts in this way, growing increasingly convinced by their arguments and grasping fully how skilful and ingenious the Pentateuchal redactor has been. The stage is then set for the trick to begin.

The trick is simply this. The more impressive the critic makes the redactor's work appear, the more he succeeds in showing that the redactor has, by subtle and delicate artistry, produced a simple and coherent text out of the diverse materials before him; the more also he reduces the evidence on which the existence of those sources was established in the first place. No conjuror is required for this trick: the redaction critic himself causes his protégé to disappear. If, say, Genesis 2 follows on so naturally from Genesis 1, then this is indeed evidence for the skill of the redactor *if we know that Genesis 1 and 2 were originally distinct*; but the only ground we have for thinking that they were is the observation that Genesis 2 does *not* follow on naturally from Genesis 1. Thus, if redaction criticism plays its hand too confidently, we end up with a piece of writing so coherent that no division into sources is warranted any longer; and the sources and the redactor vanish together in a puff of smoke, leaving a single, freely composed narrative with, no doubt, a single author. It may be remembered that we casually conceded that the author of the Pentateuch may just as well be called Moses, since he does not exist to trouble us; but it is not difficult to imagine that the trick we have just described is particularly dear to the hearts of fundamentalist opponents of non-conservative biblical criticism, and in their hands it can well become a convenient means of showing that the critics are hoist with their own petard, or (to give our analogy its last run) that when the magic box that contained the redactor is opened, not only is the redactor gone, but Moses himself has stepped into his shoes: a very frightening prospect indeed for a higher critic of any kind.

I do not think we need to fear this last twist in the tail of the trick; but that there is substance in the vanishing act itself should be plain. Evidence that will show how sources have been edited to the point where all inconsistencies between them have been removed is also evidence that there never was a diversity of sources in the first place. It would be different, of course, if we possessed the Pentateuchal redactors' raw materials in an unedited form. Then we could indeed say what their contribution had been, just as we can say, broadly speaking, what the Chronicler has done, because we have most of his sources in Samuel and Kings. But the peculiar difficulty of the Pentateuch is that we have only the finished product; and we cannot argue *both* that it is so full of inconsistencies that it must be highly composite *and* that it is so consistent and well-integrated that the redactor must have had a masterly touch with his source materials. One or other must be given up: and I have no doubt at all (against the fundamentalist position just described) that it is the consistency of redaction that must yield. While it is undoubtedly sometimes possible to see that a redactor has tried with some success to bring order out of chaos, it is in the nature of the case impossible to identify a *perfect* redactor, since *ex hypothesi* his perfection would consist in having removed all the inconsistencies which enable us to know that he exists at all.

In principle, then, redaction criticism is a perfectly reasonable approach; and in practice there are texts even in the Old Testament where it can be remarkably illuminating (I have instanced Chronicles). But more often than not it is either unnecessary, because the text is a unity anyway, and we are competent to read it, or unsuccessful, because the inconsistencies that remain, the very inconsistencies that enable us to know the text is a redacted one, are such that we remain in doubt as to how it should be read in its finished form. If we knew what the compiler of the Pentateuch was trying to achieve – if we knew what kind of book the finished Pentateuch could be classified as – then we might be helped to read it by seeing what the redactor had done to his source material. But we do not really know; the redactor's mind is far more opaque to us than we should like to think.

Is the Old Testament Unreadable?

With this conclusion we may seem to have run ourselves into a blind alley. We have seen, certainly, that much can be known on the historical level about how Old Testament literature is to be read appropriately, about its conventions and genres, and about the kinds of meaning it is capable of having within the context in which it was produced. But this knowledge seems to be linked to a need to analyse and break up biblical books into their component parts. Attempts at reading larger complexes, such as have been made by redaction critics, seem likely to meet with only very partial success. The problem which gave rise to 'literary' criticism, the earliest of the methods here surveyed – the problem that most Old Testament books cannot be read *as* anything, that they cannot be classified in any system known to us – seems as far as ever from being solved.

Does this mean that we are doomed for ever to a competence in reading this literature which does not reach beyond the parts of which it is composed, and that we can never become competent to read a whole book, a collection like the Pentateuch or, least of all, the Old Testament as a whole? It is not difficult to imagine that biblical critics feel unwilling to acquiesce in so gloomy an estimate of the possibilities open to them and have begun to look for ways out of the corner they have talked themselves into. It seems to many that the only way forward lies through acknowledging that not much more *can* be achieved at the purely historical level – that we cannot know what the Pentateuch as a whole *meant* to its final redactors – but then shifting our ground so that the historical level is transcended, and we can ask 'What does the Pentateuch *mean*?' But such a question has a very large range of possible meanings, and there are many different literary and philosophical backgrounds against which it can be asked. The rest of the book will consist largely of an attempt to explore some of these and to evaluate the prospects for biblical study of taking them into account.

First, however, I propose to pause, and to spend a chapter illustrating further the methods already discussed. We shall see how, when they are applied to a particular book – in this case, Ecclesiastes – they throw up all the problems that we have already seen arising in general terms. We shall also see that, if thought through consistently, they bring us back to just the same difficulty with which this chapter has concluded. This difficulty is essentially that we can see many possible meanings in the text, but hardly know to whom to attribute them: to an author, a redactor, a community or even, in some ill-defined sense, to 'the text itself'. This last possibility will lead us directly into the question raised in the last paragraph, whether a text can mean (now) something that was not meant (then). And so we shall be ready to tackle the most recent additions to the techniques of biblical criticism: canon criticism and literary structuralism.

Further Reading

M. Noth, *The Deuteronomistic History*. Sheffield 1981

R. E. Clements, 'Patterns in the Prophetic Canon' in *Canon and Authority*, ed. G. W. Coats and B. O. Long (Philadelphia 1977), pp. 42–55

N. Perrin, *What is Redaction Criticism?* Philadelphia and London 1970

5

AN EXAMPLE: ECCLESIASTES

Stars, I have seen them fall,
  But when they drop and die
No star is lost at all
  From all the star-sown sky.
The toil of all that be
  Helps not the primal fault;
It rains into the sea,
  And still the sea is salt.

A. E. Housman, 'More Poems' in
The Collected Poems of A. E. Housman. London 1939

If the high counsels of the Lord of Thunder
Seek'st thou to know with singleness of heart,
Look to the highest of the heights of heaven,
See where the stars still keep their ancient peace.

Boethius, de philosophiae consolatione iv. 6. 1–5,
tr. Helen Waddell in <i>Medieval Latin Lyrics.</i> London 1939</div>

Preliminary Reading

Ecclesiastes
G. von Rad, *Wisdom in Israel* (London 1972), pp. 190–206, 226–37
J. L. Crenshaw, *Old Testament Wisdom: An Introduction* (Atlanta 1981),
    pp. 126–48

A Sample Study

It is generally easier to grasp the essential differences between various methods of study if one sees them being applied to the same subject matter. With this in mind I shall try in this chapter to consolidate our discussion so far by showing how the various methods we have been examining work in practice when they are applied to one comparatively short text, the book of Ecclesiastes or Qoheleth. Since in my experience discussions of biblical methods rarely use this book by way of illustration, there may be some advantage in choosing it for our purposes; it has hardly ever been a focus for serious controversy, and (by the standards of Old Testament study) not very much has been written about it. Nevertheless, the purpose of this chapter is by no means to present an original, or even a personal, interpretation of the book, but simply to see what has been or might be said about it if the methods so far discussed are applied. The reader is not being asked to accept one interpretation of the book rather than another, but only to take note of what is involved in deciding among the different interpretations made available by various kinds of criticism.

Most people who are familiar with Ecclesiastes will think of it as a rather pessimistic or even cynical book, expressing the conviction that very many of the normal activities of life are ultimately pointless and unsatisfying, and that death levels all differences. On the other hand, they may also think of it as a work rich in shrewd observations about human foibles, which puts forward a recipe for contentment in the midst of ultimate pessimism by stressing the need to accept that all things happen in an appropriate way and at an appropriate time: the most famous passage being, of course, 3:1–8, 'For everything there is a season, and a time for every matter under heaven; a time to be born, and a time to die . . .'. Despite the repeated assertion that 'all is vanity' (i.e. pointlessness, emptiness), the book ends with the advice to 'fear God, and keep his commandments; for this is the whole duty of man' (12:13), thereby providing the title of one of the most popular books of moral advice and devotion of the seventeenth century (*The Whole Duty of Man*, 1658). But before the rise of critical scholarship this juxtaposition of scepticism and moralism was not, apparently, felt to be particularly puzzling or to require explanation: the mixture was simply part of the author's make-up.

Literary Criticism

The earliest critical discussions appeared when scholars trained in Pentateuchal studies began to notice inconsistencies and changes of direction in Ecclesiastes reminiscent of those that had been found in the Pentateuch. Even if it was possible to read the book as fairly consistent, this meant playing down both some very sceptical passages (e.g. 3:19) and some very orthodox ones (e.g. 12:13), thus failing to do justice to either.[1] The assertion that 'one fate comes to all, to the righteous and the wicked, to the good and the evil, to the clean and the unclean, to him who sacrifices and him who does not sacrifice' (9:2) is surely deeply subversive of basic Old Testament faith in divine justice and the moral ordering of the world; while 3:1–9, on closer inspection, proves in its context to be more nearly a statement of a rather gloomy determinism than a serene acceptance of the regular cycles of life and nature. On the other hand, the concluding verses of the book do not simply add a note of stern piety; they effectively undermine the book's message, by assuring the reader that 'God will bring every deed into judgment' (12:14). According to this, the free choices of men *do* matter to God, and the same fate does *not* befall all alike. With these observations the way was clearly open for some sort of 'literary' analysis similar to that which had proved so successful in handling the inconsistencies of the Pentateuch.

On the whole, however, early critics did not conclude that Ecclesiastes was composed of two or more separate sources, but preferred a hypothesis akin to what in Pentateuchal studies was known as the 'supplementary hypothesis': that a basic text had been supplemented by the additon of fragmentary extra material of a different character.[2] The original Qoheleth was a work of considerable though not wholly unacceptable scepticism, which had been touched up in places to bring it back within the orthodox fold by the addition of such verses as the conclusion, which we have already mentioned, and 3:17: 'I said in my heart, God will judge the righteous and the wicked.' The first scholar to attempt a more radical analysis, which is recognizable as a piece of full-blown 'literary' criticism, was C. Siegfried.[3] He, too, thought in terms of a basic text to which material had been added, rather than of parallel sources, as for the Pentateuch.[4] Siegfried was convinced that the original Qoheleth was a very sceptical work indeed, so radical in its attack on normal Jewish piety that it would never have been accepted as canonical by either Jews or Christians.

According to Siegfried, Ecclesiastes passed through six separate major 'recensions' or editions, and in each the additional material that changed the book's overall emphasis can be isolated and assigned with reasonable accuracy to a particular circle in post-exilic Israel – just as, say, the 'P' material in Genesis can be assigned to 'priestly' circles in the period of the second Temple. The version of Siegfried's theory that established itself most widely in Britain, however, was a simplification by A. H. McNeile,[5] and it will make our task easier if we work with this: it preserves all the essential ideas of Siegfried's work, but greatly simplifies its details. McNeile made the labour of his readers even lighter by printing the sections of Ecclesiastes in different type-faces to mark the sources.

McNeile tries to establish three major stages in the redaction of Ecclesiastes. (1) His first editor is a scribe or 'wise man', the sort of person (or group) who taught in the schools of post-exilic Judaism where much of Proverbs was produced, and from which, indeed, Qoheleth himself had come – though he had surely been something of a renegade. The first editor has diluted Qoheleth's pessimism by inserting a number of innocuous proverbs – e.g. 4:5; 4:9–12; 8.1 – and adding comments which twist the original material in such a way that it supports stock 'wisdom' positions. (2) Secondly, a later editor has tried to save not just Qoheleth's acceptability within the 'wisdom' tradition (the system of common-sense platitudes represented in Proverbs or Ecclesiasticus), but also his religious orthodoxy as judged by the criteria of the Judaism current in the last couple of centuries B.C.: the religion of devout legal observance and absolute trust in divine justice and retribution. He has added highly theological material such as 11:9b and 12:1a, which qualify Qoheleth's advice to have a good time while one is young enough to enjoy it by reminding the reader of coming judgement by God; 8:2b, on the sanctity of oaths; and 7:26b, which ascribes deliverance from seductive women (a favourite theme of ancient Near Eastern wisdom literature) to the help of God. (3) Finally, an editor of a more prosaic sort has added the title (1:1) and, probably, the biographical note about the author in 12:9–10.

Already in trying to decide between the earlier theory of a basically unified book and McNeile's hypothesis of a three-fold redaction, we are confronted with the question how this work should be read, and hence with the question of genre, what *kind* of book it is. Scholars who take the work to be substantially unified do not see any great problem in a book that contains both radical questioning of traditional religious values and more or less unquestioning acceptance of them: for them, 'wisdom literature' is a category broad enough to include such a work, and there is no need to explain it by resorting to theories of multiple authorship or redaction.[6] After all, Proverbs itself contains passages that seem, taken out of context, scarcely less pessimistic than the gloomier parts of Ecclesiastes: see, for example, Proverbs 14:10 and 14:13. For McNeile, on the other hand, the inconsistencies are too great to permit such an interpretation, and the work is too puzzling to be understood as the work of a single author. It must therefore be seen as composite: an original, very radical work, which could best be described as a *parody* of a stock 'wisdom book', which has been forcibly turned into a conventional work of proverbial wisdom and then into a 'holy' book by successive redactional additions.

Overtly, the question to be resolved is whether certain verses or passages ought to be (in the traditional terminology) 'deleted' as later additions to the original text, and it is very tempting for a scholar who is aiming at scientific rigour in his work to say that this question must be decided *before* any attempt is made to interpret the work: first establish what the original book contained, and only then can you hope to say what Qoheleth himself meant. But to come to a decision about the original extent of the work, we must first decide the question of genre. Is the book possible or impossible as it stands? Could it have been read by its first readers as making coherent sense, or do the joins show through? Indeed, we must make some preliminary decisions about *content*, which according to a purist view of biblical method (as we find it in Richter) can be allowed to come up for consideration only when every type of critical method has already been applied. After all, the reason why McNeile felt forced to postulate a series of redactions was not just that this provided a better explanation of universally recognized inconsistencies than other methods could provide. It was at least partly because the inconsistencies seemed to him far more glaring than people had generally thought them. But then again, it was no doubt because explanations of biblical books in terms of glossing, redaction and revision were in the air that he allowed his initial sense that there were major inconsistencies such full rein. Once a critic has begun to formulate a 'source' or multiple-recension theory (or indeed any other kind of theory), the evidence which can be held to point to it is likely to grow in weight in his mind. None of this is to say that McNeile was fudging the evidence to prove his case, but rather to point out yet again the inevitable element of circularity in all literary judgements. Ecclesiastes itself undoubtedly contains tensions – no one would deny that – but if we are aware of the possibility of multiple authorship, we are bound to feel less sure that there must be some way of resolving the tensions than we should if such a possibility had never occurred to us. Conversely, it is because the tensions, here and in other biblical books, genuinely do exist that scholars stumbled upon the idea of multiple authorship in the first place.

The circularity here must mean that there can be no possibility of constructing a knock-down argument – based on an assessment of the textual evidence that any unprejudiced reader would be *bound* to accept – to show that one or other of the theories we are examining is correct. In the end, informed intuition about what is likely and reasonable must decide. But the intuition must be informed, and is not at all above the reach of certain rational and empirical tests, provided it is understood that such tests are not a matter of infallible verification. For example, we have seen that the argument in favour of a position like that of McNeile comes down to a judgement about what is thinkable within the genre 'wisdom book'. It is impossible, the suggestion runs, that anyone could have produced a single work which so mixed radical scepticism with conventional aphorisms. Obviously it will be relevant when assessing this suggestion to look at other examples of 'wisdom' in Israelite and related literatures and to see whether there are any precedents for such a mixture. If there are, we may want to conclude that the inconsistencies pointed out by McNeile are really evidence, not that Qoheleth is the work of more than one hand, but that the genre 'wisdom book' needs redefinition, that our competence in it was less perfect than we supposed. On the other hand, we may argue that the level of inconsistency is not so high as McNeile thought: that the tensions have been exaggerated. Some scholars, indeed, might wish to construct such a counter-argument by maintaining that the 'consistency' being demanded is not found in wisdom books or proverbs in any case; or even that it is not found generally in ancient Semitic cultures, being a 'modern Western' preoccupation.

They would probably point to (arguably) self-contradictory maxims such as Proverbs 26:4–5: 'Answer not a fool according to his folly, lest you be like him yourself; answer a fool according to his folly, lest he be wise in his own eyes.' All such arguments can be assessed and evaluated rationally; none of them constitutes 'proof' in a simple sense.[7]

Form Criticism

So far we have treated Ecclesiastes as the work of one or more 'authors' or 'editors' and have spoken of one or more 'hands' having been at work on it; in other words, we have been thinking of it as a literary work. But of course there are a good many proverbs or aphorisms in Ecclesiastes, and the proverb is widely held to be in origin an oral genre. So it is not surprising that Ecclesiastes, like other wisdom books, has been of considerable interest to form critics. K. Galling[8] argued that one could divide it up (in much the way that Proverbs 10:1—22:16 can be divided up) into a large number of originally independent sayings. In this Galling did not in fact depart far from traditional, literary-critical estimates of the book's composition, since he thought that Qoheleth himself was both the 'author' of all the independent sayings and also the editor who had collected them together. His suggestion nonetheless had very far-reaching consequences for the sort of discussion about consistency and integrity of genre that has just been surveyed, for he argued that Qoheleth had simply uttered or composed a great many sayings in traditional aphoristic forms, some conservative and some radical, and at a later time had collected them together, in no particular order, into an anthology. If this were so, we should be on a quite false trail in using the criterion of consistency of content in trying to come to a judgement about the literary growth of the book; for an anthology of sayings (even sayings by one man) need not display any consistency of viewpoint or even of theme at all.

Indeed, a committed form critic might well think Galling's attachment to Qoheleth himself as the source of all the sayings was the sign of a rather faint heart, rather like Gunkel's continuing belief in individual 'psalmists' even after he had shown that psalms were basically anonymous, cultic texts. Such a form critic might suggest that many of the sayings were really old proverbs, with no authors, current in Israel from time immemorial, each having an interesting prehistory of its own.[9] The inconsistency between many of them would then be evidence of diverse currents of thought within the movement known as 'Israelite wisdom', but would not point to any inconsistency in the mind of Qoheleth, who merely collected them all together. Still less could it form the basis for any literary-critical hypothesis about multiple recensions of the book.

Once again, a question of genre is at the forefront of the argument. A great deal rests on the analogy with works such as Proverbs 10–22. On the one hand we may argue: since there is no unity of theme or consistency of approach in Ecclesiastes, it must be a work of the same kind as Proverbs 10—22, i.e. an anthology of originally independent sayings. On the other hand, someone could reply (most readers of Ecclesiastes probably *would* reply) that Ecclesiastes is rather unlike Proverbs 10—22. It is impossible to read it without being struck by a certain common style, atmosphere and theological theme – the transcendence of God and the randomness of human existence; whereas Proverbs 10—22 seems to lack any kind of thematic unity. Consequently the inconsistencies that do occur cannot be explained on a form-critical basis, as only to be expected in this genre, but must have some other explanation.

But it is easy to see that a form-critical style of hypothesis could, in only slightly different circumstances, have considerable explanatory force. Suppose Proverbs 10—22 were the text being considered. How complicated that would seem, if approached with purely literary-critical presuppositions! But how simply it can be accounted for, once we have grasped the fact that maxims circulated *orally* in the ancient world, so that compilers of anthologies could set them down without regard for consistency or literary artistry. Most readers will feel that such a hypothesis is not very well suited to Ecclesiastes; but if it were, it would undoubtedly undercut a great many of our earlier discussions of the book and would mean that *both* McNeile *and* those opposed to him had quite misunderstood the kind of literature they were dealing with.

Redaction Criticism

Suppose, however, that we accept for the sake of argument that some theory of more than one edition of Ecclesiastes does most justice to the work; and that even if it contains some proverbs or aphorisms that had an independent, oral prehistory, these have been incorporated into the present form of the text intentionally, in order to alter its excessively radical tone, rather than merely as isolated units in a formless anthology. It will remain to ask what can be deduced from the text about the detailed intentions of the redactors. We have already said a certain amount about the broad aims of the first two redactors postulated by McNeile, and indeed there is a sense in which even in his literary analysis elements of what would now be called redaction criticism necessarily creep in – a further example of the practical impossibility of keeping all the methods in watertight compartments. But a good deal more than this can be extracted, if we look carefully at the differences the redactors have made to the original text simply by adding to it.

We may begin with the first, 'wisdom' redactor and look at what he has done in 4:7–12. Verses 7–8 make the point, very characteristic of Qoheleth himself, that all labour is pointless when there is no one to inherit the fruits of one's labours: why work to earn more than one needs to live, if there is no one to pass it on to? One might as well work less, and enjoy the extra leisure. Verses 9–12, however, which appear to come from the first redactor, make a very different point, although they use the same illustration: heavy manual labour. The point here is the much more commonplace one that 'many hands make light work'. The problem in being alone is not the profound one of having no one for whom to care, no goal which makes one's work meaningful and worthwhile, but the practical disadvantage that there is no companionship to ease one's immediate burdens and no physical help available when work becomes difficult or accidents happen. Where there *are* two people working together, they 'have a good reward for their toil'. This (a redaction critic will say) is surely not what Qoheleth meant. The problem in verses 7–8 is not lack of success or companionship, but pointlessness and 'vanity'. But by adding verses 9–12 the redactor largely draws the sting of this complaint, by constraining us to read the passage as a single whole. We are led to submerge the fleeting impression that the author is speaking about the pointlessness of work in general under the conviction (which the later verses confirm) that he is simply reminding us that being alone is an evil and having company is a great good – indeed (v. 12b) if two's company, three are irresistible. Thus Qoheleth's words of profound desolation find themselves pressed into the service of a fairly banal conclusion, which is fully at home in the Israelite tradition of proverbial wisdom: life in the society of faithful companions is far better than lonely toil.

If we examine the other insertions made by this redactor, we shall see that they generally have much the same effect: not only do they correct Qoheleth's pessimism and scepticism by the message they themselves convey, *they also force the reader who is trying to extract a coherent meaning from the end-product to read the words of Qoheleth himself as far less radical than they seem if taken alone.*[10] Redaction criticism, thus applied, makes it plain that the same words can have a different meaning if they stand in a different context – a vital point for the understanding of all texts, to which we shall return[11] – and that it is only by attending closely to the work of the redactor that we can discover how the text ought appropriately to be read. Hence redaction criticism has consequences for exegesis: once again, we cannot say, Get the exegesis right *first*, and *then* go on to ask about the intentions of the redactor. The process of understanding is not so simply linear.

The second redactor (assuming that McNeile is correct) has sought to transform the still fairly secular wisdom book that reached him from the two-stage development just described into a piece of religious wisdom, somewhat after the manner of Ecclesiasticus. The transformation he has achieved can best be seen in 11:9—12:14, the concluding section of the work. If we remove the small portions likely to be his contribution, we find that the original text takes on a dramatically different sense. The additions are 11:9b, 11:10b and 12:1a; and without these the text reads:

Rejoice, O young man, in your youth, and let your heart cheer you in the days of your youth; walk in the ways of your heart and in the sight of your eyes [i.e. 'wherever your fancy takes you']. Remove vexation from your mind, and put away pain from your body, before the evil days come, and the years draw nigh, when you will say, 'I have no pleasure in them'; before the sun and the light and the moon and the stars are darkened . . .

A haunting reminder that life is short, certainly, but a clear invitation to enjoy what one can: *carpe diem*, in fact. There is nothing here about God, no attempt to set the advice to enjoy life within a larger religious or moral context, no suggestion that the remembrance of coming death (and judgement) should make the reader sober in his enjoyment of the pleasures life affords: only an injunction to live while one can.

Now it is clear enough that the insertion of the second redactor's fragmentary half-verses completely changes the course of the passage. We now have a profound reflection on the brevity of life and its inevitable end in divine judgement, and the author's advice is to enjoy *what God gives*, for as long as he gives it; to remember that man is made for joy as well as for judgement, but at the same time to remember the God to whom, in the end, his spirit will return; and so to savour the pleasures of life, not unadvisedly, lightly or wantonly, but reverently, discreetly, soberly and in the fear of God. The recognition that death and judgement are coming is not to blight present joys, but to deepen them and make them more serious, and so more truly satisfying.

It is not surprising that the work as it left the second redactor should have struck many writers in the past not as an incentive to hedonism, but as a model of poetic reflection on the transitoriness of all human affairs and a spur to moral endeavour and piety in the pursuit of the 'whole duty of man'. One of the greatest works inspired (at least in part) by its ideas is Samuel Johnson's *The Vanity of Human Wishes*, whose pattern of thought, though naturally tinged with Christian sentiments, represents a by no means strained or unnatural reading of the book as we now have it; and it can well serve to make one realize how great must have been the achievement of the second redactor, considering the materials which (if McNeile is correct) he had before him:

> Where then shall Hope and Fear their objects find?
> Must dull Suspence corrupt the stagnant mind?
> Must helpless man, in ignorance sedate,
> Roll darkling down the torrent of his fate?
> . . . Enquirer, cease, petitions yet remain,

71

Which heav'n may hear, nor deem religion vain.
Still raise for good the supplicating voice,
But leave to heav'n the measure and the choice.
. . . Pour forth thy fervours for a healthful mind,
Obedient passions, and a will resign'd;
For love, which scarce collective man can fill;
For patience sov'reign o'er transmuted ill;
For faith, that panting for a happier seat
Counts death kind Nature's signal of retreat.
These goods for man the laws of heav'n ordain,
These goods he grants, who grants the pow'r to gain;
With these celestial wisdom calms the mind,
And makes the happiness she does not find.

To a book which can be read in this way the last verse forms a fitting climax, and instead of being a platitude it takes on a certain profundity: 'Fear God, and keep his commandments . . . for God will bring every deed into judgement, with every secret thing, whether good or evil' (12:13–14). The apparent cynicism or scepticism (it was real, of course, for Qoheleth himself) has ceased to be an ultimate value and has become, we may say, penultimate: not an attitude to be encouraged for its own sake, but a temperamental disposition which prepares one to take seriously the fact that God alone is the really worthwhile end of human life, and all merely human pursuits ultimately unsatisfying.

Beyond Redaction Criticism

Now the reader may well share my own feeling at this point, that such a statement of the meaning of Ecclesiastes in its final form is all very well, but that it is doubtful how far it can really be called redaction criticism. First, and rather superficially, we may suspect that there is some danger of the redactor's disappearing in the manner described in the last chapter. The unity of theme, the subordination of pessimism to a higher religious sentiment, is so successfully achieved, that one begins to wonder whether the separation into an original text and two or three redactional strata was really justified in the first place. It is, of course, possible to construct a secular or even anti-religious work by judiciously removing little pieces, as in the analysis of 11:9—12:14 above; but it is hard to feel much confidence that one really is *re*constructing an earlier stage in the history of the text, when the finished product reads so smoothly.

This point, however, could easily be exaggerated. There undeniably are passages where the text contains quite sharp inconsistencies, or proverbial sayings very loosely anchored in context, but supplying rather conventional wisdom that is hard to reconcile with the more sceptical utterances elsewhere in the book. And this makes it entirely sensible to think in terms of several redactors. Indeed, a much more serious objection may begin from this very observation. Even if 11:9—12:14 evinces very careful and successful redaction, there are many other places in the work where one can hardly feel that the redactor has reshaped Qoheleth's meaning with the degree of subtlety and profundity to be seen in that rather impressive peroration. For example, in 5:4 the 'religious' redactor may certainly be said to 'temper' Qoheleth's scepticism about the notice God takes of what men do, by insisting that he does care about the fulfilment of vows. But it seems more natural to me to say that he is flatly contradicting Qoheleth, rather than subtly modifying him. It would be hard to argue that Qoheleth's near-agnosticism is being taken up into any kind of higher unity here, as we have argued it is in 11:9—12:14. The same may be said of 3:17, which simply denies what in 3:19 is asserted, that God makes no distinction between the fate of beasts and men, good and evil. There is certainly a redactor at work in these places, but it is difficult to make a case for regarding him as a creative genius, or to argue that he has a message of his own which is expressed through the redaction.

All this suggests that redaction criticism probably cannot establish a profound meaning in the final text of Ecclesiastes. The attempt to read a whole book, as opposed to its component parts, seems once more to have come to nothing. And yet there have always been enthusiastic readers of Ecclesiastes who thought they knew what they were reading. And many of them have felt that, taken overall, the book does indeed have some such meaning as Johnson captured in *The Vanity of Human Wishes*. Could we do justice both to professional critics and to ordinary readers if we said that Ecclesiastes *does* indeed have some such meaning, and yet that there never was an author or 'redactor' who gave it such a meaning by consciously writing or reordering it with that in mind? Could the text *mean* what we have taken it to mean, without anyone having *meant* it?

If the reader is prepared to contemplate such an idea, two possible lines of approach may suggest themselves. (1) First of all, one may well ask *why* so many readers of Ecclesiastes (Johnson would be a good example) have read it as a statement of the pointlessness of merely human aims *by contrast with* divine providence, even though no author or redactor intended this and the original author intended almost the opposite. Little reflection is needed to convince one that it was because they were reading the book as part of Scripture, interpreted through the Judaeo-Christian tradition of belief in providence, retribution, divine justice and so on. These were the themes they were prepared to find in a biblical book; these provided the context of expectations within which they read it.

Now many critics in the past, when biblical criticism of a historical sort was carrying all before it, would have said that this mode of reading was precisely the error from which the historical-critical method could set us free: it could give us 'the original Ecclesiastes', undistorted by later tradition. I hope I have shown that this aim is not so simply achieved as they supposed. But may it not be that it was in any case a false ideal, at least in its claim to a position of exclusive privilege? It has begun to look as though Ecclesiastes really does mean what (say) Johnson thought it meant, in some sense or other of 'mean'. Perhaps we could say that this is its meaning 'within the canon of Scripture', and that such a meaning does not need anyone to 'mean' it. It is the meaning the book is constrained to have by being set within the context of a corpus of religious literature belonging to a certain tradition. There would be an analogy here with the way particular passages within a work may be constrained (by their redactors) to have a certain new meaning, when they are placed in juxtaposition with new material composed for the purpose. Just as, to revert to an example discussed above, Ecclesiastes 4:7–8 means something different once 4:9–12 is tacked on to it, so we may say that the whole book of Ecclesiastes means something different once it is placed in a canon, or corpus, which operates with certain theological ideas about providence and judgement.

Such an idea, I believe, is not manifestly absurd, but it is difficult to evaluate. We should need, for example, to ask questions about genre and competence: what kind of work is 'part of a canon'; how do you decide with what conventions such a book operates, and what sorts of question it is appropriate to ask of it? At all events, this way of looking at the meanings of biblical books is now being seriously proposed as an approach that ought to take over the supremacy that has until recently been given to 'historical' ways of reading the text (redaction criticism being the most recent example), in which the critic is looking for the intentional meanings implanted in the text by its authors or editors. The 'canonical approach' associated with the name of B. S. Childs seeks instead the *canonical* meaning, and in the next two chapters we shall try to show in more detail what this may be. Our discussion of the finished form of Ecclesiastes may be useful as a foretaste of the kind of thing that is in store.

(2) Secondly, however, some people may wish to go even further than this in abandoning the historical dimension and its interest in authors and compilers. It may be said that Ecclesiastes has the overall meaning we have attributed to it irrespective of what the compiler meant *and* irrespective even of the context in which it stands: the meaning can simply be read off from the book, without going into questions of authorship, history of composition, literary context or any other issue extrinsic to the words of the text itself. We may say that to be competent in reading literature is, precisely, to be able to find thematic and artistic unity within literary works. Once a book exists as one work, the task of criticism is to read it within conventions that will ensure it does have a coherent content. Thus the evidence that Ecclesiastes means what we have suggested is simply that it can be read consistently in this way, and that it cannot be read consistently in any other way. Considerations about what the putative author or redactor may or may not have meant are strictly beside the point.

This way of looking at literature is likely to strike few chords in the hearts of English readers, who inherit a long tradition of asking historical questions about all literature, not just the Bible, and who will very naturally suspect that on such principles you can make a book mean anything you like. However, an approach which adopts some such guiding principles has made serious headway in biblical studies. Its source lies in French literary 'structuralism', which we have already encountered in passing and laid under contribution for the term 'literary competence'. It will require some much more detailed exposition if we are even to begin to do it justice. But I hope that, by approaching it as I have, I may have led the reader to see that it deals with possibilities that may well suggest themselves unprompted to a thoughtful student of more conventional biblical criticism; and so that it will get a fair hearing as a very sophisticated and conscientious attempt to resolve the question how literary competence may be attained in biblical literature.

Further Reading

M. Hengel, *Judaism and Hellenism*, vol. i (London 1974), pp. 115–28
J. L. Crenshaw, 'The Eternal Gospel (Eccl. 3:11)' in *Essays in Old Testament Ethics* (J. Philip Hyatt. In Memoriam), J. L. Crenshaw and J. T. Willis, eds. (New York 1974), pp. 23–55

6

THE CANONICAL APPROACH

Oh that I knew how all thy lights combine,
   And the configurations of their glorie!
   Seeing not onely how each verse doth shine,
But all the constellations of the storie.
This verse marks that, and both do make a motion
   Unto a third, that ten leaves off doth lie:
   Then as dispersed herbs do watch a potion,
These three make up some Christians destinie:
Such are thy secrets, which my life makes good,
   And comments on thee: for in ev'ry thing
   Thy words do finde me out, & parallels bring,
And in another make me understood.
   Starres are poore books, & oftentimes do misse:
   This book of starres lights to eternall blisse.

George Herbert, 'The Holy Scriptures (II)'

Preliminary Reading

E. B. Mellor, ed., *The Making of the Old Testament* (Cambridge Bible
Commentary on the *New English Bible*. Cambridge 1972),
pp. 105–201

J. Barr, *The Bible in the Modern World* (London 1973), pp. 1–34,
150–67

Back to the Canon

In the last two chapters I have tried to create a feeling of unease
with the historical-critical approach to the Old Testament. All its
methods – literary, form and redaction criticism – can take us some

way towards a better understanding of what lies behind the biblical text, but they all seem to fail us if we look to them for help in reading the text as it actually meets us when we open a Bible. Indeed, the method that looks most promising from this point of view – redaction criticism – also seems the most fragile. The claim that any of these methods, or even all of them together, constitute the one 'valid' way of handling the Old Testament seems to have an obvious flaw in it. The flaw is that there are questions we want to ask that none of these methods can answer for us. The methods we have got will simply not tell us what we want to know.

Yet, on the other hand, the discussion of Ecclesiastes has thrown up the possibility that we sometimes stumble on the kind of answer we are looking for without actually using any method, or at least without using any of the methods described so far. We have found a way of reading Ecclesiastes which seems to make plausible and coherent sense of the book as we now have it, even though it cannot be shown that any redactor ever intended it, even though it certainly was not intended by the 'authors' of the various strata within the book, or by those who composed the (oral) aphorisms that may underlie it. So perhaps we ought to say that the text has meanings that no one ever meant. But if so, how can we get at such meanings? We may say 'by intuition', but that sounds a very unsystematic, careless approach. Besides, even intuitions have some shape, some structure. Perhaps it would be best to *begin* with intuition, but to go on to ask under what conditions we would have intuitions like the one about the meaning of Ecclesiastes with which the last chapter ended. In what spirit would you need to be approaching the text, if you were to perceive its meaning in the way that Dr Johnson and his contemporaries generally did? I argued that there are in effect two approaches that may lead to that kind of perception of meaning. One, a very radical approach, would argue that the meaning of a text is entirely a matter of the constraints within which it is read. The fact that Ecclesiastes is (now) one book means that it has to be read as one book: in other words that its inconsistencies have to be ironed out, and its extremes of piety and scepticism moderated, so that a single coherent message can emerge. This message will necessarily be about scepticism-in-the-interest-of-piety: no other interpretation can prevent the book from falling apart. We shall be looking at this approach in chapters 8 and 9. But the other approach sees the eighteenth century understanding of Ecclesiastes as resulting from the context within which it belongs: the canon of Scripture.

To say that a writer such as Johnson read Ecclesiastes as conducive to piety, because he read it as part of inspired scripture, may sound like no more than a piece of historical information about Johnson. As I suggested before, early exponents of historical criticism would have seen this merely as a way of explaining why he so seriously *mis*read it: the fact that it was Scripture insulated his mind from the chilly scepticism within it. But some Old Testament scholars are less sure now that right was always wholly on the side of historical criticism. If even redaction criticism leaves us baffled by the final form of some biblical books, may it not be worth reviving the idea that their meaning has something to do with their place in Scripture?

Reading the Bible as Scripture: B. S. Childs

A major programme for reorientating Old Testament studies towards a 'canonical approach' or 'canonical method' can be found in the work of B. S. Childs. It was set out in 1970 in his *Biblical Theology in Crisis*[1] and developed in several articles; and it was illustrated in practice in his commentary on Exodus[2] and in *Introduction to the Old Testament as Scripture*.[3] I have been arguing that historical-critical methods are not completely adequate from a literary point of view, but Childs's primary thesis is that they are unsatisfactory theologically. From the point of view of a believing Christian or Jew, the achievement of critical scholarship has been to treat the Old Testament as merely a collection of ancient texts, to apply all sorts of critical methods to it in an attempt to discover more about its original meaning and setting, and only then to go on and ask about its possible value for the contemporary community of faith. Critical scholars have insisted that biblical books should be 'freed' from their context in the Church's canon of Scripture – a context artificially imposed on them in the past – and studied in their own right. But the price has been to create (equally artificially) a problem about the relevance of books whose original context is obviously so different from our own:

The modern hermeneutical impasse which has found itself unable successfully to bridge the gap between the past and the present, has arisen in large measure from its disregard of the canonical shaping. The usual critical method of biblical exegesis is, first, to seek to restore an original historical setting by stripping away those very elements which constitute the canonical shape. Little wonder that once the biblical text has been securely anchored in the historical past by 'decanonizing' it, the interpreter has difficulty applying it to the modern religious context.[4]

Child's own suggestion for avoiding this 'hermeneutical impasse' was shaped by his dissatisfaction with the ways in which American biblical scholars of the 1950s and 1960s had tried to avoid it, at the time of the so-called 'Biblical Theology Movement'. But it is quite possible to give some idea of his programme without for the moment going into its antecedents.

Instead of treating the Old Testament as *prima facie* simply an ancient text, and asking about its possible religious meaning and value only as a kind of surprised afterthought once critical study is complete, Childs's canonical method *begins* with the datum that the Old Testament as we now have it is part of Scripture, and seeks to interpret it with that always in mind. He does not deny that the historical-critical method may be able to elicit some real (historical) information from the text, or to discover what its original authors meant. It is not the possibility or efficacy of historical criticism that he calls in question, but its claim to unique validity. The 'original meaning', even granted that it can sometimes be discovered, does not have a uniquely privileged status for our own theological endeavours. As well as asking what the text meant, we should ask what it *means*, given that it is part of the canon of Scripture received by the Church and by the synagogue. If we insist on asking (as most critical scholars who are also believers do ask) how the modern Christian can assimilate the meaning of a reconstructed *original* text, we shall find ourselves in hopeless straits. But the question we should be asking is what the text *in its canonical form* has to say to the modern Christian; and here questions of historical distance do not arise in the same way. For the modern Christian is still part of the community for which the text has been and remains canonical;

and in its final form the text is contemporary with each new generation of those who accept its authority. The meaning which is 'canonical' for the Christian is the meaning the text has when it is read as part of the canon, with full allowance made for the other texts that also form part of that canon, in their overall, coherent pattern.

This must suffice as a description of the canonical approach; in the rest of this chapter it will be illustrated in detail, and evaluated critically in the next. It will be clear that it is a proposal as to how biblical texts ought to be read, as opposed to being interested in what their authors meant by them[5], and in this it does, as Childs correctly perceives, represent a really decisive break with traditional modes of biblical criticism. It has many affinities with literary criticism outside biblical studies, however, and these we shall investigate in some detail.

Ecclesiastes as Scripture

How does the canonical method work in practice? We have already glimpsed the kind of conclusions it might reach in examining Ecclesiastes, and have seen that it does not suppress but rather makes overt the context of general biblical assumption and even of Christian doctrinal belief within which the biblical text is read. In Ecclesiastes 11:9—12:8 there really is a tension, *even at the level of the final redaction*, between 'Rejoice, O young man, in your youth' (11:9) and 'Remember your Creator in the days of your youth' (12:1). The kind of redaction criticism that would argue for a redactor who reconciled these alternative pieces of advice into a single message would be so over-subtle as to destroy itself. No one 'intended' us to read these verses as even compatible, still less as 'really' making the same point. Yet as it stands the text does convey a unified message, and within this message 11:9 means what no one ever *meant* it to mean: that one should be joyful in youth in a way that takes account of coming judgement and of the claims of God. This message is the message the book conveys at the canonical level. Because it is a 'biblical' book – because it stands alongside other religious wisdom books, and indeed other works that remind the reader of the judgement and demands of God (e.g. the books of the prophets) – the reader is constrained to take it as reducing the joy of youth and the cynicism of old age alike to penultimate values,

81

and as coming to rest in neither of them, but rather in the unerring purposes of God to which youth and age must both submit.[6]

Of course, in order to establish that this is the canonical meaning, we need to have already seen what are the fixed points or leading themes of the Old Testament, in terms of which Ecclesiastes is to be read. An unkind critic could construct a *reductio ad absurdum* of the method, purporting to show that, since the same must be true of every other part of the Old Testament, including those parts that supply the criteria for reading this one, the process can never get started. We need to have read every part of the Old Testament with understanding, before we can begin to read any part of it, and this is self-contradictory. But this is to press the idea of canonical reading too far. In any case, as we have seen, *all* reading of texts does in fact have some such circularity inherent in it. If the canon critic moves back and forth between the parts and the whole in order to grasp either, he is no different in this from any other kind of critic. And however difficult it may be in practice to establish what are the 'main themes' of the Old Testament, once one begins (as the canon critic does) to treat it as in effect a single book, there is no more difficulty *in principle* than in extracting the main themes of any other very long and diffuse work. We may not be able to say with confidence exactly what these themes are, but we can certainly rule out some suggestions as obviously implausible. For example, it would be implausible to suggest that the Old Testament, taken as a whole, encouraged people either to indulge in the cynicism of the original Qoheleth, or to follow the advice that was originally intended in 11:9 (do as you like while you are young enough to enjoy it). Whatever the Old Testament as a whole 'means', it surely does not mean *that*.

It seems reasonable, then, to suggest that in reading Ecclesiastes 'as part of the canon' we are bound to read it so as to mitigate such extremes of advice, and to integrate it into its biblical framework in such a way that both hedonism and scepticism are held in check by religious faith. To insist on the 'original' meaning is to wrest the work from its context; it is to refuse to take seriously that, whatever it may have been once, we encounter it now only as part of Scripture. There is something a little naive about thinking that we can read part of the Bible as though it existed all on its own; at least, it is hardly surprising that, when we try to do so, we are then faced with the question how this isolated work can possibly have anything to say to today's Church. It is as though one were to remove a pillar from a great cathedral and insist on studying it in its own right; and then were to ask what use such a detached fragment could possibly have. The problem would be of one's own creation.

Psalm 8: Man in the Bible

To define a little more closely how the canonical approach works we may outline one of Childs's own examples, a discussion of the theology of Psalm 8:

> O LORD, our Lord, how majestic is thy name in all the earth! . . .
> What is man, that thou art mindful of him, and the son of man,
> that thou dost care for him? Yet thou hast made him little less
> than the gods (*or* angels), and dost crown him with glory and
> honour.[7]

Once the 'original sense' and *Gattung* of this text have been established (it is a hymn of praise to God for his creation, and a reflection on the unique privilege of mankind within it), we can go on to ask the two questions that will help to establish its 'canonical meaning'. First, what do other parts of the canon make of this text? Second, how do the ideas in this text fit into the context of other biblical discussions of the same theme? In both cases we shall inevitably be drawn into an examination of some New Testament passages.

First, the use of the Psalm elsewhere in Scripture. The most important place is clearly Hebrews 2:5–9, which cites Psalm 8 in the Greek version and develops a christological reference for it: Jesus is the one 'made *for a little while* lower than the angels' but 'crowned with glory and honour' because of his sufferings. This is not simply a misreading of the Psalm; rather, it plays back on to the original text a new level of meaning. The Psalm is both originally, and in its citation in Hebrews, about the 'glory of man'; but the Christian writer sees Jesus as the key to a doctrine of man, and by narrowing the reference of the Psalm from man in general to Jesus in particular he makes it possible for us to go back and reread the Psalm, within the context of the Christian Scriptures, as implying more profound ideas about human nature than the psalmist himself had in mind. Within this context, the Psalm speaks of a glorification of man's nature which is already actual in Jesus, and potential for all mankind.

Secondly, we must look at other scriptural discussions of the same theme. Obviously pride of place is likely to be given to Genesis 1—3 (which the psalmist may well actually be alluding to), and perhaps to the Epistle to the Romans, with its extended discussion of the redemption of man's fallen nature. It is not a matter of reading ideas from Genesis or Romans into Psalm 8, but of reading the Psalm in a context defined by these texts, letting them specify the kinds of meaning it can have for the Christian reader. The Christian will not read the Psalm as the uncomplicated joy of the 'natural' man, rejoicing in his powers of domination over the created world, but rather as the more complex wonder of the man who knows himself to be bought with a price, who sees his value as the value God has set on him in consideration of the price he has paid in the death of Christ. Thus we may bring in Romans 5:7–8: 'One will hardly die for a righteous man – though perhaps for a good man one will dare even to die. But God shows his love for us in that while we were yet sinners Christ died for us.' Man is precious – little lower than the angels – because, in Christ, God has made him so. Thus the canonical way of reading the Psalm integrates it into a general Christian view of man which is derived, not from this or that text taken in isolation, but from the general drift of Scripture, read as a unified work.

Is the Canonical Approach Anti-critical?

But doesn't all this amount simply to a return to pre-critical exegesis? If we are to read Scripture as a unified work, doesn't that mean that we are going back to all the old abuses – allegory, harmonization, typology, even downright falsification of the text – from which the historical-critical method freed us? It can indeed be argued that this is the practical effect of Childs's method, but there is no doubt that he himself sees it as quite different from all these pre-critical approaches. (In fact, the canonical method should be called post-critical, rather than pre-critical: see the discussion in the next chapter.) Childs is certainly anxious to hear the whole of Scripture as giving a coherent witness, but he is not prepared to purchase this at the cost of using absolutely any technique that may come to hand. He specifically rules out allegorical and typological exegesis in their patristic, medieval and rabbinic forms. We may want to argue that he is not actually *entitled* to rule them out, according to his own principles, but he undoubtedly wishes to do so. The rule which excludes them is quite a simple one on paper, though desperately hard to observe without begging the question. It is that the critic must concern himself with what a given passage is actually *saying*, with its 'plain sense', not with merely verbal details or merely formal resemblances to other texts.

For example, in Psalm 8:4 the phrase 'son of man' appears, and a commentator concerned with the surface of the text might well start to ask questions about its relation to the 'Son of Man' in apocalyptic literature, and in the Synoptic Gospels. But attention to the 'plain sense' of the text makes it clear that this phrase here means simply 'man', in parallel with the 'man' of the first half of the verse. (How Childs would react if the New Testament itself used the phrase in this verse for christological discussion is not clear.) True to these principles, in a sample study of biblical texts about human sexuality he discusses the Song of Songs in its 'literal' sense, but does not so much as mention the long tradition in both Judaism and Christianity of interpreting it allegorically; nor does he mention the allegorical use of marriage imagery in Ephesians 5. Though the canonical context affects, even determines, how a given text should be read, it cannot force a passage which is not allegorical in its plain sense to be read as an allegory, nor twist its words so that they relate to a different subject-matter. I am not myself at all sure that there is any good reason, on Childs's own principles, why this should be so; but there is no doubt that in his practice of the canonical method he always strives to avoid this kind of distortion.

On the other hand, we might think that the canonical method would produce excessively 'synthesizing' interpretations of the biblical material, smoothing out all differences between the biblical writers. There is no doubt that it has a tendency in that direction. But the danger is always well in view, and Childs tries to show that his method does not entail this kind of harmonization. Fundamentalists, we may say, think that all the Old Testament books speak with a single voice because they were all written by one author – God – who may be supposed to have a highly consistent mind. But Childs, by contrast, is not saying that, as a matter of historical fact, all the biblical writers thought the same way about everything; nor is he suggesting that God is what might be called the Ultimate Redactor – though he is sometimes understood as implying this. He is well aware that there are diversities of belief attested within the Old Testament. He is suggesting, rather, that the Old Testament must now be read, not perhaps as a *wholly* consistent work, but at least as hanging coherently together. When the synagogue and the Church canonized the Scriptures this was tantamount to laying down a rule for interpretation: interpret each of these texts on the understanding that it is part of a larger whole; do not read them in such a way that they flatly contradict each other.

Now it has to be conceded that this seems very close to the provision made in Article 20 of the Church of England's thirty-nine *Articles of Religion*, that 'it is not lawful for the Church' to 'expound one place of Scripture, that it be repugnant to another' – which would generally be taken as a considerable impediment to modern critical study of the Bible. But Childs himself plainly has no wish to impose a doctrinaire, harmonizing edict on biblical scholarship; only to urge that the canonical context of a biblical book ought to be allowed a prominent place in its interpretation. He wants to maintain that the meaning established by reference to the canon has a reasonable claim to priority over a meaning that would make it altogether impossible to integrate the book into the canon at all, even if this could be shown to be the 'original' meaning.

I think we can see that, if we leave aside the element of prescription in Childs's proposals, he is right to say that the canonical level is at least one *possible* level of meaning in a text. The idea is coherent, even if we can't see why it should be normative. At the very least, the canonical approach extends the range of methods available to the student of the Bible and suggests new questions that we may ask of the text.

The Canonical Approach and Literary Competence

How does all this relate to our theme of literary competence? In one sense it would be fair to say that Childs is not concerned with specifically *literary* competence, but with something that may be described as *theological* competence. He is asking how we should read the biblical text, if we wish to take seriously the fact that it

forms a canon of religious literature within a particular tradition –
a tradition[8] to which we ourselves belong. But it would be short-
sighted to see this as having no consequences of a literary sort; for
we may say that 'religious literature' is itself the description of a
literary genre, so that in trying to establish appropriate conventions
for reading texts within a sacred canon Childs is not only contribu-
ting to theology, but also helping to clarify what are the distingui-
shing marks of canonical religious literature as against other types
of writing. One condition, we might say, of describing a text as part
of a religious 'canon', is that it must be read as cohering with other
texts recognized as canonical within the same religious tradition;
and this is a fact about what we could call the 'sociology of literature' just as much as about theology.

Once the matter is put in this way, a committed Christian is
almost certain to feel that it has a debunking tendency. Surely, he
will say, the reason why our canonical texts must be read in this
way is not that *we* have conventions for 'canonicity', but that the
canonical texts are given by God and therefore must in reality (not
just by convention) be consistent? But Childs, as we have seen, is
not prepared to say this: and it seems to me best that our discussion
also should 'bracket out' the question whether these particular texts
ought to be canonical, and to accept that, if they are, that fact
constrains us (so long as we are working within the tradition in
question) to read them in the ways he outlines. In other words, the
'canonical approach' does indeed provide in principle a way in
which the reader can become competent in reading texts of a
particular genre – the genre 'canonical religious literature'. We shall
see in the next chapter, however, that there are very considerable
difficulties in applying the method in practice; and that to be fully
coherent it probably needs to move even further than Childs would
accept in the direction of styles of literary criticism that are wholly
indifferent to historical questions.

In short, canonical approaches are attractive but somewhat
unstable. They tend, if they are not willing to embrace an exceedingly high view of biblical inspiration, to require the support of
such extremely conventionalist and even determinist theories of
textual meaning as are characteristic of 'structuralism'. Their desire
to move beyond the traditional insistence on 'the original meaning
of the text' lands them in some strange company; and it may well

be that in the end the price of contemporary relevance will again be found higher than it looked at first glance, and higher than a critic such as Childs is prepared to pay.[9]

Further Reading

B. S. Childs, *Introduction to the Old Testament as Scripture*. Philadelphia 1979

J. Barr, 'Childs' Introduction to the Old Testament as Scripture' *JSOT* 16 (1980), pp. 12–23

7

CANON AS CONTEXT

Two statements are made as if they are connected, and the reader is forced to consider their relations for himself. The reasons why these facts should have been selected for a poem is left for him to invent; he will invent a variety of reasons and order them in his mind.

William Empson, *Seven Types of Ambiguity*
(London 1930), p. 25

Preliminary Reading

B. S. Childs, *Introduction to the Old Testament as Scripture* (Philadelphia 1979), pp. 46–106

Beyond Historical Criticism

Any group of texts that form a canon – even in the purely literary sense of the 'canon' of a given author's works – will be partly misunderstood if they are read as isolated units. Although we can study each of Shakespeare's plays separately, and indeed for some purposes must do so, most literary critics would say that they must also be read as parts of Shakespeare's complete works. Questions about the way each contributes to what we mean by 'Shakespeare' are not the only questions worth asking, but it would be a strange approach to literature that never asked them at all. In this sense, B. S. Childs is plainly correct in adding a question about meaning at the canonical level to the agenda for biblical criticism, and in insisting that we cannot regard our study of an Old Testament text as complete until we have asked what it means now that it is part of the Old Testament canon, as well as what it meant at a pre-canonical stage. For the Old Testament is not a random collection of

89

heterogeneous texts: it has been constituted (through the Church's decision to 'canonize' it) a unified corpus: a canon.

But, as we have seen, Childs himself does not understand his canonical approach as simply another, hitherto neglected, area of historical literary criticism; he understands it as different *in kind* from all previous methods. That is why he refuses to speak of 'canonical *criticism*', as if it were on a level with 'form criticism' or 'redaction criticism'.[1] In this chapter I shall strongly support Childs's claim to be original, but shall argue that the most original parts of his thesis are also the most questionable.

We begin by noting that the difference between the canonical method and the various kinds of historical criticism has two aspects. (1) First, the canonical approach is conceived as a *theological* mode of study. It is an attempt to heal the breach between biblical study and theology, and it assumes (at least for the purpose of method) that the interpreter is not a detached, neutral critic free from religious commitment, but a believer, trying to apply the biblical text to the contemporary life of the Church.

(2) Secondly, the canonical approach clearly belongs more to the realm of what in ordinary usage would nowadays be called 'literary' criticism than to that of the 'historical' study of texts, in that it is concerned with what the text *means* rather than with what it *meant*. All the other methods we have considered so far are historical, in the sense that they ask about the intentions of the person or group that produced the text we now have, and seek to reconstruct these intentions on the basis of what can be known about the historical and social context in which the texts were written. The canonical method, on the other hand, is not primarily concerned with what was in the mind of the final compilers of the canonical text; if it were it would be simply a branch of redaction criticism. It is concerned with the meanings each part of the text is constrained to have by its juxtaposition with all the others. Canonical meanings are a function of the shape of the canon and do not depend on our being able to reconstruct the minds of the canonizers. For the same reason, they have a certain permanence and timelessness that bypasses the problems of the cultural gap between ourselves and their 'original' authors, which has so preoccupied modern biblical scholarship.

On both these counts, Childs's approach is genuinely new. Any criticism of it which assumes that it is merely a minor addition to existing methods will be bound to miss the mark. In what follows, I shall try to suggest that, while the recovery (or perhaps discovery) of a canonical dimension is a solid gain which biblical scholars ought to take into their system, there are problems at both theological and literary levels in Childs's statement of the correct approach to it. And I shall develop the hint at the end of the last chapter, that a thoroughgoing pursuit of the 'canonical' meaning of texts ought probably to lead to a position much closer to that of many biblical structuralists than we may wish, on other grounds, to adopt.

Which Canon?

We may begin at the theological end with a question that will quite quickly be found to have literary implications, too: how are we to define the limits of the Old Testament canon? There are two major 'canons' of the Old Testament, the Hebrew and Greek, which differ very widely; indeed, from a 'canon-critical' perspective it is probably more accurate to say that there are *three* canons, among which the canon critic must choose. Jews and Protestant Christians, it is true, share the same canon in the sense that they accept as canonical only the books of the Hebrew Bible, excluding those books of the Greek Bible called 'apocryphal' by them and 'deuterocanonical' by Catholic and Orthodox Christians. But of course they differ in their overall canon of Scripture, in that for the Jewish community this does not include the New Testament, which for all Christians forms part of the canonical context for reading even Old Testament texts (cf. Childs's discussion of Psalm 8).

The historical problems surrounding the acceptance of the canon and the definition of its extent in each community are enormous, but do not immediately concern us here. Childs holds that for Jews and Christians alike the text which ought to be regarded as normative when practising the canonical method is the Masoretic text of the Hebrew Scriptures. But this is one of the parts of his case that many readers have found least persuasive. It is hard not to be swayed by the purely historical arguments of scholars such as A. C. Sundberg[2] – writing before Childs had developed his theories – to the effect that before the Reformation there had never been a time when the Christian Church acknowledged any canon

91

but that of the Greek Bible; so that the attempt by the Reformers to 'restore' the Old Testament canon to its original limits was hopelessly anachronistic. If it is true, as seems now to be widely agreed, that at any time when it made sense to draw a distinction between 'canonical' and 'non-canonical' books Jews and Christians have recognized different canons, then Childs's argument that we must take the Masoretic text as our norm, because it is the one form of the Old Testament that Jews and Christians have in common, is bound (for all its ecumenical attractiveness) to seem rather perverse.

In any case, whatever we believe are the 'correct' limits of the *Old* Testament canon, the fact that all Christians see it within a larger canon that includes and indeed is dominated by the New Testament must surely put paid to any possibility of large-scale agreement between Jewish and Christian scholars on the 'canonical meaning' of many, perhaps most, Old Testament texts.[3] For the Christian, it is *on Childs's own principles* a mistake, closely analogous to that persistently made by traditional historical critics, to read an Old Testament text without regard to the canonical context defined by its juxtaposition with other texts in both Old *and New* Testament canons; the Old Testament, for the Christian, is only *part* of the canon, just as for both Jews and Christian Genesis, say, is only part of the Old Testament/Hebrew Scriptures.

Ecclesiastes: a Case in Point

The effect of this argument is not, I believe, to weaken the case for the canonical approach in itself, but rather to suggest that it would be better if it could become a specifically *literary* approach, rather than a *theological* tool for reuniting biblical criticism with Christian faith. What the canonical method can do is to establish what meanings a given text can have within a given canon, and to show how these meanings would change if the limits of the canon were differently defined. The book of Ecclesiastes once again provides an instructive illustration of this.

As is well known, the Hebrew Scriptures contain very little material that suggests the existence of a worthwhile life after death: certainly nothing that could serve as the basis for arguing that Qoheleth's pessimism about man's ultimate fate needs to be read against a background of assurance that one day there will be a glorious resurrection of the righteous, or that their souls will live on in an exalted spiritual realm. But if our Old Testament canon includes the deuterocanonical book of Wisdom, as is the case for the Catholic or Orthodox Christian, then the canonical context of Ecclesiastes is quite different. If, as Wisdom claims, 'the souls of the righteous are in the hand of God, and no torment will ever touch them . . . for though in the sight of men they were punished, their hope is full of immortality' (3:1, 4), then Qoheleth's insistence that man and beast have the same empty fate must, at the canonical level, be read with different eyes – perhaps as the kind of gloomy reflection that one must pass through before one can fully recognize the goodness of the God who in the end *will* reward the righteous; as the question to which Wisdom provides the answer.[4] An even more marked shift of meaning would be introduced if the New Testament passages about resurrection were allowed to colour our reading, and we have seen that this has often historically been the case when Christians have read and pondered on Ecclesiastes. Childs's own sample studies show with admirable clarity how such shifts occur.

Criteria for Canonicity

We seem to have established that canonical criticism 'works', in the sense that it is possible to ask about the 'canonical meaning' of texts. We can find out what a work must mean, given that it stands within a particular canonical context. I cannot see, however, that the canonical method itself can establish which of the many possible canonical contexts is the 'correct' one. This is a question that belongs more properly to systematic or dogmatic theology. There are no methods 'internal' to biblical study that will enable us to decide what ought to be in the canon. The canonical approach seems to be far more neutral theologically than Childs intends. Just as redaction criticism can tell us what was the theological belief of 'J' or the compiler of Ecclesiastes, so the canonical method can tell us what theological beliefs these works can sustain within any given collection of texts accepted as canonical; but there are a number of possible canonical collections, and Childs's approach does not help us to choose between them.

Indeed, by an unkind paradox, the one approach to questions of canon that does at least claim to use internal biblical criteria rather than ecclesiastical edict as the test of canonicity is likely to be peculiarly hostile to Childs's method. Luther insisted – and the Lutheran Churches have traditionally followed him in this – that ultimately the only criterion of canonicity was the extent to which a given text bore witness to Christ. It has often been pointed out that this in practice can reduce canonicity to an entirely subjective matter: who is to be the judge of what bears witness to Christ? But the important point to note here is that the criterion can be applied at all only if it is possible to read each book of the Old or New Testament on its own terms *without regard* to its canonical context, and to decide whether its 'plain sense' is compatible with the Christian gospel. The Christian's decision about this will then determine whether or not it should stand in his canon. If Childs's method is applied, then it becomes impossible *ex hypothesi* for any book that already is in the canon to be read as incompatible with the canon's general drift, since the canonical method consists in applying the principle stated above: do not read biblical texts as conflicting with each other. For the method to work, therefore, the canon must be taken as given, and it cannot be justified on any grounds internal to itself – say, as consisting of those books that are in fact worthy expressions of Jewish or Christian faith – without begging the question.

Again, then, the approach proves to be theologically neutral at best: once we have a canon, we can use the canonical method to interpret it, but in order to decide what should be in the canon we need to rely on some other criterion. For a Catholic Christian, or for a Reformed Christian such as Childs, this may be found in an appeal to the authority of the Church, or in a high view of scriptural inspiration. But for anyone in the Lutheran tradition it would need to be grounded in some way of discovering what the texts in question originally meant (their 'plain sense'), in order to go on and test how far this bears witness to Christ. It is hard to see how this can be done without some use of the historical-critical approaches we have previously examined. This is why, in Lutheran biblical scholarship, the historical-critical method is regarded as having a high theological importance: it is not at all the 'problem' for theology that Childs portrays it as. Its practitioners are seen as true heirs of the Reformers.[5]

Seen from within this tradition, Childs's approach is not just neutral, but positively a retrograde step from a theological point of view. It entails an insistence on reading the text so that it fits in with what we take to be an acceptable meaning: in effect, using it as a peg on which to hang theological beliefs that are actually derived from a confessional allegiance. To many Lutherans, there would be little to choose between 'the canonical approach' and a traditional Catholic insistence that the Bible may only be read in accordance with Christian tradition – even that the Church as *ecclesia docens* is its only and infallibly inspired interpreter. It is not surprising that Childs has little following in Germany. One misses in his proposals the sense so dear to the heirs of the Reformation (including many in his own Calvinist tradition) that the biblical text is something with rough edges, set over against us, not necessarily speaking with one voice, coming to us from a great distance and needing to be weighed and tested even as *it* tests and challenges us: *adversarius noster*, in Luther's phrase.

Pre-critical or Post-critical?

It seems, then, that the limits of the canon that is to form the context for interpretation are set by some authority other than the texts themselves. But in that case this authority is likely to have opinions about the proper reading of the texts within its canon – opinions which may not always coincide with the meanings a canon critic extracts by analysing the inherent shape of the canon. If it is essentially the Christian or Jewish community that defines the limits of the Old Testament canon, does this not mean that the interpreter is under some constraint, not just to read the particular *form* of the Old Testament his community accepts, but also to read it *in the manner* his community regards as normative?

At times it seems that Childs is prepared to accept this corollary of his approach. His commentary on Exodus contains, in addition to the usual historical-critical discussions of the text, a fairly comprehensive treatment of the history of its interpretation; it is one of the first critical commentaries ever to allow such a major place to the exegesis of Augustine, Calvin and rabbinic commentators. Nevertheless Childs does not wish to be misunderstood as equating the canonical approach with the study of the history of biblical interpretation. In his *Introduction*, he makes it clear that the study of patristic or medieval exegesis is only a means to an end, a tool to help in understanding the canonical text's *inherent* meaning. The usefulness of the great commentaries of the Fathers and the Reformers lies primarily in the fact that they, like Childs himself but unlike most scholars since the rise of the historical-critical method, worked in conscious awareness of the canonical dimension. Like him, they were asking questions about the text's meaning *as Holy Scripture*, rather than about the intentions of its putative original authors. But they do not themselves form a further 'canon' within which the text is to be read. We are not to go on and establish a further rule of the form: read the text so that it coheres with the theology of Augustine/Calvin/Maimonides/*et al.*

Now at this point it becomes clear that the canonical approach is ultimately unconvincing at the theological level, and that it can carry its case only if it accepts the limitations of becoming purely a technique for a *literary* reading of the Old Testament text. There are two reasons for this.

(1) First, Childs insists that we should read the biblical text only at the canonical level. We must ignore all earlier, 'pre-canonical' stages and interpret it only within the web of meanings constituted by the final form of the canon as the early Church and synagogue established it. But if those decisions of the early Church and synagogue were so important, why are we not to trust their judgement a bit further? Why must we establish a cut-off point that will exclude later stages in the theological tradition of the Church or of Judaism? Childs's argument looks, on the face of it, very curious. First he says that we must read each Old Testament book from the point of view of its place within the canon, because that is how the Church/synagogue decided it should be read, by fixing the limits of the canon. But in the next breath he denies that our interpretation should be guided in any way by the exegetical tradition the Church/synagogue actually developed in the succeeding years. What rational grounds are there for this volte-face? It would be quite possible for a Jewish reader to argue that there is nothing specially new in Childs's approach, because the Scriptures have always been read by Jews within an interpretative tradition that observed the principle already outlined ('do not read biblical texts as conflicting with each other'). The framework ensuring that the canonical text

will be read 'canonically' is provided by the traditions codified in Mishnah, Talmud and other rabbinic collections. (Very similar traditions exist in the Christian Churches.) But Childs would say, I am sure, that this wholly misunderstands what he is saying. For him, this is not 'canonical' reading, it is the subjugation of Scripture to external authority. Scripture must continue to exercise a regulative role *against* tradition, as in classical Protestant theories; the 'canonical' meaning, established by examining the Old Testament text itself in its finished form, must be allowed to correct tradition.

It seems to me, as to many readers of Childs's work, that in this he is trying to have it both ways. On his view it is in principle possible that the very same generation of Christians who fixed the main outlines of the canon is also a hopelessly unreliable guide to the correct way of reading that canon. Indeed, it is more than possible, it is in fact the case, for early patristic exegesis was notoriously given to practices Childs would outlaw, such as allegorization and the exploitation of merely verbal quibbles.[6] In other words, if we practise canon criticism on the understanding that we are thereby being true to the mind of the Church that gave us the canon, we shall need to explain why our actual conclusions are so different from theirs. If we are not prepared to say that tradition furnishes any guidance to the correct way of *reading* the text, then why should it be considered normative when it tells us what the *limits* of the text are to be?

(2) Secondly, the suggestion that the canonical approach is required by a theological appraisal of the Old Testament is linked (rather paradoxically, in view of what has just been said) with an argument that it was at the canonical level that the Bible functioned for Christians before the rise of the historical-critical method. Childs is suggesting that our best hope of 'saving' the Bible for the Church is by a (consciously and properly critical) return to this way of looking at it. Now it is quite true that the Church (and synagogue) in ages past did indeed read the Old Testament as a coherent corpus, rather than in the fragmented condition historical criticism may be held to have reduced it to – even if in the process they used the dubious methods referred to just now. But to see them as therefore canon critics before their time is, I believe, seriously anachronistic. The great commentators – Augustine, Chrysostom, Calvin – to whom Childs appeals would have made little of the

suggestion that they were concentrating on the text in its canonical form *rather than* on what the writers of the biblical books had 'originally' intended. This contrast is a completely modern one, possible only for a reader to whom the principles of historical criticism are second nature; and this observation justifies us in calling the canonical method a *post-critical* approach, rather than a return to the days before historical criticism. An analogy may help to make this point clearer.

The 'anti-critical' stance of Childs's *Introduction* has led some to accuse it of giving succour to fundamentalists – even of being fundamentalist itself.[7] Whether fundamentalists will indeed draw comfort from Childs I am not qualified to judge; whether they do or not, it is manifestly plain that Childs himself cannot be called a fundamentalist. But the structure of his arguments bears an interesting *analogy* to those used by fundamentalists, and it is this I should like to draw out. Just as Childs suggests that many 'pre-critical' commentators were exponents of a sort of 'canonical method', so it may be argued that all pre-critical Christians were 'fundamentalists'; and fundamentalist scholars themselves often argue that the doctrine of Scripture they maintain is nothing new or eccentric, but simply the pure gospel as it was held by all in ages past. There is truth in this suggestion, if it means that Christians in times gone by took the Bible to be inerrant in what it asserted in all spheres – not only in theology but in history, geography, science and so on. But this was more a matter of its not having been suggested that there might be mistakes in Scripture, than of anyone's feeling a need to assert inerrancy polemically as an article of faith. Readers who assumed that the history of the world had been just as the Bible described it were not championing the biblical record against alternative theories; they were simply treating the Bible as the natural repository of all kinds of truth, somewhat as many modern readers treat reference works such as encyclopedias.[8] Fundamentalism properly so called is quite a different matter: a polemical assertion that the Bible is always right whatever other evidence may be or become available, in which inerrancy has become a dogma to be defended against a strong body of opinion that has consciously formulated a rival theory. As such, fundamentalism is a post-Enlightenment phenomenon and is as far from a naive acceptance of the biblical record at face value as it is from a naive scepticism about it. People can only be fundamentalists in this strict sense, if they live in a culture where it is possible to be a non-fundamentalist: fundamentalism is a 'post-critical' development.[9]

Canon criticism has many formal similarities with fundamentalism. The two systems share this feature, that they represent a response to questions that only occur within a context where the historical-critical method has come to be taken for granted as part of the landscape. Neither could survive the demise of historical criticism, for they draw all their strength from being able to wage war on it. It is the enemy they love to hate. In both cases the claim to be recapturing a pre-critical approach is attractive but specious. The Fathers were 'canon critics' only in the same measure as they were 'fundamentalists'. When they maintained that the whole Bible hung together and was consistent in all its parts, they were not taking a text which they knew or felt to be composite – the work of many authors from diverse and incompatible cultural and religious backgrounds – and proposing that it be *read as* a single coherent whole. They were asserting that it was the same God who spoke in all its parts, and seeking to find what was his word for the Christian reader. This word must be internally consistent, simply because it was spoken by a God who could not lie or change his mind. This approach, for all that it throws up strange and pleasing anticipations of canonical reading which Childs rightly, and with great skill, presses into service, is actually different at almost every point from the canonical method. Whatever else Childs may be doing, he is not taking us 'back to the canon', for no one has ever been aware of the canon in this way before. It is only after we have seen how varied and inconsistent the Old Testament really is that we can begin to ask whether it can *nonetheless* be read as forming a unity. To put it briefly: the canon critic is asking whether the Bible may not have a unity *after all*, just as the fundamentalist is asking whether it may not be right *after all*; and it is the 'after all' that defines the gulf – widest very often when it looks least daunting – which separates the modern critic of whatever persuasion from even the greatest of the pre-critical commentators.[10]

A Literary Interpretation of the Canonical Method

The upshot of all this is that we should not be swayed too much by Childs's own conscious perceptions of the significance of his new approach. Often he presents it as at least partly historical in orientation – an investigation of the mind of the early Jewish or Christian communities that defined the canon – or as a study of how Scripture has in fact been read. But he also insists that the canon critic should *not* use the interpretative techniques that were used, in pre-critical days, to preserve the unity of the canon; and this makes it difficult for him to sustain the claim that he is somehow recovering the mind of the canonizing community, or returning to the methods of the Fathers. His attempts to justify a Christian adherence to the Hebrew rather than the Greek canon on historical grounds seem similarly strained and could be suspected of special pleading.[11] Almost certainly, therefore, Childs is on firmer ground when he stresses – as in *Biblical Theology in Crisis* – that his approach is a new one. It would have been impossible before the rise of critical scholarship; indeed, it presupposes that critical scholarship is already established as the norm and that we can distance ourselves enough from it to question its basic assumptions. Theologically, the canonical method is brand-new.

But if it is new, it is also theologically unsatisfactory, for the reasons already outlined. Is there any way of modifying the method, perhaps giving it a narrower and less ambitious scope, that would nevertheless do justice to our sense that its innovations are sometimes fruitful, not always perverse? Here we may take up the suggestion made a few pages above that canon criticism may be best seen as a *literary* rather than as a theological approach to reading the Old Testament. It may not solve the riddle of how to hear the Bible as the Word of God in a new generation; but it may, more modestly, help us to understand what can be meant by calling a collection of religious texts a canon. I began the chapter by using the word canon in a completely secular sense, of the 'canon' of Shakespeare's plays, but it is clear from Childs's discussion that that would be too weak a sense to do justice to the Bible or indeed to any other religious canon. The canon of an author's works is no more than a list or catalogue; the reader is prepared to find unity and coherence, or disjointedness and muddle – though he will tend to prefer readings that detect at least a common style or character. But a canon of religious literature, which has existed within a particular tradition over a long period, and to which the adherents of that tradition subscribe even in the loosest way, raises a strong expectation that the books in it will cohere, illuminate each other, be of one mind. Childs may not be correct in claiming that this has always been the case. I suspect that the expectation of coherence owes much more to modern literary assumptions than he realizes, and that in 'canonizing' Scripture the Church gave far less thought to the contents and mutual relations of the biblical books than he implies. But if we are to continue to think of these books as 'the canon', it may well be that we shall need to read them in some such way as he proposes. This is not a matter of theology; it is merely a consequence of our belonging to a certain sort of literary culture. I shall go on in later chapters to make some suggestions about how this culture arose.

Our conclusion, then, is that Childs has made explicit, and skilfully illustrated, some rules for reading 'canonical religious literature'. By this means he has increased the biblical scholar's *literary* competence, enabling us to read larger complexes – up to and including the whole Old Testament – than we could cope with using historical-critical methods. Theologically, less has been achieved, far less than Childs claims. But there is no reason why we should not accept what we can accept, and be grateful. Childs's fascinating insights into what it is to read a canon need not be rejected merely because they claim too much for themselves. Perhaps, after all, it is better not to have a canon; perhaps Christianity should have resisted the temptation to become in any sense a religion of a book; perhaps the canon is a curse. But if we have one, and if we read it through twentieth-century, post-critical eyes, we shall find ourselves asking many of the questions Childs asks and looking for the same internal coherence and harmony that he seeks. We are likely to do these things much more carefully and, in the end, self-critically, for reading Childs.

From Canon Criticism to Structuralism

Childs's 'canonical method' logically implies that the biblical text, or indeed any other text, can be read without paying any heed to the intentions of authors, compilers or even canonizers. It is not a sub-type of redaction criticism; it is an attempt to read 'the text itself'.[12] We have already seen that it is sometimes possible to give an interpretation of a text which will strike many readers as plausible, and yet which can be shown not to have been intended by any of the people to whom the text owes its existence. Canon criticism suggests one framework for reading within which such interpretations may emerge. We may say, Given that a particular set of texts form a religious canon, each of them can reasonably be read as having a meaning whose result would be that all of them, taken collectively, formed a single coherent work. One could almost formulate the interpretative principle involved here as follows: Read all these texts as if they were written by one author (say, God) at a single sitting; set out what he must have meant by each of them if he also wrote all the others, and had a consistent purpose in doing so; then delete all references to the author from your final statement of their meaning. We know (from historical criticism) that the biblical texts did not in fact have a single author; but the meaning they have as a canon is the meaning they *would* have had if they *had* had a single author.

On such a view of literature, authors, whether real or merely notional, do not ultimately matter. The meaning of a text inheres in the text, or in the setting within which it is read, not in the intentions of those who wrote it. The text an author writes has a life of its own, and what it means will depend on the context in which it appears. If the book of Ecclesiastes had been lost from all copies of the Bible, and were then discovered among the Dead Sea scrolls as a 'non-canonical' text, its meaning would be different from what it is now.[13] This is one conclusion that plainly follows, once we abandon the author's intention as the criterion of meaning: that one and the same text can change its meaning, according to the context in which it is read. This is far from making meaning a subjective matter – quite the reverse. We cannot, as Childs justly points out, read Ecclesiastes merely as a piece of pessimistic wisdom even if we want to, once we take seriously its canonical setting. So determined by context is the meaning that the author himself cannot force the text to bear a meaning that the setting will not allow: Qoheleth may well be gnashing the teeth he would not have expected to find in Sheol over the way his bitter words have lost their edge by being included in the orthodox framework of sacred Scripture.

All this may seem quite bad enough to readers accustomed to historical-critical investigations, especially if it is their first taste of 'text-immanent' exegesis. It is all, I believe, implied in Childs's position, but he does not make it explicit, and he is not really very much interested in literary questions: for him, they are a mere side-effect of the theological issues with which he is wrestling. Once we have teased them out, however, we may ask whether it may not be possible to go further still down the road that leads away from authors and their intentions and into what may as yet look like swirling mists of abstract speculation. The answer is that there is indeed a long march still ahead of us, and by the end of it we may well look back to Childs as a reassuringly familiar, even rather old-fashioned friend. But an acquaintance with him may at least have loosened up some of our ideas, and made us ready to contemplate the themes, obsessively embraced by some biblical scholars and disdainfully dismissed by others, of structuralist criticism.[14]

Further Reading

A. C. Sundberg, 'The Bible Canon and the Christian Doctrine of Inspiration', *Interpretation* 29 (1975), pp. 352–71

J. Barr, 'Childs' Introduction to the Old Testament as Scripture', *JSOT* 16 (1980), pp. 12–23

J. A. Sanders, *Torah and Canon*. Philadelphia 1972

B. S. Childs, *Old Testament Theology in a Canonical Context*. London 1985

8

STRUCTURALIST CRITICISM

Said the Red Queen, 'Do you know Languages? What's the French
for fiddle-de-dee?'
'Fiddle-de-dee's not English,' Alice replied gravely.
'Who ever said it was?' said the Red Queen.
Alice thought she saw a way out of the difficulty, this time.
'If you'll tell me what language "fiddle-de-dee" is, I'll tell you the
French for it!' she exclaimed triumphantly.

Lewis Carroll, Through the Looking-Glass, ch. 9

Preliminary Reading

Genesis 32
J. Culler, *Structuralist Poetics* (London 1975), pp. 3–54

The Road to Structuralism

We have arrived at structuralism *via* canon criticism, but it should
be said at once that this is a very winding route, a route possibly
never taken before. 'Structuralist' studies of the Bible had appeared
well before Childs wrote his first book on biblical interpretation. It
is simply that, for anyone who has studied the Bible in an Anglo-
Saxon context, his approach is much more obviously the next logical
step after redaction criticism, whereas structuralism seems bizarre
and 'foreign'. By pressing the canonical approach to its limits, we
can start to see issues emerging which only structuralism, among
existing biblical methods, makes any attempt to deal with. So the
order of presentation is not historical, but logical – and logical
within the terms of my own argument, not in a way accepted by
the wider scholarly community. As a matter of fact there seems to

be rather little contact between structuralists and 'canon critics';[1] certainly both sorts of critic would repudiate suggestions of influence by the other!

At any rate it is now time to present structuralist criticism on its own terms. I hope that the winding route will be vindicated as the reader finds that some of the concepts and categories involved are, because of the discussion of canonical method, already old friends (or perhaps enemies). We should begin by asking what led biblical scholars – first in France, but then in the United States and even in Britain and Germany – to think that this movement in contemporary philosophy and literary criticism might be profitable in studying the biblical text.[2]

I believe that there are two main reasons why biblical scholarship has begun to move in the direction of a structuralist approach to the Old Testament text. (1) The first is a sense of disappointment and disillusionment with the traditional historical-critical methods. This disappointment is very close to that felt by Childs. It arises as soon as we turn from a detailed attention to historical methods and ask ourselves this question: when we have analysed the text in all these ways, are we any closer to understanding it and being able to read it as it stands? My own discussion in chapters 1–5 above seemed to end in the same kind of unease. The structuralist movement in literary criticism itself arose from a certain discontentment with the lines of approach traditionally adopted by critics, and in particular from the realization that there are certain kinds of text (particularly traditional, orally transmitted texts such as myths, legends and folk-tales) into which conventional criticism, with its concern for authorship, style and artistic technique, affords very little insight. As one of the clearest exponents of structuralist literary theory, Jonathan Culler, puts it, 'we . . . do not know how to read myths'[3] – we have lost the recipe, in fact. The closely similar feeling that has led some biblical scholars to embrace structuralism is well summed up by J. W. Rogerson:

Could we substitute 'the Bible' where Culler has used the word 'myths'? . . . Would it be fair to say that 'we do not know how to read the Bible'? With regard to some parts of the Bible, this would be quite untrue. In the case of the so-called Wisdom Literature, and especially a book like Proverbs, we can read it in the light of comparable literature from the ancient Near East, and understand it as an instance of a wider class of writing. Again, in the case of books like Daniel, we can learn something about the 'enabling conventions' of what we call 'apocalyptic'. It would be fair, though, to say that although we know much about the individual items which might make up a prophetic book, we do not know how to read a prophetic book as a whole; and the same could be said for parts of the Pentateuch. . . . The standard 'Introductions to the Literature of the Old Testament' often tell students something about the individual literary forms which can be found in the Old Testament – lament, messenger formula, law speech, and so on, but I know of no 'Introduction' which among other things suggests to the student how he might *read* the Old Testament. Perhaps this accounts for the common experience of examiners in the Old Testament, that the content of the Old Testament is often less well known than the critical theories about it.[4]

(2) Secondly, there is a persistent awareness among biblical scholars that the ways in which they have traditionally studied the biblical text are now in important respects out of line with what is going on in the wider literary world: an awareness which literary critics sometimes painfully reinforce by acid comments on their professional competence.[5] Though this sometimes results in a rather uncritical desire to trail along after the latest literary fashion, it also produces a (surely desirable) determination to seek some common ground with critics in other branches of literary study. Biblical structuralism should not be simply dismissed out of hand as a fad. The question whether these new methods could be applied to the biblical text was bound to be asked, sooner or later.

Structuralism and Semiotics

I have already touched on a number of the leading themes of structuralist criticism, especially in the initial description of 'literary competence'. But structuralism is not just a theory about literature; it is a general style of interpretation that can be adopted in almost all kinds of inquiry, in science and in the humanities alike. In biblical studies structuralist *anthropology*, of which C. Lévi-Strauss is the leading exponent, has had considerable influence,[6] and structuralist *linguistics* has made its mark on the study of Biblical Hebrew. Our inquiry is limited fairly tightly to structuralism in its *literary* applications; but even to introduce these it will be easier in many ways if we begin by looking at a few non-literary aspects of the structuralist approach, from which its distinctive flavour can be appreciated more readily.

Some of the most accessible of these aspects can be found in what some structuralists call *semiotics*. This term is sometimes used as a synonym for 'structuralism', or (more recently) for what is also called 'post-structuralism',[7] but it is often applied more narrowly to structuralist theories about social conventions of various sorts, and this is the sense I am concerned with at the moment. A semiotics of human behaviour can provide an illuminating (and usually rather entertaining) way of codifying and analysing many fairly common-sense intuitions about human social life, and it is as such that it can help us to feel our way into the more austere world of literary structuralism.[8]

A structuralist approach to the understanding of human social life begins with the observation that man, unlike other animals whose environment and way of life are fixed for them in ways beyond their control, to a great extent makes his own world. The human world is created by *culture* at least as much as by nature. It is within a culture that actions, words and gestures have meaning. For example, all normal human beings can clasp each other's hands, and so can all normal chimpanzees: but it is only within human culture, in which certain conventions obtain about how such gestures are to be interpreted, that it is possible to 'shake hands'. The expression 'shaking hands' does not merely describe a physical action; it interprets it as having a certain significance, and that significance varies with different human cultures. In English society, a handshake normally signifies that an introduction is being effected; whereas in most continental European cultures it has a much less specific meaning and is a normal accompaniment of all greetings. It is this cultural difference that makes possible a well-known piece of misleading advice to visitors to Britain: 'In England it is normal when entering a railway carriage to shake hands with all those already present.'[9] Such a joke would be impossible if all human cultures were the same; but, more to our purpose, it would also be impossible if the 'meaning' of a handshake were determined by nature, or (we could say) by biology. The joke is possible precisely because, on the one hand, the meaning of such gestures as a handshake is entirely a matter of convention within a given culture (it *could* be the custom to shake hands with all one's fellow-passengers, and in some countries it probably is); and, on the other hand, their meaning is *determined* by the conventions obtaining in the given culture, so that they cannot normally be used to mean anything other than what they do mean within that culture. A handshake has no 'inherent' meaning: it is a purely conventional sign whose meaning derives from a general agreement as to what it shall mean. Yet we cannot use it to mean what we like, unless we do not mind being persistently misunderstood; and when we shake hands, we convey certain impressions and expectations, whether we wish or intend to or not. A handshake conveys a greeting, whatever my feelings towards the owner of the other hand, because it is part of a conventional code: it has a *public meaning*, which attaches to it irrespective of any private meanings I might like to be able to use it to convey.

A second example may help to reinforce these points. When botanists classify plants, they are trying to provide a system of classification which corresponds to distinctions really existing in nature: they are not, that is, expressing value-judgements or suggesting that certain plants have particular 'meanings', but trying simply to reflect various natural distinctions in their classification. But this is very different from the way in which plants are classified in the non-scientific world of human culture. In our culture, at least, one of the most important distinctions between plants has no connection at all with the distinctions recognized as botanically significant. This is the distinction between flowers and weeds. There is, as the old saying has it, 'no such thing' as a weed: a weed is simply a flower in the wrong place. It is a matter of pure human convention which plants are to be regarded as 'flowers' (and therefore desirable) and which as weeds (and therefore evil), and it is quite possible to imagine cultures in which convolvulus was highly prized and exhibition dandelions carefully cultivated. But this does not at all mean that everyone is free to decide for himself what he will count as a flower or as a weed. One's intentions will be misunderstood if one insists on sending bunches of dandelions by

Interflora; the neighbours will not be swayed by the argument that their roses are spoiling the appearance of a field of giant hog-weed. The distinction between weeds and flowers is at the same time both *conventional* and *determined*.

There is one further aspect of cultural 'systems', such as the conventions about social gestures or about the significance of various types of plant, which must be mentioned before we shall be in a position to see how a structuralist or 'semiotic' approach can be applied to literature. I argued that the distinction just mentioned, between flowers and weeds, is ultimately an artificial one; but it is worth noticing that the artificiality applies to our use of *both* terms. It is not just that a weed may be defined as 'not-a-flower': a flower, in its turn, is 'not-a-weed'. In a culture where there were no weeds – that is, where it had not occurred to anyone to designate some plants as undesirable – there would not be any 'flowers' either, in the evaluative sense we give to the word. Similarly, a handshake can only convey the meaning it does because it is part of a *system* of physical gestures, the meaning of each being defined by contrast with all the others. It is a handshake because it is not a kiss, not a slap on the face, not a clap on the shoulder; and it is as one possibility within a cultural system in which these are also possibilities that it has the meanings it has. In itself it is empty, or meaningless: it draws its meaning from the other options available, with which it is contrasted. When we shake someone's hand, we are at the same time *not* kissing him, *not* patting his head, *not* clapping him on the back; and the meaning that will be conveyed by the handshake depends very precisely on which of these other possibilities would have been thinkable under the circumstances. We cannot 'read' the significance of such a gesture until we know the conventions of the cultural system in which it takes place: notoriously, as in our railway-carriage example, the handshake has a different place in the overall system of gestures in England than it does in France or Italy.

Structuralism and Language

This aspect of meaning, as a function of contrast within a given system, has its clearest illustration in language; and it is, indeed, from the study of linguistics that 'semioticians' have borrowed it.

Words or sentences in a language do not have any 'inherent' meaning: this is an absolutely fundamental principle in the modern study of language.[10] The meaning they have is a function of the system or structure of which they form a part, and of the other words and sentences within that system with which they contrast.

This is clearest, perhaps, at the level of *sound*. In English, and in other European languages, the distinction between the sounds we represent as 'l' and 'r' is significant for meaning: thus 'lot' and 'rot' mean different things, and English speakers have to listen for (though they have no difficulty in picking up) the difference between the 'l' and 'r' at the beginning of the two words. One can easily suppose, naively, that the distinction has some sort of 'natural' existence – that any language would be bound to give a different meaning to words beginning with the two letters in question, even if they were identical in other respects. However, countless jokes about the Japanese will remind us that this is not so. In English the sounds 'l' and 'r' are contrasted, and the contrast is semantically significant (in other words, it makes a difference to the meaning); but in some languages one sound is perceived as a semantically insignificant variant of the other, much as in English we do not attribute any semantic importance to whether or not an 'r' is trilled.

The same principle extends to the meaning of words and of whole sentences. John Lyons points out that even so apparently simple a sentence as 'The cat sat on the mat' can present almost insuperable difficulties if one tries to translate it into French, because in French certain contrasts are marked in the language which English does not always make explicit. For example, is 'the cat' here male or female? We need to know, before we can decide between *le chat* and *la chatte*. Does 'sat' mean 'was seated' (*était assis[e]*) or 'sat down' (*s'est assis[e]*), or 'was in the process of sitting down' (*s'asseyait*)? In other words, the sentence 'the cat sat on the mat' does not correspond exactly in meaning to any possible French translation of it, because the other possible sentences with which it contrasts in English are not the same as the other possible sentences with which such a translation would contrast in French. 'Cat' itself in English contrasts with only one set of alternatives – dog, horse, sheep, etc. – whereas *chat* contrasts *both* with *chien, cheval, mouton, and* with *chatte*. Its more precise or narrower meaning is a function of this double contrast.[11]

The idea that meaning is a function of contrast within a given system – that we cannot say what a word, a sentence, a gesture, or an action *means* until we know what system or structure it is part of, and with what it is to be contrasted – is at the root of one term encountered frequently in every kind of structuralist work: 'binary opposition'. Structuralists tend to argue that all structures within which meaning can be generated, whether they be linguistic, social or aesthetic, can be analysed in terms of pairs of opposites. Although it may be going too far to make so much of the *binary* character of the contrasts through which meaning is produced (since, as we have seen, it is often a matter of multiple contrast), it is surely right to see contrast as such as of the essence of meaning. To be able to say what meaning is to be attached to an utterance, a gesture or an object, we need to know what it is not, as well as what it is: to know from what range of possibilities it has been selected, and what was excluded when it was chosen. We need to know how it could have been different, if we are to understand the significance of its being how it is.

Indeed, it is of the essence of things which are said to have 'meaning' that they could have been otherwise. We read off their meaning from our perception of what is significant about their being the way they are. We can say that a house 'means' something, in that its architect could have designed it differently, and chose to design it as he did out of a range of possible options: its being like *this* and not like *that* is therefore (at least potentially) significant. We can hardly ask in the same way what a mountain means, because it does not form part of a cultural system: it just is. Significance seems always to depend on the possibility of a thing's having been otherwise. If I have a normal voice, then in any conversation the volume I speak at conveys meaning, over and above the meaning of the actual words I use: by speaking in a whisper I can convey secrecy; by shouting I can convey anger or irritation or aggression. But if I have had an operation on my throat, and I can only speak in a whisper anyway, then the fact that I am whispering ceases to be contrasted with any other possible state of affairs, and thereby it at once loses all significance. Nothing can be deduced from it, because it is not part of any system of contrasts: I am no longer whispering *and thereby not shouting*, I am simply speaking in the only way I can. The principle of binary opposition, therefore, however

111

curious it may sound, does touch on something fundamental in our perception of what meaning is.

Structuralism and Systems

It will be seen from all this that structuralism is, in its essentials, not a method of inquiry, but a general theory about human culture and its various branches: language, social life, art. This theory asserts that *meaning is a function of the structures of a cultural system*. The primary question to ask about meaning, whether it be linguistic, social or aesthetic, is not 'what did the speaker/acquaintance/artist mean by that?' but 'what does that sentence/gesture/work of art mean?' Meaning is not something that has an independent existence deriving from an intention on someone's part, which is then *expressed* through some specific medium, verbal or social; meaning is an effect which *inheres in* certain combinations of sounds, or of gestures, or of artists' materials, within a given cultural setting. It depends wholly on agreed conventions, both in the sense that it cannot exist outside a conventional structure, and also in the sense that private individuals cannot choose to convey meanings that their culture does not make possible. One can of course flout conventions, but one cannot work in the absence of any conventions. To revert to the example we used briefly in chapter 1: the 'meaning' of a move in a game of chess is determined wholly by the rules of the game, even though these rules are entirely a matter of convention. To discover what a given move 'meant', or what significance it had, in a particular game, we need to be in command of (be 'competent' in) the game of chess; we do not need a knowledge of the psychology of the players. The possible meanings of moves at chess are determined completely by the structures of the game; and though players can make 'original' moves in the sense of moves that *exploit* to the full the possibilities the rules make available, they cannot make moves that contravene the rules (for example, moving a knight as if it were a rook) without ceasing to play the game altogether. Such a move has literally 'no meaning' within chess: it is not a real move at all. The meaning that a genuine move has is determined by its contrast with other possible moves, just as the value of the pieces on the board is a function of their relation to each other. Thus a queen has a high value only because it is part of an ordered structure

112

within which it can make a wider variety of moves than any other piece. If the rules were changed so that all pieces could move as the queen moves, it would cease to have this special value; and if one removed it from the board, which is its own cultural context or 'world', it would have neither meaning nor value, but would become simply an oddly-shaped wooden object.

Structuralism and Literature

The contention of literary structuralists is that literature is a cultural system exactly analogous to a language, a society or a game.[12] The fact that we are able to understand and to extract meaning from literature shows that we are, in the sense defined in chapter 1, competent in literature, just as we may be competent in a given language, in a set of social conventions, or in a game such as chess. We have some command of the structures within which literary works are capable of having (not just linguistic but) literary meaning, of existing *as* novels or lyric poems or whatever. It is important not to be misled by the word 'structure' here into thinking that structuralists are interested in the internal structures which authors implant in their works, in 'well-constructed' plots or effects of structure such as dramatic irony or tension – the concern, of course, of much traditional literary criticism. Structuralists do indeed interest themselves in the shape of works and can be found writing about narrative patterns, the shape of novels and so on; but they are interested in them only insofar as they throw light on the much larger issue of the structures of literature as a whole – in other words, as clues or pointers to the character of the *ordered system* which constitutes literature. Structuralist criticism is only secondarily concerned with investigating particular works for their own sake. Its primary concern is, in Daniel Patte's words, with 'showing *how* texts "make sense", that is, what are the "mechanisms" through which a text is meaningful'.[13]

A structuralist, then, is not necessarily bent on detecting new meanings in a particular text – though often he will in fact claim to have done so, in passing – but rather with showing how it is that a text comes to have the meaning that it evidently has, with explaining why the reader is likely to perceive it as bearing that sort of meaning.[14] He will suggest that texts have the meaning they do

113

because literature forms a cultural system operating according to certain conventions; and he will claim that the main importance of most texts is the insight they give us into what those conventions are. In other words, we do not study literature in order to understand particular texts better: we study individual texts in order to understand 'literature', taken to be a cultural system. It can easily be imagined that the place of the author in such an analysis is fairly minimal. Patte again puts it very clearly when he says that traditional literary criticism has thought of man as author as 'a creator of significations', but that structuralism teaches us to think of literature as a system in which 'significations are imposed upon man'.[15] For the structuralist, the meaning of a text is a function of the type of literature it is, and the sorts of significance that the words composing it are capable of bearing, given that it is *this* kind of work rather than some other kind. What the author may have intended is, no doubt, an interesting question to those concerned with history or psychology, and sometimes may even be discoverable: but it is of no particular interest to the literary critic.

'The Morphology of the Folktale'

Structuralist studies both outside and within biblical studies have tended to concentrate on narrative texts, and especially on narrative material that has been transmitted orally in traditional cultures – in other words, the kind of literature we generally call folk-tale. The structuralist indifference to authorial intention is an obvious strength in studying such literature, for whatever 'meaning' a traditional folk-tale has can hardly be attributed to an 'author' in any case: it must in some sense inhere in the tale itself. Indeed, folk-tales are a great problem for any critic who wishes to argue that meaning always requires someone to mean it, for it is clear that most folk-tales have some kind of existence which transcends any given version of them. Thus all versions of *The Sleeping Beauty*, however varied in style, length or artistic skill, are in a real sense 'the same story'; and the essential tale cannot be said to have an author at all (not even a group or community), since it will have developed over a long period and, in some cases, in many different cultural settings.

It is because the Old Testament contains so much material that has obvious affinities with folk-tale that structuralism initially seemed so attractive to many biblical scholars. If we are to speak of the 'meaning' of folk-tales, it cannot be a matter of asking what someone meant by them: their meaning will have to be read off in some way from the tales themselves. Now one aspect of such tales which strikes most people who are familiar with them, in whatever culture, is their very high degree of stylization. They use certain 'stock' characters and situations, recurring motifs and plot-types. One needs no literary training to have a good idea of the conventions with which folk-tales operate, and to recognize at once whether or not a given story sounds like a folk-tale. For example, we should have little hesitation in deciding that *Cinderella* was a folk-tale, however long and circumstantial and 'novelistic' a version we might meet it in, but that *War and Peace*, even if reduced to a two- or three-page plot-summary, was not. How does this come about?

Long before literary structuralism was an organized movement an attempt had been made to provide an explanation of the properties that define 'folk-tale' and make it recognizable, in the work of the Russian formalist critic Vladimir Propp. His *Morphology of the Folktale* appeared in Russian in 1928, but it is only since the Second World War that it has been available in English and has become a major influence on literary structuralists.[16] Propp tried to show, by analysing a hundred examples of Russian folk-tales, that it is possible to reduce all the characters who appear in folk-tales to a finite number of types or 'roles', each defined by its relation to the others; and that all possible folk-tale plots may be generated by allowing these characters to interact in certain specifiable ways. Propp found, in fact, that the plots of all the folk-tales he examined could be reduced to a quasi-algebraic formula, and that any attempt to combine the characters in ways that transgressed this formula would produce stories that were instantly recognizable (intuitively) as 'not proper folk-tales'. In other words, he succeeded in showing that folk-tales form a closed system, rather as we argued that chess forms a closed system, which is entirely rule-governed.

The rules that determine what is or is not a 'well-formed' folk-tale are of a high order of generality, and we are normally not consciously aware of them, though through an analysis such as Propp's it is possible to *become* aware of them. Such an analysis does not make us able to understand or to be competent at reading folk-tales, where before we did not understand them; in this sense it conveys no fresh information. What it does is to explain how it comes about that we do understand these tales, by showing that they conform to certain patterns which are generated by a structured system. A knowledge of the syntax of a language enables us to see what are the mechanisms by which sentences can have the meaning we intuitively perceive them as having: Propp's analysis provides a sort of syntax of the folk-tale, by which it is possible to see what it is that makes a true folk-tale, and what is wrong with stories that we should intuitively recognize as 'breaking the rules'. For example, no one would have the slightest hesitation in denying the name 'folk-tale' to a version of *Red Riding Hood* in which the woodcutter freed the wolf, shot the grandmother and married Red Riding Hood. It will come as no surprise that Propp's rules declare such a plot to be impossible – though it may come as a relief.[17]

Once the full implications of Propp's work are realized, it is not surprising that other critics should have sought to extend his principles to cover the whole of literature, arguing that what applies to 'authorless' texts such as folk-tales is true also of literary genres traditionally regarded much more as the work of individual genius, such as novels or lyric poems or tragedies. Why can we not have a 'morphology of the novel' which will similarly account for the sense, which is undoubtedly familiar to most experienced readers of novels, that some works 'count as' real novels and others do not? In a way, this would be little more than an attempt to make more explicit and objective the principle of genre-recognition which (as we saw in chapter 1) is fundamental to all understanding of literature. However, before moving on to such far-reaching applications of the structuralist approach, I shall conclude this chapter by outlining one application of a method akin to Propp's to an Old Testament text. This is now a stock example: the discussion of Genesis 32 (Jacob wrestling with the angel) by the French literary critic, Roland Barthes.

Jacob, the Angel, and Roland Barthes

Genesis 32:22–32 has been, of course, the subject of a great deal of scholarly discussion by all the methods described so far.[18] Barthes' analysis examines it from the point of view of the grammar and syntax of folk-tale, and this produces some strikingly new insights.[19] I suspect that many readers of Genesis will share the experience that, however often they read this passage and however much they may try to ask only historical-critical questions about it, it never fails to give them a certain *frisson*, a blend of fascination and repulsion that sends a tingle down the spine: an effect it shares with such passages as 2 Kings 6:15–19 and Exodus 3:1–6. Though Barthes' discussion of the passage is not in the least concerned with the reader's psychological reactions – the subject is anathema to a committed structuralist – one very impressive side-effect of it is to account in some measure for the peculiarly numinous quality of the story; and this may well persuade the reader that he really is on to something important.

Barthes' analysis begins by defining the participants in the Genesis narrative in terms of their functions within the tale. They are stock items from the 'vocabulary' of folk-tale. Jacob is the Hero, who is on a Quest – one of the commonest of all folk-tale plots. God stands behind the present narrative as the Originator of the Quest. The 'man' or angel with whom Jacob wrestles is the Opponent, who waylays the Hero and tries to prevent him from accomplishing his mission. There are various 'syntactic' possibilities for combining these three characters in the plot. One standard pattern is for the Originator of the Quest to step in and help the Hero, either in person (as in stories where the Hero is given a magic horn or other device with which to summon the Originator's aid) or through intermediaries called Helpers (often friendly animals or people otherwise extraneous to the plot, such as the woodcutter in *Red Riding Hood*). Another is for the Originator to be present again at the end of the Quest – as when the Hero is sent by a lady to perform some deed, with her own hand in marriage as the prize for successfully accomplishing it.

But once we have become aware that the story of Jacob and the angel belongs to such a stock pattern – that it is to be read within the system of folk-tales – then certain very extraordinary features become apparent. The crucial factor, which gives Genesis 32 its peculiar flavour, is that here (in contravention of the rules) the Originator of the Quest and the Opponent turn out, in the moment of disclosure, to be one and the same. It is God who sends Jacob on his Quest, and God who (in the form of the 'man') opposes him at the fords of the Jabbok and seeks to destroy him.

This kind of transformation is, at the literary level, potentially very frightening, for it upsets the ordered 'world' in which folk-tale plots are played out. It throws our mental grasp of the story into confusion, making us wonder whether we have misunderstood the whole story of Jacob from the very beginning. Barthes argues that at the theological level it reveals a great deal about how the God of Israel was understood, and suggests that this story belongs, in effect, to the general movement of thought in pre-exilic Israel that we may call 'the avoidance of dualism'. Because Israelite theology is from quite early times aggressively monotheistic, it is impossible to countenance any forces opposed to God that have enough power to hinder God's chosen servants, in the way that the angel here hinders Jacob. Hence the story will be 'permissible' within Jewish monotheism only if the angel is identified with God, even though this destroys the story as a folk-tale. Barthes' suggestion is formally rather similar to the sorts of argument used by von Rad, when he tries to show that earlier mythological stories were 'demythologized' by those who used them as the basis for the primeval history in Genesis.[20] Just as, on von Rad's view, 'true' myth is impossible within Yahwism, so, Barthes seems to be saying, 'true' folk-tale cannot survive in the austerely monotheistic atmosphere of the faith of Israel. We may also be reminded a little of discussions about the possibility of true 'Christian tragedy'.[21]

It seems to me less clear that such *theological* conclusions follow from Barthes' work on Genesis 32, though they are certainly appealing. The point that surely does stand is the literary one: that Genesis 32 is able to have the effect it observably does have on most readers only because it *first* constrains us to read it as if it were a normal folk-tale, and *then* turns the tables on us by illicitly exploiting the conventions of such tales. The result is a surrealistic sense of disorientation. A parallel from modern literature would be a detective novel where the detective himself turned out to be the murderer. Indeed, detective stories have exercised much the same fascination as folk-tales on structuralist critics, and it is easy to see why: in both cases the conventions of the genre are limited and precise, and therefore readily exploited.[22] But it is not hard to find the same technique in other periods and types of literature. Consider, for example, the Middle English poem *Sir Gawain and the Green Knight*, where in the moment of disclosure we (and Gawain) learn that Sir Bertilak, his host, and the Green Knight, his adversary, are one and the same. The reader is likely to experience just the same shudder as in Genesis 32, and for the same reason: confusion of roles undermines our confidence that we know what we are reading.

A structuralist analysis such as Barthes' lays bare the mechanism by which the story of Jacob and the angel achieves its effect, in a way that no other discussion known to me has even attempted to do. It is only when we have properly understood that, within the system of the folk-tale, Originator and Opponent are defined by their binary opposition to each other and are therefore mutually exclusive that we can see why the story is so powerful. If the meaning of a folk-tale is a function of the conventions of the genre, then the meaning of *this* tale is a function of the flouting of those conventions. It is, in effect, parasitic on the true folk-tale

If Barthes is right, much of the distinctiveness of Old Testament literature may well lie in the way it exploits conventions. We have become accustomed to seeing the prophets as parodists, taking up secular or orthodoxly religious forms of speech (the lawsuit, the popular song, the priestly oracle) and filling them with new and surprising meanings;[23] but perhaps a great deal more of the Old Testament is 'prophetic' in this sense than we have hitherto suspected – including much of the narrative material. In passing, we may note that we owe such ideas of the prophets to form criticism; and form criticism, the least self-consciously 'historical' of our three traditional methods, might well have arrived at a more or less structuralist understanding of literature in time if it had been left to its own devices and not pressed into the service of traditio-historical reconstruction. At all events, there may well be much fruitful work to be done along the lines of Barthes' study of Jacob and the angel.

However, not all structuralist work on the Old Testament has been so concerned with large questions of the nature of literature or the distinctiveness of Israel; very often, like other kinds of criticism, it has been interested in the exegesis of particular passages for their own sake. In the next chapter I shall move on to this 'practical' structuralism.

Further Reading

D. Robey (ed.), *Structuralism: an Introduction.* Oxford 1973

D. Robertson, *The Old Testament and the Literary Critic.* Philadelphia 1977

9

BIBLICAL STRUCTURALISM

It has been said of Boehme that his books are like a picnic to which the author brings the words and the reader the meaning. The remark may have been intended as a sneer at Boehme, but it is an exact description of all works of literary art without exception.

C. Northrop Frye, quoted in E. D. Hirsch Jr,
Validity in Interpretation (London 1967), p. 1

Preliminary Reading

D. J. A. Clines, *The Theme of the Pentateuch.* Sheffield 1978

Convention and Constraint

The transition from structuralism as a theory to structuralism as an exegetical method is not a very smooth one. 'Structural(ist) exegesis' is certainly very common now,[1] but the expression sounds odd in the context of literary structuralism outside biblical studies. In principle, structuralists are concerned with *analysis* rather than with exegesis: they are not so much proposing new interpretations of texts as trying to show how *any* interpretation, old or new, comes to be an appropriate reading of a text. It is hardly surprising, however, that structuralist critics often do produce novel interpretations of familiar passages. Structuralism is interested in constraints – the constraints of the literary system within which any particular text has meaning – and often a structuralist analysis will show that works have been written and read within constraints that neither author nor reader is likely to be aware of. In such cases the structuralist will claim to be pointing out what the text has always meant, not to be producing novel interpretations; but his readers will probably find the proposed meaning very novel indeed.

Often, for example, the critic will make suggestions about the meanings that the text communicates to the reader at a subconscious level, by tacitly involving the reader in a particular system of values. Thus nineteenth-century novelists (both English and French) tend to have passages of 'realistic' writing in which it is assumed by both writer and reader that an 'uninterpreted' picture of reality is being presented: Balzac would be a good example in France,[2] and Trollope in England. Structuralist studies will often try to show that the impression of 'realism' depends on all kinds of conventions, assumptions shared by the writer and his intended readership. In some cases, the text is only 'realistic' if both of them belong to the same social class, with the same view of the world and the social order, and it can be argued that the novelist 'canonizes' this social outlook by making it seem simply a part of 'reality', unchanging and unchallengeable. Now ostensibly this is not an attempt to find new meanings in novels, but merely an attempt to show us meanings that we had already perceived, though at a subconscious level. But the fact remains that most readers react with great indignation to the suggestion that 'realism' in novels is only a matter of convention, and that by trying to pull the wool over our eyes about this novelists are guilty of bad faith, even of conniving at repressive social systems. It is not surprising that some structuralists are also Marxists, and that most structuralists are suspected of being so.[3]

All this is a long way from most biblical structuralism, but here too the structuralist interest in conventions and constraints, in implicit meanings and unstated presuppositions, produces interpretations that claim simply to highlight what the text is 'bound to' say to us, but which strike most readers as entirely novel. And in that sense we are fully justified in speaking of 'structural exegesis'. Here is an example.

Genesis 1—2

One of the earliest attempts to apply structuralist theories to the interpretation of the Bible was P. Beauchamp's *Création et Séparation*, a study of Genesis 1—2. Rather than beginning with questions about sources or redactors, in the manner of traditional commentators on Genesis, Beauchamp insists that we must begin with the text as it now lies before us. Its meaning resides not simply in what we might want to call its 'content' – what it actually asserts – but just as much in its shape, in the relations between its parts. Indeed, just as at the linguistic level we may say that we need to understand both the meanings of the words in a sentence *and* the rules of syntax before we can see what the sentence as a whole means, so we may say that we need to understand not only the 'ideas' being communicated directly, but also the 'literary syntax' of the passage in question, before we shall be able to extract its full meaning. (To understand a poem you need to know both what it 'says' and also *that it is a poem*: compare my discussion of the clerihew in chapter 1.) Just so with Genesis 1—2; we need to know not just what it asserts but also what kind of work it is.

So much might be agreed even by some traditional critics. What is more novel is the technique Beauchamp uses to establish what sort of text this is, a technique which involves analysing its shape just as it now stands without any regard for the history of the text's composition. He takes as the unit for analysis Genesis 1:1—2:1. Within this he finds ten 'words of creation', that is, ten instances of the clause 'and God said'. These fall naturally into two balancing groups (a classic case of binary opposition), each containing five 'words', and the two groups are of almost exactly equal length: 1:1—19 contains 207 words, in the Hebrew text, and 1:20—2:1 contains 206. The account of the fourth day concludes with a statement of the purpose of the luminaries (1:18): 'to rule over the day and over the night' the second half of the passage reaches its climax in describing man as created 'to rule (have dominion) over' all the natural world. Now, as with any kind of binary opposition, each half can be understood only by way of contrast with the other; so we may expect the two groups of five words to convey, by their juxtaposition, some meaning which brings out the parallel or tension between them. According to Beauchamp, this takes the form of a contrast between the inanimate created order, whose climax and highest achievement is to be seen in the stars, and the world of living beings, whose crowning work is mankind. By means of this contrast, a parallel is set up between animate and inanimate orders, and between man and the highest of the inanimate creatures.

123

This parallel is highly significant theologically; yet it is conveyed, not by any overt statement, but simply by the *structures* of the passage. We could say that what Genesis 1:1—2:1 is 'really about' cannot be discovered by any traditional exegetical or interpretative methods – source criticism, or redaction criticism, or comparisons with other ancient cosmogonies – but only by analysing its structure. And what emerges as the real subject-matter of the passage is *the status of man in the creation* – a status as exalted in the animate sphere as that of the stars in the inanimate.

But there is another, complementary structure in Genesis 1:1—2:1. As well as being composed of two parallel sections, each building up to a climax, it has as a whole a circulate shape: it forms a self-contained unit that ends where it begins. Genesis 1:1 reads 'God created the heavens and the earth'; 2:1 'Thus the heavens and the earth were finished'. In 1:1 God acts, in 2:1 he ceases to act: he rests from his labours, and so institutes the sabbath. Creation thus forms a complete cycle. The world comes forth from God in an act of creation on God's part, and returns to him in the act of worship on the sabbath day, in which man restores God's works to him by observing the sabbath rest – that is, by refraining from asserting any creative purposes he may have himself, so that God's may shine out more clearly. The binary structure underscores this point, for if the climax of creation is the sabbath, the climax of the first four days of creation (the first half) is the establishment of the luminaries to mark sacred dates and times, of which the sabbath is one.

Here is a whole theology of creation and of worship, allegedly implicit in the structures of the passage; and it can be extracted by an almost mathematical division, by an analysis which could more easily be illustrated with a chart than by lengthy pages of 'literary criticism' of the old *explication de texte* variety. Indeed, nothing is a surer indication for most readers that a book belongs to the structuralist fold than frequent, and complicated, charts and diagrams. It may well be this addiction to diagrams, in preference to readable prose, that has contributed more than anything to the bad name structuralist exegesis has among many biblical scholars. I think it is very questionable whether structuralists need to offend traditional sensibilities in this way, but maybe they think the shock is good for us.

Whether or not we find Beauchamp's discussion of Genesis 1:1—2:1 convincing, it will be agreed that it constitutes *exegesis* of this passage rather than, in the manner of Barthes on Genesis 32, using the passage as an illustration of the structures of literature in general. But it is exegesis of a very unusual kind. Two points in particular need to be stressed.

(1) First, anyone trained in traditional biblical criticism is likely to feel an immediate sense that all is not well on noting that Beauchamp takes Genesis 1:1—2:1 as the unit for investigation. How crucial this is to his conclusions can be seen quite plainly from the fact that the division into balancing halves depends on counting the words in the Hebrew text. This of course would not work if the unit extended further into chapter 2. Again, the important phrase 'the heavens and the earth' marks the beginning and end of the passage only if these are indeed its limits! But on no traditional division of Genesis 1—2 is there a break after 2:1. As we saw in discussing the account of creation from a redaction-critical point of view,[4] the exact status of 2:4a is debatable; but that the priestly account extends at least to 2:3 there was never any doubt.

Beauchamp, of course, is well aware of this, and his indifference to it is an excellent illustration of the difference between structuralism and the historically orientated approach of conventional literary criticism. He is not proposing that 2:1 represents the point where, historically speaking, the priestly author's work broke off, nor is he suggesting that an editor *intended* us to see it as rounding off the opening section of Genesis. He is simply saying that, as the text now stands, a division at this point exists. The text constrains the reader to make a break here, and to interpret 1:1—2:1 as a closed unit. If we ask how one can tell that this is so, he would no doubt reply that the very fact that the unit thus defined divides readily into two halves of exactly equal length is demonstration enough. Of course for the historical critic such an answer is hopelessly circular: if the limits of the unit dictate our interpretation, but our interpretation itself is the only evidence for the limits of the unit, then either the whole process cannot get started, or else we can prove anything we like. But Beauchamp would no doubt retort that traditional source analysis suffers from just the same circularity; and we saw in chapter 2 that there is an uncomfortably large measure of truth in this. His own structuralist approach may be more frank in acknowledging the circularity (that is its strength!), but it is not in this respect different in kind from the approach of a traditional source critic, who also (as we saw) fixes the limits of each source according to a prior understanding of what constitutes a coherent and self-contained passage. It is not that source criticism is objective while structuralism is subjective, or circular; there is a sliding scale in such matters, and no form of criticism exhibits either characteristic in a pure form. Indeed, the structuralist approach at least does not *claim* to be discovering truths about the author of Genesis 1:1ff. and his intentions, but only to be commenting on the text as we have it; and it is not hard to see how a plausible case can be made out for regarding such an approach as more, not less, objective than the historical-critical approach. Beauchamp's analysis appears, at least, to eschew appeals to 'literary intuition' or any other subjective sense, and to rest its case on hard fact – even *numerical* fact, as we have seen.

(2) Secondly, this deliberate inattention to what the original author may or may not have meant brings into prominence the extent to which structuralism represents a *theory of reading*, rather than a theory about *writing*.[5] It is not concerned with how authors write books, but with how readers read them; not with what meanings are intended, but with what meanings it is possible to perceive. However much we may think we have taken to heart the structuralist understanding of literature, we are still likely to find the idea of a criticism which is interested in the correct way of reading a text, rather than in what the text 'originally' meant or 'really' means, quite a difficult one to assimilate. The feeling that this makes criticism subjective, or lacking in rigour, will continually assert itself. It is vital to see that an analysis like Beauchamp's, as a structuralist perceives it, is the very opposite of subjective or vague. It looks subjective, because we are used to criticism that concentrates on what lies behind the text; but in fact it is an attempt – probably the first ever – to prescribe 'correct' methods, not for reconstructing what the author of Genesis 1:1ff. *meant*, but for producing a contemporary reading of what he actually *wrote*.

When Beauchamp sets out the structures within which Genesis has to be read if it is to make sense – with binary oppositions, circular movements, balancing parts and so on – one must remember that he is not making historical statements about the conventions within which Jewish literature of (say) the sixth century B.C. was *written*. He is suggesting conventions within which it may meaningfully be *read*; and these are modern conventions, because he is writing for modern readers. That the conventions in question were unknown in ancient Israel may or may not be true (it will certainly occur to many readers of Beauchamp), but it is essentially an irrelevance, because he is not practising *historical* criticism: he is telling us how to read the text *now*. No doubt many people will find such a mode of criticism deeply irritating, even disturbing; but it is extremely important to see that this is what structuralism is, and not to judge it as if it had the same aims as traditional criticism.

Naturalization and 'Holistic' Reading

A point on which biblical structuralists and their counterparts in other branches of literary study agree is that the proper object of criticism is the text *in its finished form*, as it lies before us, and not in hypothetical earlier stages in its growth. In this there are certainly similarities to the canonical approach, as we have seen, however different the underlying theory that produces the two movements. A structuralist theory of reading begins with the conviction that any text which exists as a text, i.e. which is perceived as a complete text within a given literary culture, can be read: all one has to do is discover or devise conventions of reading which will enable it to have meaning. However odd or disjointed a text may appear, it can be *naturalized* – that is, perceived as belonging to some genre with statable conventions – and so made sense of. As an extreme example of this possibility, imagine a 'novel' composed entirely of gibberish. Even this could be naturalized, once you knew that you were meant to read it as a novel, by being understood as a first-person narrative set in the mouth of someone suffering from aphasia.[6] It may be doubted whether you would get much out of such a work, even then. But the limiting case serves to establish the point, that the sense a work makes depends on what it is read *as*.

In describing source criticism I tried to show that one conviction underlying the suggestion that some texts in the Old Testament were composite was that they could not be read intelligibly as they stood. This was a mildly structuralist way of stating an idea that, in itself, most students of the rise of critical method would probably agree with. But of course source critics were saying that *historically* speaking a book like the Pentateuch was an impossibility, because it belonged to no genre that *existed in ancient Israel*, and therefore was comprehensible only as the conflation of several smaller, possible works. The structuralist does not necessarily deny this. As a statement of the genre-possibilities in ancient Israel, it may well be true (though he may wish to ask how we know). But the structuralist's idea is that the Pentateuch does exist *now*, and exists as a single work, whether we like it or not. To read it, we do not need to construct more or less plausible theories about the kinds of literature that were thinkable for ancient Israelites. We need to discover or devise conventions within which it will now make sense as a unified whole: to 'naturalize' it, in fact, and to read it 'holistically'.

An impressive attempt to devise a 'holistic' reading of an entire section of the Old Testament is D. J. Clines's short study, *The Theme of the Pentateuch*. Clines uses very little structuralist terminology and would not, I think, describe his work as structuralism; nonetheless, it concerns itself with questions that lie at the heart of the structuralist approach. Clines raises the question: if we are to read the Pentateuch as a single, coherent work, what must we read it as meaning? Once this has been asked, a wide range of possible methods is available by which we could seek an answer; and among these one is an examination of the way the Pentateuch may be divided into sections, and of the shapes and patterns it manifests. (Affinities with Beauchamp should be clear.) We can look for recurring motifs or formulas which constrain us to pause over certain sections in preference to others, or to perceive very diverse events recorded in the narrative as manifesting the same pattern of divine or human activity. By such techniques Clines seeks to show that the 'theme' of the Pentateuch – what it has to be read as conveying, if it is to be read as a whole at all – is *the divine promise to the patriarchs and its partial fulfilment*. Whatever other points some sections of the Pentateuch may originally have been intended to convey, and however much some passages may once have contradicted others, we cannot now read the Pentateuch as a whole without perceiving it as meaning some such thing as this.

Whether or not we agree with Clines's particular statement of the theme of the Pentateuch, we ought at least to concede that such an attempt to 'read' a complex work makes sense. It is perfectly possible to see what is meant by looking for a theme that inheres in the final form of the text; and it is quite plain that it is not the same as *any* of the historical-critical questions about the purpose or intention of authors, transmitters or compilers that are asked by source, form and redaction criticism. It is far from being an objection to Clines's work that what emerges as the 'theme' of the Pentateuch is not at all surprising, and that it conforms (though it is stated much more exactly) to the impression gained by a quite untechnical reading of the text, such as may be undertaken by a Christian or a Jew with no knowledge of biblical criticism. On the contrary, it is a mistake to think that a structuralist approach should be expected to throw up novel or bizarre interpretations. In many ways a structuralist reading gains in plausibility if it begins with possibilities of meaning that might occur even to an 'innocent' reader, since – to reiterate the point – structuralism is not in principle a method for uncovering new meanings; it is an explanatory framework to account for meaning that is already perceived.[7] The explanation will convince more people if it explains a meaning that they really *have* already perceived, than if the structuralist produces the meaning and the explanation together from the same hat. This is not to deny, though, that it is sometimes necessary to dig quite far beneath the surface of a text before it can be seen as having any coherent meaning at all. In such cases the critic is bound to present his interpretation and his explanation at the same time, and no one should complain. There are parts of the Pentateuch, for example, where the uninitiated reader simply does not extract *any* meaning. Here the structuralist may well delve into minute details, and even diagrams may come into their own.[8]

Ecclesiastes for Structuralists

The contrast between structuralism as a *method* for extracting meaning from texts and structuralism as an explanatory *theory* about how meaning occurs can be made clearer by yet another look at our standard sample text, Ecclesiastes. This will also give us a chance to see how the application of structuralist ideas to the Bible has run itself into a cul-de-sac by losing interest in the theory altogether in its enthusiasm for an exciting new method. As an example of the structuralism-as-method approach, I shall discuss

J. A. Loader's *Polar Structures in the Book of Qohelet*; for a structural-ism-as-theory treatment of the book I shall have to depend on improvisation, since I know of no published study that will serve the purpose.

Loader's book attempts a structuralist analysis of Ecclesiastes by examining what may be called its 'internal structures' – to put it loosely, how it hangs together. His argument, profusely illustrated with analytical charts, is that Ecclesiastes is full of antitheses, contrasts and chiastic arrangements which may be described as 'polar structures'. Opposed themes such as 'risk and assurance', 'talk and silence', 'the worth and worthlessness of wisdom' are discussed by Qoheleth in passages whose shape points up the contrast. None of Qoheleth's sayings can be properly understood, unless it is seen that the book is so constructed that another, opposed saying is to be read in antithesis to it. Indeed, the very use of traditional wisdom forms in order to oppose traditional wisdom ideas is itself the overarching 'polar structure' of the whole book and has the effect of relativizing all that is explicitly said within it.

This means that traditional source- or form-critical analyses of the work (such as those discussed in chapter 5), in which the inconsistency between different sayings serves as a criterion for postulating plurality of authorship or an original independence of the short units that compose the work, miss the point entirely. They make a problem of what is in reality the book's deliberate design; for Qoheleth's whole purpose is to proceed by self-contradiction and antithesis to his ultimate conclusion, a conclusion which is not so much sceptical as relativistic.

At first sight one would have little hesitation in describing Loader's very original work as structuralist; and he himself stresses its interest in 'text-immanent' features rather than in the extrinsic, historical questions with which traditional biblical methods deal. His 'polar structures' are clearly an *avatar* of the structuralists' 'binary opposition', and his charts are a familiar part of structuralist equipment. Nevertheless, it seems to me only in a very qualified sense that we can call this a structuralist study. Loader is plainly quite concerned with the intentions of Qoheleth, the author, and he is anxious to integrate his own work into the wider context of the study of ancient Near Eastern wisdom literature. We may say that, on his view, Qoheleth's intentions are manifested in the structure of his work as much as in any individual saying within it. The book can be understood only if its shape or structure is taken full account of, and precisely analysed. If this is true – as it may well be – then it is an adequate answer to a source-critical analysis, which would see the contradictions between different sayings as evidence of more than one author. But (and this is the important point) it is essentially an answer on the same terms. Loader is saying, in fact, that Ecclesiastes has been misread because scholars have failed to see that the repertoire of techniques available to a wise man in post-exilic Israel included apparent self-contradiction in the interests of relativizing traditional dogmas. This is a *historical* suggestion, which if true undermines other historical suggestions, such as that wisdom books manifest a high degree of internal consistency. In spite of its structuralist terminology it does not depend in any way on a characteristically structuralist view of literature; and it strikingly fails to share the structuralist indifference to authorial intention and to the historical circumstances of composition. It is not necessarily the worse for that: but it is not structuralism in the strict sense. It merely adds structuralist ideas to the historical-critical tool-box.

By contrast, we could sketch a treatment of Ecclesiastes that adhered more closely to the pure structuralist gospel without offering a new *interpretation* of it at all. We could begin by merely stating the data with which any interpretation whatever has to cope, and then analysing what the process of interpretation involves. The data are curiously contradictory. On the one hand, a careful reading reveals Ecclesiastes to be a puzzling work. It is jerky and disjointed; many passages are mutually contradictory; and, above all, it is a riot of different genres. There is some autobiographical narrative (1:12—2:17); there are some poems (3:1–9; 7:1–13); some aphoristic sayings, many inconsistent with each other (3:17, 3:19); a couple of short 'tales' (9:13–16; perhaps 4:13–16); and some comments on the author in the third person (12:9–10). On the other hand, almost all readers agree that it is a book with a distinctive and readily recognizable flavour and message, which is coherent enough for some people to make it (or at least believe they are making it) a major part of their personal philosophy of life. This message was summarized briefly at the beginning of chapter 5, above. It says that we should enjoy life in a moderate and sensible way, knowing that in the end all men come to a common grave, and no pleasure or pain endures for ever.

How is this contradiction to be resolved? The structuralist insight that helps us here is that Ecclesiastes is not really unusual in being a chaotic work out of which readers effortlessly bring order: on the contrary, in this it may serve as an ideal paradigm for how reading works. To read any work holistically, as having a unified, coherent 'message', we have to naturalize it, to assign it to a genre, to set conventions within which we are going to understand it. When we read a light, realistic novel the process is so effortless that we pay it no attention; we even imagine that realism and coherence are a property of the novel itself. But when we are faced with a work like Ecclesiastes, we have a chance as it were to watch our own eyes moving.

How does it come about that so complex and muddled a text can communicate so satisfactorily unified a meaning? How, for example, do we know that the weight falls on the aphorisms about the recurring cycles of life and their relativizing effect on human plans, rather than on the biographical material about Solomon (1:1; 1:12—2:11)? Why is it, in fact, that we read the work essentially as a piece of proverbial wisdom, and not as a short story about Solomon with some of his sayings thrown in for the sake of verisimilitude? It can only be because in literature as we understand it, it is acceptable for works of a didactic or reflective kind to have a brief narrative framework, but not for narratives to be so overweighted with sapiential advice. Again, we seem to be constrained to read the sceptical warnings about the pointlessness of life, and the much more affirmative sayings which assert that judgement is coming, in such a way that a synthesis is formed between them; and this is because in 'literature' (unlike casual conversations) it is a strong convention that a given work is to be read as consistent with itself. If we insist that Qoheleth is contradicting himself, then the work becomes 'unreadable', unless we construe it as belonging to a derivative genre – say, as parody, or as an exercise in paradox.

We could, no doubt, read it as literature of the absurd, as an attempt to subvert literary conventions by constructing a deliberately unreadable work: indeed, almost any work can be read in this way by being placed within a literary system whose conventions of reading are quite different, and meaningful works can thus be rendered meaningless and vice versa.[9] But if we wish to keep to our original intuition about the meaning of Ecclesiastes, it may be best to say that we are constrained to read it in that way because we wish to understand it as a coherent and meaningful part of a larger complex, the Scriptures of the Old Testament; and that within that context it must be seen as an example of the genre 'religious wisdom book' (which there are strong conventions for reading as conveying a generally cool but pious outlook on life), rather than as either a work of protest or a historical romance.

Once we have reached this point, it should become clear why I suggested that the 'canonical approach' of B. S. Childs ought logically to be seen as a form of structuralism, if it is to be more than merely redaction criticism in an advanced form. For as soon as we start to think in terms of *conventions for reading*, rather than of historically determined, fixed genres, we are moving onto structuralist ground whether we wish to or not. Canon criticism, like structuralism, works with the very pregnant idea of 'reading *as*'; and to justify this, a theoretical foundation such as that on which structuralism rests is needed – *theological* appeals to 'canonicity' will not suffice.

For a structuralist, then, the meaning of Ecclesiastes would be a function of the system of conventions within which we read it – conventions which, being who we are, we cannot change. An analysis of the internal structures of the book may help us to understand better how these conventions work – and a study such as Loader's may be helpful here – but it is incidental to the main structuralist task of showing what are the conditions that must be met if Ecclesiastes is to have meaning for us.

Structuralist Dogma and Structuralist Style

When arguing that canon criticism could be fully consistent only if it was prepared to adopt a structuralist theory of reading, I suggested that the price of this might prove too high for B. S. Childs and his followers. It should now be clear just how high the price is. Full-blown structuralism offers an approach to the interpretation of literature that has few points of contact with the historical-critical method familiar to students of the Old Testament. True, it is possible to analyse the internal structure of Old Testament books by a selective use of structuralist techniques, without in any way abandoning historical-critical principles. Loader's book on Ecclesiastes and some of R. M. Polzin's studies work along these lines; and their conviction that meaning is conveyed by the patterns and 'structures' of a text as well as by its 'content' or 'subject matter' is a most important one.[10] Nevertheless, as I have suggested, they are 'structuralist' only in a qualified sense. Whatever the origins of the terms they use, such studies belong conceptually to the upper reaches of redaction criticism. And my own feeling is that it is scarcely worth bothering with the immense complications of the structuralist approach, unless we are going to take matters further than this. Much that goes under the name of 'biblical structuralism' could be paraphrased without using any structuralist terminology, to everyone's gain. A really fruitful use of structuralist insights can only come, I believe, from a serious engagement with the more fundamental ideas of the movement. It has been possible to give only the faintest impression of what these are, but two, at least, have emerged as particularly important.

First, I have already made extensive use of the idea of *literary competence*; and this carries with it the centrality of *genre*, and the notion I have called 'reading as'. This complex of ideas is central to a structuralist theory of literature and its meaning. Second, there is the understanding of meaning as *a function of the conventions of a structured system*. If taken to their logical conclusion these principles produce a theory of literature which is both *determinist* – so much so, that the author has no control at all over the meaning of his own work – and also wholly *conventionalist*, in the sense that 'meaning' has no existence outside the arbitrary conventions of human society and its aesthetic systems, and changes as society changes. These large-scale ideas are what should be engaging the attention of biblical scholars, if they really want to take structuralism seriously. The charts and schemes, the word-pairs and chiasms and intricately numbered paragraphs which seem to obsess much 'biblical structuralism' are just window-dressing unless there has been a fundamental change in scholars' outlook on the study of texts, and I suspect that is much more rarely the case than one might suppose at first glance.

To take structuralism seriously, however, is not the same as to think it infallible. Indeed, it is probably because many who would describe themselves as convinced structuralists have not really tried to let full-blown structuralist principles transform their whole outlook that they are so comparatively uncritical of it. To take it seriously is to be aware of its radical challenge to one's assumptions, and perhaps to feel more compelled to put up some resistance than if one perceives it as merely an attractive new set of exegetical tools. It will probably be clear from the tone of my discussion that I find structuralism at once attractive and repellent, and should be glad to resolve this tension by limiting its claim in some way – yet not by ignoring the theory in favour of the techniques, since for me the theory is where the interest lies. A tentative suggestion along these lines may be to bracket out, for the time being, the structuralist claim to provide a total *explanatory framework* for the whole of human culture (and the claim is no less), and to observe that there is at all events a structuralist *style* of looking at literature and art and other cultural phenomena, which systematizes and raises to a conscious level matters that normally remain at the level of presupposition and unexamined assumption. This style is certainly not the same as a historical-critical mode of thinking; but let us leave aside the question whether they are actually incompatible. Then we may be able to describe some of the benefits that could accrue from it.

First, structuralist categories may help us to see more clearly what we are doing in practising *any* kind of biblical criticism. Though we are only now looking at this possibility explicitly, this whole book is in a sense an application of it. Our central theme has been *literary competence*, a structuralist idea, of course, and one which has proved a useful tool for characterizing all the methods used in biblical criticism, including the historical-critical ones. It has made it possible to ask what various biblical critics have been aiming at in literary, not just theological, terms; and to avoid the student's common feeling that the various methods are essentially incommensurable, by establishing a common ground of a high order of generality on which they can meet and clash. So far as I can see this has neither committed us to embracing structuralism as a dogma, nor, on the other hand, merely twisted structuralist terminology for an alien purpose (as in some 'biblical structuralism').

Secondly, a structuralist style of criticism makes us aware of ourselves as readers and forces us to consider our own assumptions and prejudices. This can hardly be undesirable on any terms. It is easy for us to assume, for example, that we know what would constitute a coherent or consistent piece of writing in any literate culture, and to forget how far ideas like consistency – which figure so high among the criteria used in historical-critical work – are dependent on conventions that vary from culture to culture. Again, we can easily ask questions about what the author of an ancient text meant without paying enough attention to the possibility that he was almost wholly constrained, not just by the traditions at his disposal, but also by the literary conventions within which he worked. Structuralism reminds us that the meaning of a text is not to be equated with what was passing through its author's mind, but is defined by the range of possibilities that the genre being used made and makes available. One of the great functions of structuralist analysis is to deprive us of our innocence as readers: to make us see that the range of an author's possible meanings and of a reader's possible understandings is not infinite nor even very large, but limited by very strict constraints. Structuralism does not itself answer the question what a text means, or how it should be read. But it can keep alive in our minds an understanding of what it is to ask questions like these, and of the need to specify what sorts of answer we are looking for.

The Bible and 'Secular' Criticism

With the other methods of biblical study we have examined, it is possible to feel that the wider world of general literary criticism is miles away. Source criticism and form criticism look as though they were developed by biblical critics for biblical critics. Structuralism is another matter, for here there is a conscious intention of applying to the Bible an approach developed in the study of modern literatures. Committed structuralists will often speak as though biblical scholarship was entirely ignorant of 'secular' literary criticism before they began their work, and more traditional biblical critics will sometimes retort that contacts with literary people are best avoided, if structuralism is the kind of thing that results: ignorance is bliss.

But is it all really so simple? Are biblical structuralists really the first to have established links with non-biblical criticism, or are they just the first to have made contact with structuralist criticism? Were there perhaps more contacts or parallels between biblical and secular criticism in the past than the foreshortened perspective of contemporary propaganda allows? We cannot explore this possibility in depth or over the whole period covered by the historical-critical method; but in the remaining chapters we can at least take a second look at some of the methods already surveyed with the question consciously in mind. Canon criticism is a particularly interesting case, and a discussion of that will help to throw into stronger relief the methods it is meant to replace, showing that they were far more deeply rooted in the literary criticism of their time than is widely believed. This will involve us in ranging far afield in the literary world; but it will be far from irrelevant to our overall theme of validity in method, since secular critics have discussed the theoretical basis of their methods more fully than have biblical scholars. If these methods can be shown to have a close affinity with the methods familiar in biblical studies, we shall have a much wider range of informed discussion to draw on in trying to settle our domestic disputes, and there will be less risk that what we say about the study of the Bible will involve special pleading. My aim is to suggest that the critical issues that arise in biblical study are only a specialized version of issues that arise in all literary study and interpretation, and that the same sorts of solution must serve for the particular case as for the general. Paradoxically, there is no danger that biblical interpretation will actually get detached from general interpretation. As we shall see in the next chapter, the very critics who claim to be least influenced by secular literary criticism are often the most in its grip. The danger is that biblical critics will *think* they are operating in glorious freedom, untouched by the literary culture to which they belong. When that happens, criticism itself may continue to flourish, but discussion of critical methods becomes eccentric and introverted.

Further Reading

R. M. Polzin, *Biblical Structuralism. Method and Subjectivity in the Study of Ancient Texts*. Philadelphia and Missoula, Montana 1977

D. Patte and A. Patte, *Structural Exegesis: from Theory to Practice*. Philadelphia 1978

F. Kermode, *The Genesis of Secrecy*. Cambridge, Mass. and London 1979

Biblical Structuralism: Select Bibliography

There is an enormous literature on 'biblical structuralism'. Many structuralist works on both Old and New Testaments are published by the Fortress Press, Philadelphia. Four important collections of articles are:

1. VTS 22, 1972:
   In addition to Beauchamp's article 'L'analyse structurale et l'exégèse biblique', already cited, note also:
   M. Weiss, 'Die Methode der "Total-Interpretation" '
   R. C. Culley, 'Some Comments on Structural Analysis and Biblical Studies'

2. *Interpretation* 28, 1974: note especially:
   R. Jacobson, 'The Structuralists and the Bible'
   R. C. Culley, 'Structural Analysis – is it done with mirrors?'

3. *Semeia* 3, 1975: 'Classical Hebrew Narrative':
   R. C. Culley, 'Themes and Variations in Three Groups of Old Testament Narratives'
   D. M. Gunn, 'David and the Gift of the Kingdom (2 Sam. 2−4, 9−20; 1 Kings 1−2)
   B. O. Long, 'The Social Setting for Prophetic Miracle Stories'
   S. E. McEvenue, 'A Comparison of Narrative Styles in the Hagar Stories'
   R. M. Polzin, ' "The Ancestress in Danger" in Danger'
   H. C. White, 'French Structuralism and OT Narrative Analysis: Roland Barthes'

4. *Semeia* 15, 1979: 'Perspectives on Old Testament Narrative':
   T. L. Thompson, 'Conflict of Themes in the Jacob Narrative'
   P. D. Miscall, 'Literary Unity in Old Testament Narrative'
   R. M. Polzin, 'Literary Unity in Old Testament Narrative: A Response'
   J. Calloud, 'A Few Notes on Structural Semiotics'
   A group from Rennes, France, 'An Approach to the Book of Jonah'
   W. Gross, 'Lying Prophet and Disobedient Man of God in 1 Kings 13: Role Analysis'

Two useful books are V. L. Tollers and J. B. Maier, *The Bible in its Literary Milieu* (Grand Rapids, Michigan, 1979) and *Structural Analysis and Biblical Exegesis* (Pittsburgh 1974) = *Analyse structurale et exégèse biblique*, ed. R. Barthes and F. Bovon, Neuchâtel 1971. In the series *Guides to Biblical Scholarship*, structuralism is handled in D. Robertson, *The Old Testament and the Literary Critic* (Philadelphia 1977). *Exégèse et herméneutique*, ed. X. Léon-Dufour (Paris 1971) is an important collection of structuralist studies of the Bible in French. There is a good brief survey of various 'text-immanent' approaches (not all unequivocally structuralist) in S. Bar-Efrat, 'Some Observations on the Analysis of Structure in Biblical Narrative', *VT* 30 (1980).

As will be seen, the great majority of scholars have concentrated on the narrative sections of the Bible. Further works in this area are J. P. Fokkelman, *Narrative Art and Poetry in the Books of Samuel*, 4 vols (Assen, 1981-); J. Calloud, *Structural Analysis of Narrative* (Philadelphia 1976); R. Detweiler, *Story, Sign, and Self. Phenomenology and Structuralism as Literary Critical Methods* (Philadelphia 1978). There is a collection of structuralist studies of Gen. 2—3 in *SBL Seminar Papers* 1 (1978), ed. P. J. Achtemeier.

Much less work of a structuralist kind has been done on legal or poetic texts, though the following may be noted: B. S. Jackson, *Structuralism and Legal Theory* (Liverpool 1979); 'Modern Research in Jewish Law – Some Theoretical Issues', in *Modern Research in Jewish Law*, ed. B. S. Jackson (Leiden 1980), and 'Secular Jurisprudence and the Philosophy of Jewish Law', in *The Philosophy of Jewish Law*, JLA 5 (forthcoming). L. Alonso Schökel has handled the Psalms from a structuralist perspective: see his 'The Poetic Structure of Psalm 42–3', *JSOT* 1 (1976) and 3(1977).

10

THE 'NEW CRITICISM'

We have entered a universe that answers to its own laws, supports itself, internally coheres, and has a new standard of truth. Information is true if it is accurate. A poem is true if it hangs together. Information points to something else. A poem points to nothing but itself. Information is relative. A poem is absolute.

E. M. Forster, *Anonymity: an Inquiry*
(London 1925), p. 14

Preliminary Reading

T. S. Eliot, 'Tradition and the Individual Talent' in *Selected Essays*. London 1932.
J. Barr, *The Bible in the Modern World* (London 1973), pp. 53–74 *or* 'Reading the Bible as Literature', *BJRL* 56 (1973), pp. 10–33

The Bible and Literary Criticism

Anyone who reads the Bible is bound to be influenced to some extent by his general expectations about books, and by his experience of reading literature of other kinds. It can hardly be an accident, for example, that fundamentalist theories about the Bible tend to have a high appeal for many whose other reading consists mostly of non-fiction, and who tend to regard books therefore as primarily a source of accurate information; while people trained in the humanities are less often to be found taking a fundamentalist line.[1] However, biblical critics have traditionally been rather reluctant to make explicit connections between their own work and that of literary critics in other fields, and so it is not surprising that it is only with structuralism that we have a self-confessed attempt to bring methods developed for use with other literature into biblical studies. This is why my discussion so far has not paid any attention to wider literary parallels, except in this one case. The aim has been to present methods of Old Testament study as they are perceived by their own practitioners; and whereas structuralists are deliberately trying to commend a theory developed outside biblical studies, all the other methods tend to be seen by those who use them as a response to problems peculiar to the Bible.

But now it is time to pick up the suggestion at the end of the last chapter, and ask whether the biblical critics' self-understanding is correct in this respect. The purpose of this is in no sense to suggest that biblical criticism has been merely a slavish following of literary fashions. I believe, however, that biblical studies have in reality nearly always been more closely related to literary studies of other kinds than biblical scholars acknowledge or realize. And if this is true, much may be gained by making it explicit.

Canon Criticism and the 'New Critics'

We begin, not with the earliest type of biblical criticism, but with the most recent development, the canonical approach of B. S. Childs. The particular interest of this from our point of view is that Childs vehemently denies any non-theological parentage for his theory. He sees it as an attempt to avoid the impasse caused in biblical studies by the demise of 'Biblical Theology', not as a 'literary' undertaking in any sense. I shall try to respect Childs's own perception of his new method. But I shall argue that it does have a very close formal resemblance to many of the concerns of literary critics over the last fifty years or so, and shares many of the same strengths and weaknesses; and this may help to make it plausible to suggest that the same is true of the methods Childs is trying to supplant. From this it may emerge that structuralism is indeed not the first attempt to read the Bible 'as literature', merely the first to be frank about it. Biblical critics and literary critics always have inhabited the same cultural environment, though from a modern standpoint this is not always easy to see.

Childs himself gives a clue to the affinities in the wider literary world that he may most readily be suspected of, when he writes:

> The canonical study of the Old Testament shares an interest in common with several of the newer literary critical methods in its concern to do justice to the integrity of the text itself apart from diachronistic reconstruction. One thinks of the so-called 'newer criticism' of English studies, of various forms of structural analysis, and of rhetorical criticism. Yet the canonical approach differs from a strictly literary approach by interpreting the biblical text in relation to a community of faith and practice for whom it served a particular theological role as possessing divine authority. ... The canonical approach is concerned to understand the nature of the theological shape of the text rather than to recover an original literary or aesthetic unity.[2]

The first of the 'literary critical methods' listed here has not been mentioned before in this book. The 'New Criticism' (rather than 'newer criticism') is the name given to an important movement in literary criticism that flourished chiefly in America, but with considerable influence in Britain, in the 1940s and 1950s.[3] Its roots went back, however, to earlier critics such as T. S. Eliot, I. A. Richards and William Empson; and many of its leading ideas are widely diffused in twentieth-century criticism and shared by many critics who do not depend on the teachings of any particular school. It is now however decidedly out of fashion in the literary world – so much so that books can be written taking its demise for granted[4] – but that does not necessarily mean that it may not be influencing contemporary biblical critics. As with many literary movements, New Criticism had a number of different currents and sub-divisions, and there are disputes over what its leading ideas were. Students of the Bible will be no strangers to disputes of this type. Nevertheless for our purposes it is quite possible to draw attention to a few major trends within the movement whose similarities to the 'canonical approach', and to some extent also to other recent concerns of biblical critics, will be readily apparent.

To understand the motive force behind the New Criticism we need some idea of what it attempted to replace, for unless we realize that it was essentially conceived as a *corrective*, we shall be likely to find it rather exaggerated in its claims. (No doubt this is true of most movements in literary criticism as in theology.)[5] Very much literary criticism in the early twentieth century, in the English-speaking world, may fairly be described as both *historical* and *affective* in its interests. First, it was historical: interested in literary history, in discerning 'periods' in the development of literature and influences of one writer on another, and interested, too, in the biography of poets and writers and in the effect that the events of an author's life, and his psychological experience, might have had on his work. And second, it was affective: concerned with the emotional effect that literature had on the reader, and concerned with the emotions that the poet had experienced and of which his work might be seen as a distillation.

These two interests came together in the very high value which critics around the turn of the century set on the Romantic movement. This may be seen in the anthologies of verse that our grandparents read and, indeed, in the highly influential *Oxford Book of English Verse* (first edition 1900), with its huge number of Romantic poems as against a rather small selection from the Augustan age, or even from the Metaphysicals.[6] The critical stance embodied in such a selection, and in the historical and affective concerns we have mentioned, may be briefly stated as follows. The value of literature lies very largely in the insight it affords into the minds and rich emotional life of certain geniuses: people who have the capacity both to achieve a heightening of consciousness themselves and to convey it to others through the medium of words. The works of such men are a window onto reality, through which ordinary people can experience life in ways that would otherwise be denied to them. The poet's vocation is to distil his experience and make it available to others, so that they too may catch a glimpse of what he has seen in a moment of vision. It is hardly surprising that anyone who sees literature in this light should have a marked preference for the Romantics, since it is from them that such ideas largely derive, and should dislike writers in a more classical tradition. Keats or Wordsworth would seem the ideal for a critical theory of this sort, Pope or Dryden of very little interest.[7]

It is not difficult to see that a critic in this tradition is likely to be deeply interested in all that can be known of the life of a great writer, from whatever source. Literary biography becomes an indispensable part of literary criticism. If the aim of reading poetry is to share in the poet's experience, then the poem itself, while obviously important, is not the only thing in which the critic should be

interested: the experience that lies behind the poem may be accessible by other means as well, such as the poet's letters or diaries,
accounts of him by his friends, or the literary influences known to
have been at work on him. By studying all these we can hope to
approach closer to what the poet really meant to convey, and so to
share it more fully with him. Indeed, without some background
information we can hardly read a poem with true appreciation at
all. Unless we know something of the life and experience of the
poet, his words alone have little power to stir the emotions and
elevate the mind.

Some popular approaches to literature still preserve these attitudes, which I have caricatured a little to bring out their salient
points. Some critics still use novels, for example, as a means of
gaining insight into their author's psychology – though this is now
more often in order to dethrone an idol than to share in his sublime
emotions. But to anyone who has been 'taught' literature at school
in the last thirty or forty years the critical attitude I have been
describing will have an unfamiliar ring. Nowadays it is usual to
concentrate on 'the poem itself'; to touch literary biography very
lightly; to abstain from speculation about the poet's emotions, as
against those of his characters or the 'speaker' in his poems; even to
ask students to undertake literary appreciation 'unseen', confronting
them with unattributed passages, so that their judgement is not
clouded by irrelevant historical information they may happen to
possess about the author.

'New Criticism' is part of this transformation in taste. The reader
with a training in modern literary criticism will take many of its
tenets so much for granted that it may be difficult for him to distance
himself enough to see what the fuss was about. But from the 1920s
until about the end of the Second World War, much of what the
modern student takes for granted was very contentious indeed. We
may isolate three major theses of the New Criticism which mark it
off sharply from what went before; and it will be seen that these
have a strangely familiar appearance to anyone who has followed
the development of modern biblical criticism. They are (a) that a
literary text is an artefact; (b) that 'intentionalism' is a fallacy; and
(c) that the meaning of a text is a function of its place in a literary
canon. Once these rather cryptic propositions have been explained,
we shall be in a position to see more clearly how far Childs is

justified in saying that canon criticism is not an application to the Bible of New Critical methods. We shall also be able to ask how far it is true that the methods canon criticism claims to replace were not a product of modern literary culture, but of concerns peculiar to theology.

Texts as Artefacts

Wimsatt and Brooks, in their *Literary Criticism: A Short History*,[8] entitle their chapter on Eliot 'Eliot and Pound: An Impersonal Art'. This captures an essential point of Eliot's criticism which was taken up by the New Criticism in all its branches: the idea that a 'poem' (which may be used as a shorthand term for any work of literary art) is not to be understood as the outpouring of the poet's soul, nor as a window on to his world, but as ποίημα, a 'thing made', or artefact.[9] A poem is not a vehicle for transferring beautiful thoughts from the poet's mind to the reader's: it is a beautiful object. A poet is not a prophet or a genius, bringing messages from the Muses or from God: he is a maker, a craftsman. If we wanted to exaggerate, we might say that if some Victorian critics thought of the poet as being like a sage or a seer, Eliot thought of him as something more like a carpenter. We are not meant to look *through* poems into poets' souls; we are meant to look *at* them. Literary criticism is criticism of literature, not criticism of the emotions or experiences of writers.

The consequences of this shift in concern, from the author or poet to the work he produces, are very far-reaching indeed. Two in particular may be mentioned. (1) First, it leads to an important shift in literary taste. For the earlier view that we have already discussed, it is clear that some sorts of subject-matter are more 'poetic' or 'literary' than others. The true stuff of poetry is the sublime: elevated emotions, moving experiences, 'intimations of immortality'. Indeed, Wordsworth, both in the *Intimations* Ode and in *The Prelude*, provides us with two of the most 'poetic' poems there are.[10] But on a view such as Eliot's no subject-matter is inherently more suitable for literary or poetic treatment than any other, since poetry is a craft, a matter of making something with words.[11] Poetic beauty does not consist in saying something sublime, but in saying something – never mind what – sublimely (if we must use the language of 'sublimity' at all).

In theory this ought to mean that all poetry – *including* Romantic poetry – is now being understood in a new way; but in practice it tends to mean that Romantic poetry is devalued, and various types of classicism take its place as the preferred kind of literature. Thus, through the work of New Criticism and related movements, 'classical' poetry has returned to favour. A poet who himself thought of poetry as essentially a craft, rather than as the expression of personal emotion, is naturally more congenial to such critics than is, say, Keats. Strictly speaking, on a New Critical view *all* poets are 'classical' poets. The trouble with the Romantics was not that they *actually* expressed their emotions through verse instead of making beautiful verbal artefacts, but rather that they *thought* this was what they were doing. It is not that poetry *ought* not to be the expression of emotion, but that (by definition, we may say) it *is* not. Nevertheless it would probably be to ask more than human nature is capable of to expect New Critics to have devoted all their energies to producing 'classical' readings of the Romantics. Inevitably, they tended to promote their views by rehabilitating those poets whose theory of poetry seemed to have had most in common with their own.[12] And so the change in the general critical climate that made New Criticism possible has had most impact on readers of poetry who do not also read criticism by creating renewed interest in (and good critical editions of) the poets of the Augustan age, and the 'contrived' works of the Metaphysicals. The extent of the change may be gauged from a comparison between the *Oxford Book of English Verse* and its successor of 1972, the *New Oxford Book of English Verse*.[13]

(2) The second (and for us more interesting) result of the triumph of the New Criticism is that interest has moved away from the psychology and life-history of poets and authors and on to the finished texts that lie before the reader. We may express this change by saying that whereas older critics had taken the 'meaning' of a poem to be the emotional or spiritual experience that the author was trying to convey – which it needed considerable efforts of literary history and even delving into diaries to discover – the New Critics understood 'meaning' much more narrowly as a sense that inhered in the poem itself. A poem *might* provide information about the poet's state of mind – or it might not; his diary *might* tell us how he was feeling when he wrote it – or it might not. Such

'extrinsic' questions, as they were called, were perfectly valid and interesting, but they were no part of literary criticism, no part of the quest for the *meaning* of the poem.[14] To pursue the analogy with carpentry: the style of a chair could conceivably be evidence for the mood of the craftsman who made it, and equally his diary could help us to discover under what circumstances and in what mood he made it. This would be important, if we were writing his biography. But few people would think these questions relevant to assessing the chair as an aesthetic object. To a New Critic, there is an exact parallel with literature. The reason why we are so easily misled into confusing the two sorts of question where literature, especially poetry, is concerned is that poetry often has human emotions as its subject-matter and is often written in the first person singular, so that it is easy to confuse the *poet* with the *speaker*. But in reality a poem as a work of literary art, and a poem as historical evidence for its author's state of mind, are quite as distinct as in the case of the chair. The meaning of a poem, or of any work of literature, is a quality of the text itself. It is not some entity which the author is trying to convey through the poem, still less some experience or emotion in his soul to which the poem offers us access.

The 'Intentional Fallacy'

From forbidding questions about the author's *psychology* as a way of establishing the meaning and value of a work, it seemed to most New Critics a short step to banning also inquiries into the author's *intention*; for intention, surely, is itself a matter of psychology. This step appears to undermine not just the Romantic criticism which New Criticism supplanted, but also much older modes of historical criticism, as it had been practised in the eighteenth and nineteenth centuries. Late nineteenth-century critics, as we have seen, had focused on the poet's experiences and feelings; but almost all criticism since the Enlightenment had been concerned with establishing 'what the author meant', since that, it was held, was *the* meaning of the text. In literary studies generally, just as much as in biblical criticism, it had long been a clinching argument in refutation of a proposed interpretation that 'the author did not mean that' (or, better, 'the author could not possibly, in his historical circumstances, have meant that'). Quite apart from what a text might tell us about its author's emotions, it certainly told us something about his intentions, and its meaning was 'what he intended to say'.

All historical-critical work in biblical studies, it is not too much to say, depends on this notion. The great, and liberating, achievement of biblical criticism has been to establish, for a large number of texts, what the original author(s) meant *as against* what the text had traditionally been taken to mean by the Church, the synagogue or individual pre-critical interpreters.[15] But the New Critics believed that an interest in 'what the author intended' would prove to be the thin end of a wedge. Asking questions about the author's intention placed the critic on a slope down which he would slide inexorably towards the old Romantic concern for the poet's psychology and life-history. And in any case, they felt, texts have a life which continues after their authors are dead; texts continue to have meaning in ever-new contexts. The meaning is the sense the words can bear, not the meaning the author – who, after all, may not have been very good at saying what he meant anyway – intended them to convey. If an interpretation is clearly justified in the light of what the text actually says, it is of no use for the author to say, 'That is not what I meant': the critic will be perfectly within his rights in replying, 'Well, it's certainly what you *said*'. And with this rejoinder the author's intention as a criterion of meaning goes out, once and for all. The clearest illustration of this point may be made by citing a very well-known anecdote about T. S. Eliot; I quote it in the version related by Stephen Spender in his short study *Eliot*:

> Eliot could be less than helpful if one tried to 'explicate' him. In 1929 there was a meeting of the Oxford Poetry Club at which he was the guest of honour . . . An undergraduate asked him: 'Please, sir, what do you mean by the line: *Lady, three white leopards sat under a juniper tree?*' Eliot looked at him and said: 'I mean, *Lady, three white leopards sat under a juniper tree.*'[16]

Eliot, it may be noted, always scrupulously refrained from complaining that his meaning had been misunderstood – true to the belief that the meaning of a text lies in the text, not in its author.

The classic statement of the point being made here came quite late, in the essay 'The Intentional Fallacy' by W. K. Wimsatt and M. C. Beardsley, published in 1946.[17] In this, what had already been a guiding principle of the New Critical movement was stated explicitly, and initiated a sharp controversy which still continues. This essay clearly enunciated the belief that 'extrinsic' inquiries into what the author intended could be no part of valid literary criticism. But, in view of much subsequent misunderstanding and controversy about what Wimsatt and Beardsley 'meant', it may be as well to emphasize two points in which they do not go quite so far as is often suggested. This is particularly important for us, because it is all too easy to apply an exaggerated form of their anti-intentional stance to biblical studies, and so to create a form of criticism going quite beyond anything they envisaged. (I shall argue that this is virtually what has happened in the work of B. S. Childs.)

First, Wimsatt and Beardsley actually said that 'the design or intention of the author is neither available nor desirable as a standard for judging the *success* of a work of literary art' (my italics) – rather than ' . . . as a standard for judging the *meaning* of a work . . .'. One of their most trenchant critics, Frank Cioffi, has pointed out – almost certainly (to my mind) correctly – that they were in fact concerned with meaning, not just with how far the author had achieved his aim in the sense of producing a 'successful' piece.[18] Wimsatt later agreed that this had indeed been their intention.[19] To them, it did indeed seem that it was a fallacy to regard a work's meaning as 'what the author meant'. Nonetheless, the particular way in which they originally chose to express themselves is significant; for it reminds us that the New Criticism arose from dissatisfaction, not with a moderate belief that a work meant what it was meant to mean, but with the more extreme theory that its *value* had something to do with the value of its author's beliefs – that its success could be judged in terms of such qualities as its 'honesty' or 'sincerity'. Against this, Wimsatt and Beardsley protested that such a doctrine was little removed from praising a work because we agreed with, or even because we liked, its author. Surely, they were suggesting, a work's value depends on *the work itself*, not on whether the author was trying to do something worthwhile in it: after all, he may have been rather incompetent.

Secondly, they were not so much concerned to outlaw the author's meaning as the normative meaning, as to rule out certain illicit ways of *establishing* that meaning. It is, on their terms, acceptable to say that the text means what its author meant, provided that 'what the author meant' is understood to be discoverable from the text and only from the text – not from diaries, letters or remarks overheard on the telephone. To put the matter in another way: it is better to say that the author's intention is irrelevant to what a poem means than to speak as if we could settle a dispute about its meaning by asking the author what he meant. As the Eliot anecdote reminds us, if he could have said what he meant more clearly than the poem says it, he would no doubt have done so. Besides, he may not clearly remember what he meant; but this surely does not imply that the poem has therefore lost its meaning. But it was never supposed to follow from this that a poem is simply a freely floating collection of words whose meaning has nothing to do with its author at all. The point is that we establish what the author meant by reading the poem, rather than by asking his wife how he was feeling at the time he wrote it; the point is not that its meaning is entirely a function of combinations of words. Wimsatt and Beardsley were not structuralists! The meaning of a poem was for them still a *historical* meaning. For example, they did not reject questions about what particular words were capable of meaning in the period when a poem was written. They were concerned, however, to say that its meaning could be established only by seeing how the words were actually used – not by discovering what the author would have liked the words to mean, if only he had been better at putting them together.[20] This is a carefully nuanced position, not a root-and-branch attack on authorial intention such as we might expect from a critic such as Barthes. I have little doubt that Eliot's own position could have been stated in similar terms; he was far from wishing to imply that texts could mean just anything they could conceivably be read as meaning.

It remains true that the New Critical attack on intentionalism was, in its own day, very damaging to received notions of the aims of criticism. It established – and hardly any critic has since challenged the idea – that criticism is first and foremost about works, not about authors as people; and that the meaning of a work is to be sought in the work, not in 'extrinsic' evidence. It undoubtedly carries the corollary that a work can mean more than (or something different from) what its author consciously intended or desired; it means that authors can write more wisely than they know, and that critics can at times understand texts better than their creators can. It also opens up the possibility that the meaning of a work can depend partly on the context in which it is read: and it is this possibility, highly disturbing to a traditional historical critic, that finds expression in our third thesis.

Canonical Meaning

We have said that the meaning of a work does not, for the New Criticism, depend on the intentions of the author. On the other hand, it is not therefore wholly indeterminate, or a matter of the reader's whim. What it depends on above all is the *tradition* of which any individual work forms a part. It depends on the canon of existing literature, which both determines what meanings a new work is capable of bearing and, in turn, is modified in its overall meaning every time a significant new work is added to it. This is best expressed in a now classic passage in Eliot's 'Tradition and the Individual Talent':

> No poet, no artist of any art, has his complete meaning alone. His significance, his appreciation is the appreciation of his relation to the dead poets and artists. You cannot value him alone; you must set him, for contrast and comparison, among the dead. I mean this as a principle of aesthetic, not merely historical, criticism. The necessity that he shall conform, that he shall cohere, is not onesided; what happens when a new work of art is created is something that happens simultaneously to all the works of art which preceded it. The existing monuments form an ideal order among themselves, which is modified by the introduction of the new (the really new) work of art among them. The existing order is complete before the new work arrives; for order to persist after the supervention of novelty, the *whole* existing order must be, if ever so slightly, altered; and so the relations, proportions, values of each work of art toward the whole are readjusted; and this is conformity between the old and the new. Whoever has approved this idea of order, of the form of European, of English literature, will not find it preposterous that the past should be altered by the present as much as the present is directed by the past.[21]

As we saw in chapter 7, it makes good sense to say that a given play by Shakespeare has layers of meaning that derive not just from its internal organization, the meaning of its own parts, but also from its relation to his other plays. What Eliot is here proposing is that the same principle can be extended to the whole of a literature; so that the meaning of any work of English literature depends at least in part on its relation to all the other works in this vast corpus.

Predictably, one practical effect of this idea was the production of poetry – much of Eliot's own poetry is a case in point – which made conscious use of the awareness that meaning is thus canonically determined, by highly complex webs of allusion. In *The Waste Land* this even leads, notoriously, to the poet's providing his own critical footnotes so that the allusions are not missed. But (just as with the idea of poetry as artefact) this is not really meant as a statement of literary preference, of a *liking* for allusive verse, but as a general theory of literature, which is meant to be applicable in principle to the most apparently simple and self-contained work. Indeed, it would be fair to say that the main reason why we perceive certain poems as simple and artless is precisely that the literary tradition in which we stand has established certain conventions for what counts as 'artlessness'. We perceive poems as artless because they are like other poems we have been taught to perceive in this way, and unlike those which aim at depth and complexity. (Along this road there is a possible intersection with the conventionalism of some structuralists, rather surprisingly: compare chapter 9 above). Eliot did not wish to suggest that a work's meaning was *wholly* constrained by its 'canonical context'; but he was convinced that this was one important element in its meaning.

At first sight it may seem that there is a certain conflict between the 'canonical' aspect of the New Criticism and the idea, discussed in the previous section, that the meaning of a work of literary art inheres in itself. Can we say *both* that a poem bears its meaning in itself – so that we can read it 'unseen', without knowing who wrote it – *and* that its meaning derives from its place within the ordered corpus or canon that constitutes 'literature'? I believe that there is a real difficulty here, and that by probing it a little we may be able to suggest a way of refining the basic insight of the New Critics, so as to make it conflict rather less than may appear with more traditional approaches to interpretation. But for the moment it can be said that both the ideas just mentioned do at least share one feature which distinguishes them sharply from anything in the kinds of criticism the New Critics were attacking. This is their insistence that meaning at any rate does *not* derive from the 'original' author's intentions. The unifying theme here is the idea of literature as artefact. Whether we say that a literary work has its meaning in itself, and does not derive it from some external source (such as what the author was trying to do) or that any particular work has meaning as part of a larger complex (the canon of literature) – that will depend on how long a view we are taking. At times we may wish to consider an individual work as a finished whole; at others, to consider the whole body of English literature, or some large portion of it, as one giant 'artefact', and in that case each individual work is simply part of the whole. Sometimes we may want to say that a poet produces a poem which is self-contained in its meaning; sometimes that he adds another poem to the canon of 'poetry', thereby both altering (ever so subtly) the meaning of the already existing canon, and also causing the poem he writes to derive its fuller meaning from its place in that canon. The important point, from a New Critical point of view, is that the poet has no control over the process. He cannot make his poem mean anything other than it will necessarily mean by virtue of its internal structure and content, and by virtue of its place within the body of English (or Western, or world) literature.

New Criticism and Canon Criticism

The similarities between B. S. Childs's 'canonical approach', and the New Criticism as here briefly described are surely reasonably obvious. I must repeat: Childs himself rejects the suggestion that he is under the influence of the New Criticism, and also stresses that his proposals are essentially theological, not literary in conception.[22] Nevertheless it seems fair to draw attention to the close formal resemblance between his programme and that of the New Critics, and perhaps to see this as strengthening the suggestion made in chapter 7 that the 'canonical approach' is very much a child of the twentieth century.[23] In that chapter I tried to show that it is much more of a novelty from the *theological* point of view than it is often perceived as being, either by Childs himself or by his opponents. So far from being merely a 'return' to taking the canon seriously in theology (whether that is a good thing or a bad one), Childs's canonical approach is in reality a definite innovation. He is claiming a status for the canon greater than anyone has ever suggested before. It may look like an academically respectable version of the conservative alternative to historical-critical method; but any fundamentalists who adopt it for that reason will be deluding themselves, and will find in time that it is far more uncomfortably modern than it seems.

But we can now see, I believe, that the whole style of Childs's enterprise has from the *literary* point of view too an unmistakably modern air. Whether or not he has been influenced by the New Criticism, it is hard to believe that his proposals would have taken just this form, if the New Criticism had never existed. On all three counts – emphasis on 'the text itself' as a finished product rather than as a vehicle for expressing an author's ideas; indifference to authorial intention; and concern for the integration of individual texts into a literary canon, which contributes to their meaning – Childs stands very close to the New Critics.

This is not meant to devalue or debunk Childs's work, but simply to show where it is likely to be vulnerable. The point is that a whole range of arguments has been deployed against New Criticism, of which biblical studies are not necessarily aware; and if canon criticism has the same style and concerns as New Criticism, it may well be at risk from these arguments as well as from the theological ones we have already considered. Whether or not Childs 'depends' on New Criticism is not strictly relevant to this question. One could try to argue that there were quite specific reasons why principles broadly like those of the New Critics could be validly applied in biblical studies, even though they were unsatisfactory in general literary criticism, but this would probably not be very easy, and Childs certainly does not attempt it. On the face of it we may expect New Criticism and canon criticism to stand or fall together; and so in the next chapter I will try to probe more deeply into the New Critics' theories, and try to assess whether their similarity to canon criticism is an asset or a liability for Childs.

Secular Literary Criticism and the Historical-Critical Method

But before we move on, it will be useful to return to a question raised above. If Childs's approach is (unintentionally) like approaches to literature in the world outside biblical studies, how far is this also true of the methods it seeks to replace? We saw that the *techniques* of source and form criticism, at any rate, were developed by biblical scholars for biblical studies, rather than being taken over from other disciplines, and in this they differ markedly from those of biblical structuralism, which are deliberately borrowed from the literary world. But are the concerns that lie *behind* these techniques peculiar to biblical scholars, or are they too akin to the concerns of secular literary critics?

Our sketch of the criticism that the New Critics wanted to replace strongly suggests that there was never so great a divide between biblical and general literary studies as is sometimes suggested nowadays.[24] It is true, as we noticed at the beginning of chapter 2, that students are often puzzled to hear source-analysis described as 'literary criticism', when this means something so different in the study of English or French literature, and thereby are easily persuaded that biblical criticism is out of touch with 'real' literary criticism. But this impression is rather misleading. The retention of 'literary criticism' as a technical term for the study of sources in composite books of the Bible is little more than a historical accident. The biblical student's realization that the Bible is not studied in the way he has been taught to study Shakespeare does not show that biblical scholars are out of *touch* with literary criticism. It shows that their literary interests are somewhat out of *date*. The main outlines at least of source and form criticism were laid down in a period before the New Criticism and related movements (which have determined how literature is now taught in most schools) were a force to be reckoned with. But if we go back to this period, we find that the concerns of biblical critics and of general literary critics were not so very different then, even though their actual techniques undoubtedly differed – not least because of the great differences in character between the Old Testament and the major works of European literature.

What we now think of as 'traditional' biblical criticism shared the same essentially historical interest as literary criticism had in general, before the rise of the New Critical movement. It was unequivocally committed to the quest for the original author's meaning and intention; to studying texts in their historical context;[25] and to approaching them as vehicles through which ideas were conveyed, rather than as art-objects in their own right. (For biblical scholars, of course, these 'ideas' were likely to contain historical or theological information, not emotional experience). Traditional biblical criticism, like traditional literary criticism, is anti-canonical in approach: it asks what a given work means when restored to its original setting, when the preconceptions we have of it, as a result of the tradition in which it has come down to us, have been stripped away. In the historical-critical study of the Bible the canon is a hindrance to be removed, not an interpretative framework to be welcomed, for it obscures the true meaning of each individual text, which is the meaning it was intended to convey by its original author or authors. In the desire to get back to the words of the original Isaiah, and to be able to hear him speaking without the thick wrappings of the intervening 'Isaiah tradition' that had muffled his voice until the rise of source criticism, we surely have a close analogue to the desire of nineteenth-century literary critics to hear the poet and enter into his experience, unclouded by the mists that roll between him and us. Indeed, the idea of the Israelite prophet as a lone genius, speaking out of a direct experience of God and seeking to share his insights with others, arguably owes as much to Romantic models of criticism and poetry as to the Old Testament text.

What Old Testament scholars call 'literary' criticism may not, therefore, strike the modern student as having much to do with what *he* thinks of as the correct way to approach 'literature', but it has a good deal in common with what literary criticism was doing in the days before the New Critics redrew the groundplan of the discipline. There was a time when all literary criticism was historical criticism, of the sort deplored by New Critics and exponents of the 'canonical approach' alike.

We can now proceed to examine the rival claims of New Criticism and of the earlier historical approach to provide normative models for Old Testament study. We shall see that New Criticism has a certain instability – not surprisingly, an instability of much the sort we have detected in canonical approaches to the biblical text. From it one can go forward, to the conventionalist and deterministic theories of the structuralists; or backward, to some modified form of traditional historical criticism.

Further Reading

W. K. Wimsatt and M. C. Beardsley, 'The Intentional Fallacy' in
On Literary Intention, ed. D. Newton-de Molina. Edinburgh 1976

T. S. Eliot, 'Tradition and the Individual Talent', in *Selected Essays*.
London 1932

E. D. Hirsch Jr, *Validity in Interpretation*. New Haven and London
1967

'THE TEXT ITSELF'

What I should like to write is a book about nothing, a book dependent on nothing external, which would be held together by the internal strength of its style. . . . The finest works are those that contain the least matter; the closer expression comes to thought, the closer language comes to coinciding and merging with it, the finer the result. I believe the future of Art lies in this direction.

> Gustave Flaubert, Letter to Louise Colet, 16 January 1852, in his
> *Correspondance* 1 (Paris 1922), p. 417, tr. in *The Letters of Gustave
> Flaubert 1830–1857*, selected, ed. and tr. by F. Steegmuller
> (Cambridge, Mass. and London 1980), p. 154

Preliminary Reading

J. Barr, *The Bible in the Modern World* (London 1973), pp. 75–88

Difficulties in New Criticism

New Criticism and canon criticism stand or fall together: they are children of the same literary culture, even if they have never met. In this chapter I shall suggest that they should probably fall – encouraged in this by the knowledge that one of them has already fallen. Of course I shall not (could not) launch a rigorous attack on New Criticism; I shall merely try to indicate the sensitive spots in the theory, the places where it proved most vulnerable to attack. This will point us to similar sensitive spots in canon criticism. But I shall certainly not suggest that the whole structure of either method is faulty through and through. On the contrary, there is much that remains standing, or that is worth rebuilding, for critical theories are rarely monoliths. There seem to me to be sensitive spots in each of the three aspects of New Criticism discussed in the last chapter, and we may look at them in the same order.

Texts as Artefacts

As we have seen, the New Critics' proposal that literary works should be understood as artefacts – the products of a craft – was a reaction against an excessive emphasis on the way a poem might afford direct insight into the thoughts of a great soul. Against that background there was a good deal to be said for it. Criticism of the kind New Critics attacked is not dead yet: in 1980 a speaker on BBC television offered, according to *Radio Times*, 'a personal view of [*The Tempest*] which he describes as profoundly autobiographical – an exploration of Shakespeare's own inner nature'.[1] But almost all serious critics would now react in a hostile way to this sort of thing, whereas before the shift in critical thought that produced New Criticism and related theories it would have been scarcely worthy of notice. However, New Criticism generally went further than denying simply the belief that works of literary art were windows into the author's psychological state. By speaking of them as artefacts, the New Critics tended to suggest that literature had no referential function at all – to put it baldly, that literature was not *about* anything. A poem was not written to convey information, but simply to exist as a poem. Of course poems, indeed all literary works, have some *subject-matter* – they are not vacuous strings of words; but the subject-matter is not what a poem exists to convey. If it were, then a brief paraphrase of the contents would be as adequate as the poem itself. For example, we could replace Tennyson's *In Memoriam* by a sentence such as 'I am extremely sorry that my friend has died'. The anecdote about Eliot, quoted in the previous chapter, takes this point to its logical conclusion: the meaning of a poem is the poem, and cannot be stated in any other way. The critic's task is to read the poem, not to reduce it to the information he supposes it to convey.[2]

If it is felt that there is something unsatisfactory in denying any referential content to literature, it may seem better to say that literature is about something after all: it is about literature itself. The true subject-matter of all poems is poetry. This may seem a perverse way of putting it, but is in fact not far from many people's semi-instinctive perception of what literary art is for. The literary artist is not there to tell us things that we do not already know; he exists to show us the potentiality for beauty in the language which can be used for stating even commonplace truths. To say that a poem is about poetry, or exists in order to be a poem, is only a rather striking way of putting something that in the case of music or the visual arts we accept without too much difficulty. Programme-music, which tells a story, does exist but is rarely regarded as the musical norm; paintings may be 'trying to say' something, but more often we would be more likely to think of them in terms of their beauty of form or composition. It is because poetry is made of words, and words *also* have the function of conveying information, that we are more easily misled into thinking of it as referential in character. But in fact literature is a form of art, and art is an end in itself.

Although B. S. Childs clearly shares the New Critical belief in 'the text itself', his overriding theological interest tends to prevent him from taking the further New Critical step I have just described in handling the biblical text. He is deeply concerned with the truths that the Old Testament is meant to convey. It may be, however, that there is more difficulty than he recognizes in reconciling this concern with his stress on the text as a finished product. At all events, New Critics did not generally think the two aspects of text-as-artefact could be separated so easily. But the New Critical step is taken by another scholar, whose indebtedness to New Criticism is overt and acknowledged: H. W. Frei. Frei's *The Eclipse of Biblical Narrative* is an extremely important attempt to relate biblical study to contemporary literary criticism. New Criticism is certainly not the only important influence on Frei, but it is one of them. A sketch of his major thesis will help us to see where an emphasis on 'the text itself' can lead in Old Testament study.

Frei's book is a study of the different approaches to reading the 'historical' books of the Old Testament and the narrative parts of the New – in other words, all the books from Genesis to Nehemiah, the Gospels, and Acts – that have been current in English- and German-speaking theology since the Enlightenment. According to him, there was a time when these narrative texts caused no problem for the Christian reader, because it had not yet been seen that the world they described was other than the world in which the reader

160

was still living. In other words, it was simply assumed that these books presented correct accounts of earlier stages in world-history – that they told of earlier parts of a story that was still our story. The rise of historical criticism altered this naive assumption irrevocably. It became clear that much in the biblical books was not true as it stood, at the level of straightforward historical accuracy. People also came to realize that the world of the biblical narrators was not our world anyway, but a pre-scientific, pre-critical world which worked with different categories and concepts from ours. The historical books, like the rest of the Bible, became documents from an ancient and rather alien culture, not something to which we could relate unselfconsciously.

Frei argues that the problems this shift in understanding brought were handled very differently in the English-speaking world and in German theology. English-speaking scholarship adopted the approach which has remained characteristic of it to this day, of asking about the historical truth behind the biblical narratives. In conservative biblical scholarship this has taken the form of attempts to vindicate the historicity of the narrative at all points; in more liberal biblical study, it has usually led to a great interest in reconstructing the events as they actually happened, using the biblical narrative as evidence for historical research in much the way that any other ancient or modern historian uses his primary sources. German scholarship has generally taken a quite different course, and has been far more interested in the *ideas* being communicated by the narrative. The category of *Heilsgeschichte* ('saving history' or 'salvation history') has been one particularly popular attempt to encapsulate the meaning of biblical narrative in a quasi-philosophical concept: it emerged in the so-called *heilsgeschichtliche Schule*, a school of theologians in the late eighteenth and nineteenth centuries,[3] and in this century has been important in the work of von Rad in Old Testament[4] and Cullmann in New Testament studies.[5] It is from within the German tradition, on the whole, that attempts have been made to write histories of Israelite thought, and theologies of the Old Testament, in which the narrative books are used chiefly for what they can tell us about the thought-forms and leading theological ideas of various periods in the life of ancient Israel. A failure to see the difference in emphasis between German- and English-speaking theology leads to much misunderstanding:

161

German scholars often are, and always have been, impatient of the English tendency to speak as though the only question that mattered in studying the Gospels or Genesis was 'Did it really happen?'; and English scholars continue to be maddened by what they see as a refusal to come clean on questions of historicity. Suggestions such as von Rad's, that what matters is not the Exodus as it really happened, but the Exodus as the controlling idea in the faith of Israel,[6] tend to irritate and offend English readers.

Still, the period covered by Frei's work ends before the major developments in twentieth-century theology, and in one important movement this century we can see a certain fusing of the two concerns. The Biblical Theology movement, mentioned above in chapter 6, combined an interest in history with a concern for the 'ideas' of the Bible. The work of G. E. Wright, one of its most influential spokesmen, will illustrate the point very clearly. Wright, in his *God Who Acts*,[7] was equally concerned with the Old Testament as a source from which (with the aid of archaeology) 'real' history, hard facts, can be reconstructed – for it is in history that God is encountered – and with the Old Testament as a repository of the 'Hebrew world-view', the distinctively Israelite modes of thought which were regarded in the Biblical Theology movement as normative for Christian theology. It is probable that Wright was not very clear how these two elements were related in the system he was propounding. But it is interesting that he should have combined them, because the point to which Frei's argument builds up is that, for all their apparent difference, the interest in history and the interest in biblical ideas are united by one very important feature. Whether English scholars were concerning themselves with the historical information that could be culled from a careful study of the Old Testament narratives, or German theologians were reducing the Bible to a theological system, they shared a common conviction that the main function of the narrative books was to provide *information*. It might be information about what happened, or information about what people believed; but in either case it was information, something that could be *extracted from* the text by applying appropriate techniques, and then organized into an independent system by the scholar. The narrative books were being read for what lay behind them, or for what could be got out of them; their true 'meaning' or significance was held to lie in something that could be restated in other terms.

Now Frei's own proposal, which has fairly clear affinities with the New Criticism, is that the correct way to read a narrative text is not as a source of information, but *as a narrative*. The meaning of a narrative is its narrative shape.[8] Of course it may well be possible to use narratives for extraneous purposes – just as, today, we can use novels as sources of information about the social conditions in the period when they were written; but the true use of a narrative is simply to read it, and to take seriously its 'narrativity'. We cannot extract the 'message' from a narrative text, and then throw away the text itself; a narrative is its own meaning. Narration – story-telling – is a basic human activity, which cannot be reduced to anything else.

In Frei's book we have a non-referential theory of biblical narrative texts, which is closely akin to the New Critical theory of literature in general as non-referential. Again, we may say that biblical narratives have subject-matter (the events they describe) but are not exactly *about* this subject-matter, in the sense that we read them to discover more facts about it: narratives, like poems, simply exist, and if they are 'about' anything, it is 'narrativity'. The point is not hard to grasp if we think once more of a novel. We can summarize the plot of a novel; we can also outline its leading 'ideas'; but in neither case have we replaced the novel itself, or made it unnecessary to read it. In the end, a novel is not a source of any kind of information; it is simply a novel. In the same way, to read biblical narratives in either the English or the German mode is to miss the point. It is to treat them as reference-books, when in fact they are literature.[9]

It seems to me that Frei's suggestions can help to break a dead-lock often encountered in discussions about the Old Testament. As we have seen, the fundamentalist belief that Genesis 1—2 is to be read as a historically accurate account of the creation is sometimes countered by suggesting that these chapters are not 'really' a historical account at all, but 'a way of saying' that God is the creator. Indeed, some conservative critics can now be found maintaining this themselves, since it makes it possible to argue that Genesis is, after all, totally correct in everything that it actually affirms; the details were never supposed to be taken as historical fact anyway.

However, a number of scholars have pointed out that this is a two-edged argument. It certainly helps us not to worry about the historical inaccuracy of Genesis 1—2, but the price is rather high; for it leaves us with an interpretation of these chapters according to which they can be virtually *replaced* by the proposition 'God made the world'.[10] Surely, we are likely to feel, there must be more to it than that! Can we really believe that all the circumstantial detail, and careful construction, of the first two chapters of Genesis are just so much dispensable decoration? Frei succeeds in putting his finger on what is wrong with *both* sides of this debate. Both parties make the mistake of supposing that any value Genesis may have must lie in the information it conveys: the question is simply whether the information is historical, or theological. In fact the value of Genesis does not lie in its 'information-content' at all, but in that very narrative character which both of the parties to the debate ignore. Taking a leaf out of Eliot's book, we may say that the meaning of 'In the beginning God made the heavens and the earth . . .' is 'In the beginning God made the heavens and the earth . . .'. The critic's task is to *read* Genesis with understanding, not to *rewrite* it.

Much of this will be attractive to the biblical student with literary interests. And yet it is hard not to feel that this cannot be the whole story. Frei is correct, if we can be sure that all the narrative material in the Bible is to be classified as what we may call 'literary narrative', and not as 'informative discourse'. Suppose we concede the point for Genesis 1—2; can we be sure that it is also true of Chronicles, or of parts of Kings? Is it true that the Gospels are narrative whose value lies in its narrativity, rather than attempts to tell the reader what he needs to know about Jesus? It is not obviously foolish to take them in either way; how are we to decide which is correct? Once we ask this question, the instability both of the New Criticism and of related approaches to the Bible becomes clear, for there are, it seems, only two possible ways of answering it.

(1) We can say that the narrative texts of the Bible are to be taken as 'literary narrative' because *all* narrative is to be taken in this way: it simply is not possible to write any text in narrative form which is then correctly read as providing information. This is either plainly false – after all, very much historical writing has traditionally been narrative in form, but it has clearly been meant

to convey information – or else true merely because we choose to make it so: true by definition, in fact. It is perfectly possible to decide that there shall be a convention for reading narrative which ignores its referential content, and treats it simply as 'literature'. But it is clear that one could not reasonably call this the *correct* way of reading narrative texts, so as to be able to take to task (as Frei does) those who read them in other ways. In fact, such an approach would find its closest affinities with structuralism, as the reader will surely have seen. It would be a theory of reading, not an empirically based description of how particular sorts of text actually function.

(2) Alternatively – and this is probably closer to what Frei actually intends – it is possible to say that the narrative books of the Bible are to be *read* as narrative because they were *written* as narrative. It was always a mistake to read them as though they were meant to impart historical or theological information; they were intended to function as literary narrative, not as historiography. I am myself reasonably convinced that this is true for at least some Old Testament narratives, and it is a case that has been argued before in studies of such books as 2 Samuel and Genesis, and that is generally accepted for Jonah and Esther. But it belongs entirely to the realm of traditional historical criticism and neither needs, nor is compatible with, the theoretical framework provided by New Criticism. If we are to decide a disputed critical question by reference to what the original author intended, we are back with historical-critical method of the kind the New Critics disliked. Seen in this way, Frei's work ought to be interpreted as a form of redaction criticism, an attempt to interpret the intentions of those who compiled the biblical narrative books. Even if the materials they drew on had been meant as information, the finished works into which the redactors incorporated them had a different aim in view: to exist as literary narratives. But Frei himself certainly does not perceive his work as redaction criticism: he sees himself as saying something about the texts themselves quite apart from the intentions of their authors or compilers. And it seems to me that there is a basic incoherence in his position at this crucial point.

This attempt to apply something like the New Criticism to the biblical text appears, therefore, to fail according to its own criteria, however illuminating it may be if read as a sophisticated kind of historical criticism. But its failure suggests an inherent flaw in the

New Critical theory, which gives it the kind of instability just described – a flaw which we also found in the closely similar theory of B. S. Childs.[11] The belief that a text is essentially an artefact, rather than a vehicle for conveying information or ideas, must take one of two forms. Either it must apply to all texts, even those which their authors would want to see in some other light (say as historiography, or some other kind of verbal discourse); and in that case New Criticism becomes hard to distinguish from structuralism. Or – and this will strike most people as more sensible – only some texts are correctly seen as 'artefacts', as beautiful verbal objects, rather than as discourse conveying something beyond itself. In the second case we shall find ourselves asking how the two kinds are to be distinguished; and before we know where we are we shall be trying to find out which kind the author was trying to write. Then we shall be perfectly free to ask such natural questions as, Was St Mark trying to produce a work of art, or to inform his readers about Jesus? But we shall not be New Critics after all.[12]

In fact the New Critics were rarely guilty themselves of such exaggerations of method as seem to have occurred in Frei and Childs. Like biblical structuralists, these two scholars seem to be misled by the ambiguity of the word 'literature'.[13] 'Literature' may still mean (as it once could only mean) everything in writing – as when a man could be described as having a great deal of 'literature', meaning that he was well-read. But since the mid-nineteenth century it has come to have a much more restricted sense: roughly, the types of writing that are studied in courses in 'literature' – poetry, novels, drama and so on. The New Criticism was a theory about literature in this narrower sense. It can reasonably be accused of having had a pernicious effect, artificially narrowing what should count as literature to those kinds of writing that were most amenable to its own approach. Thus it acquiesced in banishing philosophy, and other kinds of discursive prose, from the curriculum of departments of English literature. But, consistently with this, it at least did not treat such 'non-literary' types of writing as 'verbal artefact' in the way we have described. It was essentially a theory about lyric verse, imaginative fiction, perhaps drama; not about written matter of absolutely any kind.

Now the difficulty in extending New Criticism to cover such material as biblical narrative books is precisely that we really do not know whether these are 'literature' in the narrower sense or not. That is just the point at issue. The New Criticism is a way of approaching writing generally agreed to be 'literature', and it says that such writing is not to be approached as if it were something else – philosophical prose, or historiography. It does not provide any criterion for deciding what is literature in the first place. Probably most New Critics would have accepted that the author's intention, though immaterial to the interpretation of a work agreed by all to be 'literary', is highly relevant to deciding whether a particular text should be assigned to the category 'literature'. So we may say that Frei (and Childs in his somewhat different way) may be right in their practical conclusions, obtained by using essentially New Critical tools, about those parts of the Bible that actually *are* 'literary' in the narrower sense; for these, there is a good deal to be said for asking about 'the text itself'. But the crucial question is, which parts of the Bible are 'literature'? This question is begged by Frei, just as the related question of which parts are 'canonical' is begged by Childs. Theoretical statements of New Criticism in literature generally which fell into the same trap would be open to the same objection. But in practice hardly anyone tried to apply New Critical procedures to texts whose status as 'literature' was in doubt. Like most literary critical theories – this is a familiar story by now – New Criticism may have tended to speak as though it had discovered the final truth about all possible combinations of words on paper, but in fact it was devised with quite a narrow range of texts in mind, and very quickly led to a preference for the kinds of text most amenable to its methods. Biblical critics have, I suspect, been less quick to see this than have their colleagues in literary studies, and so have applied what amounts to a New Critical approach with too heavy a hand to biblical texts for which it is rather ill-suited.

Intentionalism

As we have just seen, it is possible to exaggerate the anti-intentionalist stance of the New Critics. When Wimsatt and Beardsley said that the intention of the author was 'neither available nor desirable' as a criterion of the success of a literary work, they were thinking of *highly* 'extrinsic' intentions, such as the intention to write movingly, or to communicate emotion, rather than the intention that the text should *mean* X rather than Y. To read a text as though it had never had an author at all, but existed in a timeless state as an entirely self-contained entity, is to go well beyond what they were suggesting; though indeed it seems to be not far from what Childs thinks we should do with the Old Testament. Nonetheless there are problems even in the moderate anti-intentionalism of mainstream New Criticism, which can distort the work of biblical interpretation.

(1) New Critics, structuralists and proponents of 'canon criticism' all agree that the essential flaw in asking about the intentions of an author, rather than about the inherent meaning of a text, is that to do so is to abandon literary criticism for psychology. A question about intention is a question about the state of someone's mind. Now 'intention' is an enormous issue in philosophy, which we cannot go into in detail here. But it does seem reasonable to ask whether the matter is really as simple as New Criticism makes it. Surely questions about intention need not be so crudely psychologistic as to lead automatically to speculations about the author's 'inner life'. At the level of ordinary language usage, most people can distinguish the question 'What did the poet *mean* by saying X?' from the two questions 'What was *passing through the poet's mind* when he wrote X?' and 'What *psychological or emotional state was the poet in* when he wrote X?' To take an example: when we were considering Ecclesiastes, it turned out to be crucial whether 12:1 ('Remember your Creator in the days of your youth') was to be taken as meaning 'Spend your youth in wholesome meditation on the coming judgement of God' or 'While you are young, remember that God has assigned you only a short time on earth, and make the most of it'. It seems natural to ask which of these the original Qoheleth, or whichever redactor is responsible for the verse, really meant. But this is plainly not the same as asking how he was feeling at the time, or even what thoughts were passing through his mind as he wrote it. He may, for all we know, have been feeling deeply pessimistic, but nevertheless have wanted to give good advice to young people – the kind of advice that, he felt, would have made his own early life happier if he had taken it. No one would say that the advice must be read pessimistically, because he was depressed when he wrote it. But when we have seen that its meaning does

not depend on the state the author was in at the time, this does not mean we have abolished his 'intention' as a criterion of meaning. Whatever 'intention' is, it is not difficult to see that it is something distinct from the psychological condition that happened to prevail at the time of writing.[14]

It is true, as we have seen, that Wimsatt and Beardsley did not say a work's meaning was not the meaning the author intended: they said that certain ways of trying to establish what he meant – 'extrinsic' ways, involving evidence other than the text itself – were illicit. Nonetheless, if this doctrine is applied rigorously, it does tend to suggest that to talk of intention is necessarily to invoke external factors like psychology and emotion. In any case it is not clear why anti-intentionalism should be applied as an absolute dogma. What we can know about the author from sources other than the text itself is not a *criterion* of the text's meaning, certainly; but it can still provide useful hints as to what the text is *likely* to mean. There seems to be no reason why Old Testament scholars should take this aspect of the New Criticism, valid though it may be within reasonable limits, as placing an absolute embargo on questions about the biblical writers' intentions – as though this would inevitably lead to some kind of 'Romantic' theory of biblical inspiration. This absurdly exaggerates the perils latent in 'intentionalism'.[15]

(2) Secondly, one of the strengths of the New Criticism is that it does more justice than some older approaches to an experience all readers are familiar with: the experience that literary works often seem to have meanings that go beyond what their authors can have consciously intended. Even where it is conceded that the author's original intention can be determined with reasonable certainty, and the text can be seen to convey that meaning, we are sometimes aware that it has other layers of meaning that cannot be attributed to the author in the same way. Thus our discussion in chapter 5 led to the conclusion that Ecclesiastes could be very naturally read as having meanings that were quite far from the author's mind. Now this obviously cannot be adequately explained on any theory of meaning that makes authorial intention the *only* criterion; and it is no doubt because the Old Testament contains a relatively high proportion of texts which are either authorless or highly composite that New Criticism, like structuralism, is attractive to biblical scholars.

Nevertheless, this is not necessarily to say that the question what the author intended is *always* out of place. If traditional historical criticism errs by over-generalizing on one side, New Criticism may err equally on the other. As a matter of fact, texts may go beyond their authors' intentions in a number of ways. (a) They may come to be read in contexts wholly remote from that of the original author: and it is then that the modern approaches to meaning we have been describing come into their own. But (b) they may also be found to express ideas which their authors were hardly aware of when they wrote, but which they later came to see as a true expression of their intention. The experience of being able to say, 'I didn't realize that was what I meant, but now you point it out, I see that I really did', is not at all uncommon and does not seem to need any particularly sophisticated explanation. Or again, (c) a critic may sometimes justifiably feel that he understands a work better than the author himself does, not because its meaning is completely independent of the author's intentions, but because he is better than the author at articulating some thread or connection of thought which actually controlled the work's construction, but of which the author was not fully conscious. When we say that the primary meaning of a work, at least, is the meaning its author intended, we do not have to feel forced into such a very narrow definition of 'intention' that all these things are simply ruled out. By forcing 'intentionalists' to take the narrowest possible definition of 'intention', of course, one can make the case for New Criticism seem overwhelming. But this is a hollow victory, for it leaves almost all the really interesting cases undiscussed. It is a caricature of historical criticism to speak as if it were wedded to the author's intention in this very narrow sense of 'what the author was explicitly conscious of wanting to say at the moment of composition'; neither literary nor biblical critics have at all often been as indifferent as this to 'the text itself'. Once again the student of the Bible would be unwise to let propaganda for the New Criticism run away with him.[16]

Canon

In the last chapter I suggested that the New Critical idea of meaning as a function of a text's relation to other texts in a canon or corpus (the idea which has most affinities with biblical 'canon criticism') seems hard to reconcile with the stress on 'the text itself'. In the period when the New Criticism arose, indeed, the difference or tension between these two notions was comparatively insignificant when compared with what they had in common: namely, a rejection of the author and his psychology as the criterion of meaning. In effect, the New Critics were saying, it hardly matters whether you say that a work bears its meaning within itself, or that it draws its meaning from the corpus to which it belongs, so long as you *don't* say that what it means is what its author meant. However, there surely *is* a tension between 'the text itself' and 'the text as part of a canon', and we should note this as a third sensitive area in New Criticism. In what follows I shall suggest that the canonical approach actually undermines the concern for the finished text as an end in itself, and brings us, once again, nearer to traditional historical criticism.

Ecclesiastes (we suggested) means something different, from a canon critic's point of view, if it stands in the Hebrew canon, than it means if it is part of a collection including such books as Wisdom (i.e. the Greek Old Testament canon), or the Gospels (i.e. the Christian Bible). Its canonical context constrains its meaning. But why is this so? It is because the book can only have a place within whichever canon we are dealing with, if it *coheres* with the rest of the books in that canon. This does not necessarily mean that it must be *wholly* consistent with them, or convey an *identical* message; it does mean that it must be possible to see it as at least an intelligible part of the whole, or as one stage in a development of thought that has a definite direction. When we see Ecclesiastes as part of the canon, we are seeing it as belonging to what we judge to be a tradition or literary corpus that hangs together. And how it hangs together depends on exactly which books are reckoned as belonging to it. Different canons entail different meanings for every one of their constituent parts (even if the difference is only quite small). This seems to conform pretty closely to Eliot's theory about the relation of new works to 'the existing monuments'. It means that a book such as Ecclesiastes has no determinate meaning unless we know what we are meant to read it *as*. Until we know which canon it belongs to, we cannot read it with understanding.

Now it is very hard to see how this theory can be reconciled with the New Critical concern for the text in and for itself. This is not just because the text in itself and the text in the canon seem to be in some sense different texts: the problem is more fundamental than that. The point is that an interest in 'the text itself' is intelligible only if texts have a determinate meaning which can be read off from the words that compose them, without any concern for context or background. The New Critical approach, as enshrined in the practice of expecting students to comment intelligently on passages 'unseen' and 'as they stand', requires a view of meaning in which a particular sequence of words will always bear a certain meaning, irrespective of extraneous factors such as date of writing, authorial intention or literary context. This is diametrically opposed to the idea, which is required by a 'canonical' approach, that the words which compose a text draw their meaning from the context and setting in which they are meant to be read. A canonical approach depends on the possibility, if we may put it like this, that a text is capable of being *not synonymous with itself* – in other words, that the very same sequence of words can mean different things in different contexts. Most of our reading in fact proceeds upon the assumption that this is so. We habitually assume that you cannot tell what a remark means until you know who made it, and what the words that make it up meant at the time. Charles II, when he visited the new St Paul's during its construction, complimented the architect on producing 'so awful and artificial' a building; it is essential for our belief that Charles II was a person of refined manners that we should *not* hold sequence of words to have fixed and determinate meanings in all ages and contexts. This is a particularly striking case of semantic change, but any familiarity with the history of literature will throw up hundreds of similar examples. Canon criticism requires that meaning is indeterminate in just this way: that the same words can have a quite different meaning under different circumstances.

If this is so, it is plainly very misleading to say that canon criticism of the Bible, or the kind of 'canonical' approach to literature commended by Eliot, is taking us back to 'the text itself'. On such a view, there is no such thing as 'the text itself'. The meaning of the text is a function of the context in which it stands, and cannot serve as an independent control of any sort over our reading of it. We cannot have it both ways.

172

This point may be illustrated by referring to a *jeu d'esprit* by the Argentinian writer, J. L. Borges. In his short piece 'Pierre Menard, Author of the Quixote', he constructs an exercise in a kind of 'canon criticism' which shows very clearly how a text can be non-synonymous with itself. The hero of this piece, Menard, sets himself the task of rewriting the *Don Quixote* of Cervantes, using identically the same words as the original. Borges shows amusingly how this changes the meaning of every word of the text:

> It is a revelation to compare Menard's *Don Quixote* with Cervantes's. The latter, for example, wrote (part one, chapter nine):
>
> > . . . truth, whose mother is history, rival of time, depository of deeds, witness of the past, exemplar and adviser to the present, and the future's counsellor.
>
> Written in the seventeenth century, written by the 'lay genius' Cervantes, this enumeration is a mere rhetorical praise of history. Menard, on the other hand, writes:
>
> > . . . truth, whose mother is history, rival of time, depository of deeds, witness of the past, exemplar and adviser to the present, and the future's counsellor.
>
> History, the *mother* of truth: the idea is astounding. Menard, a contemporary of William James, does not define history as an inquiry into reality but as its origin. Historical truth, for him, is not what has happened; it is what we judge to have happened. The final phrase – *exemplar and adviser to the present, and the future's counsellor* – are brazenly pragmatic.[17]

Of course this is a sort of joke; but it has very serious implications. For it shows quite clearly that the idea of a text as having a meaning in itself, irrespective of historical context or authorial intention, is mistaken. We may say that it vindicates the canonical principle – a work means what its context in a given literary culture compels it to mean – up to the hilt, *at the expense of* the New Critics' belief that a text is an entity with a life of its own and a determinate meaning that depends only on its internal character.

But we cannot stop there. Once again, New Critical approaches prove to be unstable, and threaten to turn into something either more traditional, or more radical. If we take with full seriousness the idea that the meaning of a text depends wholly on its context, we shall find ourselves with a theory of reading such as that of structuralism; and this, in its own way, once again makes meaning determined and fixed. Neither the author nor the reader is in any way free, on a structuralist theory, to mean anything but what the conventions of literature permit or constrain him to mean. This is a coherent view, but, as we have seen, it goes further than either New Critics or canon critics want to go; we shall examine it in the next chapter. But if we pursue the 'canonical' meaning of texts in what will seem, at least to most English readers, a more natural way, we shall find ourselves asking such questions as: 'What would this text mean, if we supposed that its author was contemporary with the other texts in the canon?' 'What did Ecclesiastes mean to the people who incorporated it into the Hebrew Bible?' In effect, what the 'canonizers' of Scripture did was to take old books and *creatively transcribe* them, so that they became contemporary texts;[18] and to ask about their meaning at this level is simply to ask what they mean if we regard them as having been written in (roughly) the last century BC rather than the eighth, or sixth, or fourth century. To ask about the canonical meaning of Ecclesiastes, once we put it this way, looks like a question of a different kind from those asked by historical criticism; but this is only because the 'canonical' Ecclesiastes happens to be verbally identical with an earlier text of the same name. In fact, the question is a straightforward historical-critical question, whose subject is an unknown 'author' within Judaism of the New Testament period.

As we have seen, one possible objection to the canonical approach to the Old Testament is that there was no such person. The act of canonizing the Hebrew Scriptures was *not* an act analogous to that of Borges' fictitious writer. Ecclesiastes was not in fact 'creatively transcribed': it was recognized as an ancient book, not turned into a modern one, however little people at that time may have had the historical sense necessary for that to make much difference to their interpretation of it. As a matter of *historical* fact, the Bible has no 'canonical level'. Hence 'canon criticism' will work only if it adopts the more conventionalist, determinist form which brings it closer to structuralism. This is a point I have argued before, and we have now reached it by another route.

But the general sense of muddle which the reader will surely by

now be feeling may suggest that there is something radically incoherent in the way New Criticism set up the whole problem of
'texts in themselves' and 'canonical meaning'. A good deal of the
confusion probably stems from the insistence that it is the *meaning*
of literary works we are talking about. I have spoken, in New
Critical terms, of works which are their own meaning; of works
which do not mean what they were meant to mean; of meaning as
a function of context; and of meanings that no one ever meant.
Even granted that 'meaning' is a difficult word to handle, may it
not be that it is being made to work too hard, to cover too many
different senses? Is it not possible that the argument is starting to
talk itself into a corner, all because 'meaning' has now become
almost meaningless?

E. D. Hirsch, one of the sternest critics of the New Criticism, has
suggested that a good deal of confusion has arisen because 'meaning'
has been made to do duty for both meaning properly so called and
'significance' or relevance.[19] When we say that a work 'changes its
meaning' by being incorporated into a new context this, for Hirsch,
is an imprecise way of speaking about two quite distinct processes,
and each of these processes can be described without stepping
outside the bounds of traditional historical criticism and its concern
for the author's meaning.

(a) One possibility is that an old work is being (as we have put
it) 'creatively transcribed'. Probably there are not many cases today,
apart from downright plagiarism, where an author has taken an old
work and simply issued it as a new one (the situation envisaged in
Borges' parable); but the re-use of some parts of older works, either
by their own author or by someone else, was common in the ancient
world and is not so unusual today.

(b) The second case is where an old work suddenly becomes
'contemporary' by proving to have some unexpected fresh application, or some power to speak directly to the condition of a new
generation, sometimes after years of neglect. Here the old text
becomes, we could say, part of a new 'canon' and is read alongside
much more recent works which it both illuminates and is illumin-
ated by.

Examples of the first type would be Tom Stoppard's play *Rosencrantz and Guildenstern are Dead*, and Ecclesiastes (if it developed as
we have suggested); of the second, John Donne's *Holy Sonnets*, after

they had been rescued by Coleridge and others from their neglect in the eighteenth century, and the Epistle to the Romans, 'rediscovered' by Luther at the Reformation.

Now, on Hirsch's view, neither of these cases requires analysis in terms of New Critical theories of meaning. In type (a), what has really happened is that two different texts, with different authors, happen to be composed of the same words. This is a problem only if one starts with the New Critical assumption that any given sequence of words has a single, fixed, determinate meaning which inheres in the words themselves and has nothing to do with the intentions of the author. On this assumption, there is no way of avoiding complicated verbal contortions to explain how a re-used text can be the same yet not the same; and it is through such contortions that a theory of 'canonical meaning' emerges – though, as we have seen, this theory in the end proves *incompatible* with the assumption about 'the text itself' which made it necessary in the first place. That assumption must therefore be given up; and we must return to the older view, that the primary meaning of a text is what its author meant by it. Once this is accepted, there is no longer any problem about verbally identical texts having different meanings, for the relation of verbal form to meaningful content is no longer being seen as rigidly fixed. The words of a text do not constitute a verbal artefact whose meaning is wholly internal to itself; they are vehicles through which a certain content is expressed. Questions about the identity, period and cultural background of the author are just as relevant in determining this content as questions about the internal structures of the passage. In cases, therefore, where the biblical scholar is faced with texts that have been re-used, transcribed or incorporated into other texts, there is nothing for it but to recognize that the same sequence of words has more than one author, and that its meaning depends on which of its authors we are considering.

In type (b), on the other hand, where an old text is suddenly 'rediscovered' by a new generation of readers, we are not dealing with a difference of *meaning* at all, but with a difference of *significance*. Thus, Donne did not speak to the eighteenth century; he does speak to us. It is quite true that our own interests and cultural assumptions mean that we will not perceive Donne's meaning in exactly the same way as eighteenth-century readers did, or indeed as Donne's contemporaries did; but it is not the case that the text of Donne has actually *changed* its meaning between his time and ours. A further illustration from English literature may help to clarify this point.

The modern assessment of Shakespeare's tragedies is, as is well known, very different from that prevalent for much of the eighteenth century. Many eighteenth-century critics saw Shakespearean tragedy as severely flawed – crude and unfinished – and as unsatisfactory from a moral point of view. It would be quite reasonable to say that the significance of Shakespeare is quite differently perceived today than it was then. But this does not imply that we understand Shakespeare's tragedies as having a different *meaning*. Notoriously, many critics in the eighteenth century thought that a good tragedy should demonstrate the justice of providence, and therefore concluded that *King Lear* would be a far better play if it had what we would call a 'happy ending'. Nahum Tate duly provided a version in which Lear was restored to the throne and Edgar married Cordelia.[20] Now this undoubtedly demonstrates an enormous shift in literary taste, and in the evaluation of Shakespeare: what seems to us a sublime tragedy seemed then a sordid melodrama. But the very difference in evaluation is evidence that our perception of the play's *meaning* is not very different from that current in the eighteenth century. We agree with critics of that age that *Lear* as it stands does *not* have a happy ending; we differ in thinking this a good thing. But the doctrine that a text's meaning changes in conformity with the context in which it is read – what we have called the 'canonical principle' – would lead us to expect quite the opposite. On that principle eighteenth-century critics ought to have read *Lear* as *already* having a happy ending; they should have read it in accordance with contemporary conventions for 'tragedy', and that would have led them to interpret it as a tragedy of the kind they were used to. In fact, of course, they correctly perceived what Shakespeare intended, and found it alien and abhorrent. The need felt to rewrite the play, so as to make it conform to the eighteenth-century norms for a 'good tragedy', is the clearest possible evidence that its original meaning was more or less correctly perceived, and that this meaning had not been altered by the fact that it was being read in an eighteenth-century context.

It seems to me that the process of 'canonizing' the Old Testament books exhibits features of both sorts, and that Hirsch's categories enable us to account for them without recourse to a 'canon criticism' of basically New Critical style. The process of canonization involved little of what we have called 'creative transcription', since for the most part it was a matter of listing books already perceived as old and holy, not of producing a new text by linking together independent texts and putting them forward as a new and unified document. Earlier stages in the process, however, such as the compilation of the books of the prophets, probably did involve some transcriptions of this sort. At all events, this is an empirically testable issue, and it raises no problems that need take us outside historical criticism. Canonization is much more a matter of declaring that certain old texts are to be perceived as contemporary in the sense that they still speak today: that what Isaiah said *then* still applies *now*. It is quite true that people in New Testament times were very poorly placed to discover what Isaiah actually had said, and tended to read his writings as though they were contemporary; but it is quite mistaken to suggest that this is what they thought they were doing, or that if we do so we shall be returning to their way of looking at the matter. Neither inclusion in a literary canon, nor inclusion in the biblical canon, actually changes the meaning of a text; what it does is to declare that the text, in its original meaning, is a classic, which still has power to speak now, and always will have. Of course this may lead people to read the text in ways that actually falsify its meaning; but it is merely muddled to say that its meaning must therefore have changed.[21]

New Criticism and the Bible

There are, no doubt, problems in Hirsch's neat categories; but to me it seems that they introduce a welcome clarity into a very confused area of debate. Our overall conclusion to this long study of New Criticism and its analogues in the field of biblical studies must be that great caution is needed. At some points the New Critics clearly made their case – for example, in disposing of the psychological reading of literature, of what C. S. Lewis called 'The Personal Heresy', and in establishing that the words of a literary text are themselves the primary evidence for its meaning. But the three positive planks of the theory – texts as artefacts, authorial intention as irrelevant, and meaning as determined by canon – are all shaky, and biblical scholars would do well to avoid putting much weight on them. Above all, these critics too readily dismissed the assumption of most 'innocent' readers that a text is an attempt to communicate something, rather than an end in itself. New Criticism cut its teeth on lyric verse, where the idea that a 'message' is being communicated can indeed prove pernicious, and can lead to the quest for the poet's 'soul'; but in turning itself into a general theory about literature, it then bit off more than it could chew. And any attempt to extend it from a theory about literature in the narrow sense into a general thesis about all writing – which is necessary if it is to be applied with confidence to the Old Testament – will succeed only if some much more radical system, such as structuralism, is brought in to make it true by definition.

Further Reading

F. Lentricchia, *After the New Criticism.* London 1980

E. D. Hirsch Jr, *The Aims of Interpretation.* Chicago and London 1976

H. W. Frei, *The Eclipse of Biblical Narrative* (New Haven and London 1974), pp. 267–306

D. Newton-de Molina, ed., *On Literary Intention.* Edinburgh 1976

THE TEXT AND THE READER

Poetry can be recognized by this property, that it tends to get itself reproduced in its own form; it stimulates us to reconstruct it identically.

Paul Valéry, *Poésie et pensée abstraite* (Zaharoff Lecture for 1939. Oxford 1939), p. 18; also in *Oeuvres complètes*, ed. J. Hytier, vol. 1, Paris 1957, p. 1314; tr. from C. Butler and A. Fowler, *Topics in Criticism* (London 1971), no. 10

Preliminary Reading

E. M. W. Tillyard and C. S. Lewis, *The Personal Heresy: a Controversy*. London 1939

New Critics and Structuralists

On several occasions in the last two chapters I have closed an argument by saying something like, 'but that will only work if we accept structuralism'. The reader may be wondering why structuralism should be brought in as a dire threat, a bogey to frighten the children. Why should we *not* accept structuralism? I have already said quite a lot about the general theory underlying structuralist criticism, since there is no mystery about the dependence of biblical structuralists on the wider movement: we do not have to tease out a speculative connection, as we have had to do for canon criticism and its relation to the New Criticism. So in this chapter I shall concentrate on asking questions about the value of the structuralist approach; and I shall try to vindicate the procedure I have in fact been adopting, of making raids on structuralist terminology where it seemed useful, while remaining cool about the movement's claim to provide a universal theory of literature.

At first glance, there could scarcely be two approaches more different than those of the structuralists and the New Critics. New Criticism was (or could plausibly be presented as being) interested in 'art for art's sake'; it favoured complexity, 'richness' and ambiguity over simplicity and directness; it liked allusivenesss and believed in tradition. Structuralist criticism has been an iconoclastic movement. It has debunked 'art' by showing that all ideas about beauty rest on convention (many structuralists have said: bourgeois convention); rejected any notion of a 'canon' of 'great literature' as evaluative nonsense; and preferred works that disorientate and distress the reader by making him face up to the artificiality of all his ideas about 'realism' and 'clarity'.[1] New Criticism saw itself as a return to a classical ideal: for a structuralist, 'classicism' is a term of abuse. Yet any critic trained in the traditions of biblical study (which still belong to the age of historical criticism regarded as outmoded by New Critics and structuralists alike) is bound to see them as in many ways brothers beneath the skin. It is true that structuralism arose from modern linguistic theory, whereas New Criticism was a 'literary' movement from its inception, and that, at the deepest philosophical level, the two movements diverge. But the resemblances are still striking. Here are five of them.

(1) The first and most obvious is a concentration on 'the text itself' rather than on authors, intentions and historical contexts. As Culler puts it, 'The conclusion that literature could be studied as "un système qui ne connaît que son ordre propre" – a system with its own order – has been eminently salutary, securing for the French some of the benefits of Anglo-American "New Criticism".'[2] As he goes on to say, structuralism has in some ways avoided the worst excesses of New Criticism because its insistence on the literary *system* as primary, and as the source of each individual work's meaning, does not so easily lead 'to the error of making the individual text an autonomous object that should be approached with a *tabula rasa*'. There has come to be a consensus in literary criticism, both in Europe and in the English-speaking world, that a critic's task is to explicate *texts*, not authors.[3] This is not taken, in mainstream criticism of either tradition, to mean that one must be scrupulously careful never to mention the author; but it does mean that most literary criticism no longer seeks to gain in depth or detail by moving from the text to the author's life and emotions; instead, it

181

seeks an increased subtlety in analysing the text as it stands. This is true of very many critics who would not at all wish to call themselves either 'New Critics' or 'structuralists'. As we saw in discussing Wimsatt and Beardsley, it is not so much that critics want to *deny* that the author intended his effects, but simply that they believe we can perceive those effects only by looking at what he actually wrote: the text's the thing. The consensus is such that most biblical criticism in the traditional mould, except perhaps for the very latest kinds of redaction criticism, strikes 'secular' critics as fairly out-of-date in style. Even bothering to discuss such issues as 'intentionalism', as we are doing, would seem to them a sign of being badly behind the times.

(2) A second point of contact between structuralists and New Critics is a belief in the *non-referential* character of literature. Structuralists share the New Critical distaste for attempts to say what a text 'really' means, to extract some 'message' which it is trying to convey. Both have an abhorrence of any idea that literature is meant to convey information; though structuralists take this further, sometimes regarding even criticism itself as non-informative. Whereas in New Criticism, as we saw, 'literature' is understood narrowly (perhaps too narrowly), in structuralism it is simply synonymous with 'words on paper'. Even discursive prose may be analysed according to its structures, and its claim to be 'conveying information' thus discounted. With what the Anglo-Saxon reader will regard as terrible Gallic logic, some structuralists are consistent enough to apply this to their own works, and to say that their criticism itself is really fiction or poetry; but, as Hirsch tartly remarks, 'no English or American adherent to this French theory has yet produced a textual commentary under a fair-labeling statute [= Trades Descriptions Act], with a disclaimer stating: "This criticism is a work of fiction; any resemblance between its interpretations and the author's meanings are [*sic*] purely incidental." That would certainly reduce sales.'[4]

(3) Thirdly, in both traditions the belief that there is nothing outside a text to which it refers tends to produce a heightened concern for its shape, form and genre. A sonnet's 'meaning' lies, not in 'what it says', but in its sonnethood; a narrative need not describe events which matter in themselves, but can be content to rejoice in its own narrativity. We have already seen that there is

something in this. Even where we may feel they have exaggerated the point, we may be grateful to New Critics and structuralists alike for rescuing us from a style of criticism which is always looking behind texts or trying to extract something from them, rather than contemplating them as they are and realizing the significance of the form in which they are actually cast.

(4) Fourthly, we have noticed one rather surprising by-product of the New Critical approach, in which critical theory spills over into philosophy and linguistics. This is the belief that there is no such thing as true synonymity. At first sight there is no clear connection between a theory about the meaning of literary texts, and an issue which seems more properly the preserve of linguistic philosophers. But, as I have tried to suggest, the 'text in itself' approach can only be made to work if it can be shown that meaning is a function of the combination of the words a text is composed of, and that it does not depend on 'external' factors such as the author's intention. Now this in turn entails the doctrine that the meaning of a text can never be exactly restated. If two texts, whose wording is different, can mean the same thing, then their 'meaning' must be something that in principle is independent of either of them; they are simply vehicles *through* which a common meaning is communicated.[5] But the New Critical theory of meaning rules this out, laying down that meaning inheres *in* texts. On the one hand, any given combination of words has a fixed and determinate meaning, which cannot be changed by the intention or desire of its author or anyone else; on the other hand, no other combination of words can have identically the same meaning. These are two sides of the same coin. It follows, on such a view, that synonymity is impossible. Any difference in wording (however small) will always entail a difference (however small) in meaning. We may sometimes say, carelessly, that two passages communicate the same information or ideas in different styles;[6] but in fact the difference of style entails a difference in meaning, in what is being communicated. *How* and *what* are never separable in the study of literature: 'the medium is the message' – at least, there is no way of extracting the message from the medium and expressing it in some other way without losing something in the process.

For New Critics, then, rejection of the possibility of synonymity is a consequence of a literary-critical theory, which then turns out to have wider linguistic implications. But for structuralism, linguistics is the starting-point: structuralism is, as we have seen, the application to literature of theories about language. And the kind of linguistics with which structuralism begins is deeply inimical to the idea of synonymity. In trying to justify a conclusion essentially reached from a quite different starting-point, Anglo-American criticism has had to draw in a good deal of material from the structuralist camp; so, on this point, the two traditions may look closer than they really are. But the resemblance remains striking.

(5) Finally, it follows clearly from all that has been said so far that for both these theories the meaning of texts is *determined* – by the canon of literature, by the conventions of writing, by the structures of language – and *publicly accessible*. Objectivity is the keynote. The meaning of a text is the meaning it can be shown to have, by an analysis of its internal structures and of the place it occupies within the canon (New Criticism) or system (structuralism) of literature. This meaning has nothing to do with subjective 'feelings', or 'impressions' about meaning, and intuition has no place in discovering it. Structuralists have been more ready than New Critics to call their method 'scientific': but both have often had some such understanding of their work.[7]

If biblical criticism is to continue to have the relation to the wider literary world that it certainly had in the eighteenth and nineteenth centuries, then it will need to think seriously about these issues, on which proponents of such apparently irreconcilable theories as structuralism and New Criticism actually agree. If all the five points of agreement I have listed are correct, and the structuralist theory that justifies them is also correct, then it seems clear to me that traditional historical-critical approaches to the Bible will have to be abandoned: hence my use of structuralism as a dissuasive from cheerfully embracing new methods whose end is not yet visible. If new methods lead in the end to full-blown structuralism, the biblical critic who welcomes them as fresh and exciting may find that they lead him out of the 'sterility' of traditional study, only to deliver him into a world where the Bible is a matter of supreme indifference.

Objections to Structuralism

There are at least four points where dogmatic structuralist approaches seem to claim more than can be demonstrated.

(1) The first is the insistence that meaning is always 'public' meaning: that the text does not mean 'what the author meant', but whatever its words can be construed as meaning, within a particular set of reading conventions. It is a fair debating point (though no more than that) that the 'public' meaning of texts as reconstructed by a structuralist is usually such as no member of the reading 'public' could possibly arrive at unaided. The 'objective' interpretations offered by structuralists as part of a 'scientific' study of a text often exceed, in their divergence from anything the 'innocent' reader could imagine, even the wildest conjectures of 'subjective' (e.g. Romantic) criticism. This sort of thing gives structuralists a bad name, especially within the English-speaking tradition with its high valuation of appeals to 'common sense'; but it does not actually demolish their claims. 'Objective' is not synonymous with 'obvious'.

A more serious point is that the attachment to 'public' meaning alone can be justified only if there is a *complete* analogy between language and literature – an idea which is basic to structuralist criticism. Now it is indeed a fundamental assumption of modern linguistics that the meanings of words and sentences is not determined by the speaker's private intentions, but by the sense which his words have within the contemporary ('public') usages of the language. To be 'competent' in a language, as I defined this in chapter 1, is to be sufficiently in command of the linguistic system to be able to understand new utterances; it does not require one to have unusual powers of psychological penetration, giving an insight into the speaker's mind. If I say, 'I'm going to town today', it is quite possible that what I *have in mind* is 'I'm not going to mow the lawn today' or 'I'm going to town whether you like it or not'; but it would be odd to say that the sentence 'I'm going to town today' *meant* either of these things, or that you couldn't understand it unless you knew about my habits and temperament. The public meaning of 'I'm going to town today' is a function of the possible meanings that this particular combination of words has within the system of contemporary English. The structuralist claim is that we can be similarly 'competent' in literature: not just in the rather vague sense

185

in which I have so far used the expression 'literary competence', to mean a general grasp of the possibilities of form and genre, but in a quite strict and precise sense. The possible meanings of paragraphs and chapters within a novel are given in the conventions for novel-writing, and these are public and can be stated objectively. They have nothing to do with 'what the author meant'.

Even if we concede that a structuralist account of meaning in language is adequate, we are bound to have doubts about this extension of it to cover literature. As an *analogy* it clearly has much to commend it. We have seen more than once that a great deal more information is conveyed by the genre of a piece of writing than people naively assume; the possibilities of meaning within any given genre are quite tightly limited. If you write a novel, there is no use in complaining that people refuse to read it as a tragedy – any more than there is sense in complaining that you have been misunderstood if you insist on using words in private senses. But literature is by no means *so* tightly organized a system as language. The sorts of problem that literary interpretation involves cannot always be solved simply by referring to the conventions of the system. Literary meaning seems to exist in a space between public and private meaning. We feel we have understood a work of literature when we have *both* discovered the possible, publicly available meanings of the words that compose it *and* understood what the author was driving at. This may seem untidy or unmethodical, but it is how literary criticism actually seems to work. It is one thing to say that an interpretation ought not to impute to a work meanings that the words composing it simply cannot bear, merely on the grounds that we know from other sources that these are the meanings the author was trying (unsuccessfully) to convey. Against that sort of criticism both structuralists and New Critics are certainly right. But it is another thing to say that the meaning of a work inheres *exclusively* in its form and structure, and that questions about what the author was driving at are methodologically improper.

Why, then, should anyone subscribe to what seems so doctrinaire a theory about literary meaning? There is a paradox here. Structuralists say that meaning is wholly determined and constrained: no one can mean anything by a work except what it is enabled to mean by the literary system. But they themselves acknowledge that this theory is itself freely chosen, out of many possible literary theories.

186

Structuralists are not trying to tell us something which is eternally true about the essence of literature; they don't believe in eternal truths, or essences. They are proposing what I have called a *theory of reading*. They are saying that new ways of reading literature will be opened up for us if we decide to treat literature as though it were a tightly organized system, like language. It is vital to realize that structuralism is both determinist *and* conventionalist. Once inside the system, one cannot read a text as meaning anything other than the rules of literature permit it to mean; but the decision to embrace this particular system is a decision to accept certain conventions, which have no 'real' existence. Just as we glossed the canon-critical theory as 'Read all these works *as though* they had a single author', so we may paraphrase the structuralist principle as 'Read all works *as though* their meaning were wholly inherent'. The structuralist is asking, in effect, what it is possible to perceive certain works as meaning, once one agrees not to ask questions about their authors; how, in our culture, we shall find ourselves reading them, once we agree not to study them in their historical context. The structuralist approach does not so much propose that literature 'is' a system like a language, as that we shall have a more interesting time if we treat it as though it were. Like most English readers, I am impatient with such a suggestion. I want to ask questions about what is in fact the case, not about what is amusing or original or – a preoccupation of many structuralists – subversive of establishment attitudes. But if we are patient we may find that even this has its place.

(2) The second crucial element in structuralist theory is also borrowed from the scientific study of language, and it is the notion, already discussed, that synonymity is impossible. The meaning of a work (or of any sentence within it) can never, it is suggested, be restated, except in identically the same words. Once we rule out questions about authorial intention, indeed, it is difficult to resist this conclusion, since there is no meaning *behind* the work which could be stated in other terms: the work *is* its own meaning. One important effect is to rule out the possibility that a given sequence of words could bear more than one meaning. For if a particular work could mean two different things, then we could only distinguish these meanings by stating them in other words – which is supposed to be impossible.

On the face of it, it sounds attractive to say (as in the anecdote about Eliot and the three white leopards) that the meaning of a literary work cannot be captured in any words but the original ones, and that it can never be 'translated' into cold prose. But when the consequences are thought through, they will be found to run against other intuitions we have about meaning. Above all, the corollary just stated – that no work can have more than one meaning – rules out the kind of change brought about by what I described as 'creative transcription', as in Borges' piece about the second author of *Don Quixote*. No one can reasonably doubt that *Don Quixote* would mean something different if it were a twentieth-century work written in archaic Spanish; or, in our own field, that the book of Genesis, if it turned out to be a Christian work interpolated into the Old Testament, would have a quite different sense. The kind of 'determinacy' or 'objectivity' of meaning that a structuralist theory provides has the paradoxical effect of ruling out such intuitions. And (again paradoxically) it seems to me to be possible to establish a true 'objectivity' – one subject to real empirical controls – only if we say that the meaning of sequences of words is actually *in*determinate, and that it depends partly on 'extrinsic' factors such as historical context and authorial intention. Genesis can be read as having worthwhile meanings only if there is nothing that can be called *the* meaning of Genesis.

If we insist too narrowly on 'the text itself', we end up with a text whose meaning is eternal, but so ineffable that we can never state it or comprehend it. If, on the other hand, we allow some extrinsic elements to creep in, we get a text which (in whatever context we believe it belongs) actually does have a definite meaning that can be stated, however imperfectly. If synonymity is absolutely impossible, as on a strict structuralist view, then we can never understand anything: every piece of writing is perpetually encapsulated in its own solipsistic world. This possibility is, indeed, contemplated with equanimity by some structuralists, but it is hardly likely to be attractive to biblical scholars. At least they should realize that this is what they are taking on board.

(3) Thirdly, structuralism goes beyond even New Criticism in its distaste for the referential aspects of language and literature. The idea of verbal discourse – using words to say things, to put it crudely – is alien to it. Writing is an institution, by which are produced

texts that can be read in the ways we have described;[8] it is not a means used by thinkers to communicate thoughts. It is here, indeed, that writing differs from speech, which *is* a form of communication. Writing, on the contrary, is the production of objects, and it is only a kind of 'bad faith' that leads us to try to turn these objects into communication, to read them as though they were simply transcribed speech. Indeed, an extreme structuralist may say that when an author claims a communicative role for his writing, he himself is guilty of a similar bad faith: foisting a piece of writing on the public as though it were still under his control, when it is really an artefact with a life of its own.[9] But moderate structuralists are willing to draw a distinction between genuinely discursive writing (such as a book on structuralism) and 'literature', even though they would still define 'literature' more widely than would a New Critic. In literature, at least, they would deny any communicative function.

When discussing the New Critical idea of literature as non-referential I suggested that our main difficulty in applying it to the Old Testament is the prior question of whether the Old Testament is 'literature' or not. The New Critics, it seemed, would have allowed authorial intention to be brought in to help us decide; but it is clear that we can expect no such mercy from structuralists. A structuralist reading the Old Testament as 'writing' or 'literature' is not even saying that it actually 'is' writing; he is simply choosing or deciding to read it as such, with the appropriate conventions; and these conventions include an indifference to anything it may be supposed to communicate. We saw this with Beauchamp's treatment of Genesis 1—2. He is saying, Genesis can be read as exhibiting a certain structural pattern, which is its meaning; it can be read as not communicating 'ideas' about creation. And so it can: it is quite certain that if a text *has* been read in a certain way, then it *can* be so read. This seems, however, to get us very little further, and if we try to argue against the structuralist position we shall have an uncomfortable feeling that we are beating the air. I do not see how we can decide whether to read the Old Testament histories as information or as 'literature', once the question of their original purpose is put out of court; we can do whichever we like. No doubt this is quite a comfortable conclusion for a critic; but it hardly squares very well with a claim to have devised the one correct way of reading the Old Testament, before which all other methods must yield. It makes the structuralist approach immune from attack at the cost of making it quite 'unscientific', if not vacuous.

(4) Finally, all literary theories seem, usually inconsistently, to produce literary preferences. Romantic theories of criticism led to the study of the Romantics; New Criticism helped to rehabilitate the Augustans. Structuralism is no exception. Having shown that literary meaning is determined – entirely constrained by conventions of reading – structuralists set about producing works that deliberately exploited or exposed convention, and so proclaimed their own freedom from the bourgeois 'bad faith' that afflicted all other authors and readers.[10] Barthes seems even to recognize a forerunner in such subversive activity in the author (if we may use the word) of Genesis 32.[11] There is little doubt that structuralist criticism usually has a reforming aim. We may reasonably ask, however, whether it is entitled either to the preference or to the reformer's mantle. On its own terms, the idea that one can produce a literary work which breaks the rules is surely an illusion: the perception of a work as 'unconventional' is simply a testimony to our ability to 'naturalize' any work, however bizarre, as making some point or other. If structuralism shows literary meaning to be determined and conventional, then it shows it for all literature, structuralist literature included. As so often with literary theories, a doctrinaire application of what was originally a good idea seems to run the risk of producing paradox and self-annihilation.

The Uses of Structuralism

It will be clear by now that in using structuralist terminology for my own purposes I am not borrowing from a friendly power, but spoiling the Egyptians. But I remain convinced that structuralism has much to offer the biblical scholar who is prepared to sit lightly to its ideological commitment and illusions of grandeur. The structuralist approach is in fact a further example of something we have seen to characterize all forms of literary criticism: the institutionalizing of intuitions about meaning. Critical theory generally limps along behind actual criticism, trying to tidy up the stray ends of interpretation that critics leave behind and parcel them into neat bundles; and structuralism, for all its appearance of being rigidly derived from theoretical models in advance of any practical work on texts, is really no exception. This, to my mind though not to that of a committed structuralist, is a strength rather than a weakness. My objections to structuralism have tended to focus on places where its conclusions are counter-intuitive – especially on its unreasonable hatred of authorial intention, referential meaning, and the possibility of paraphrase or restatement. These, it seems, are points where a good idea is being done to death. But the idea *is* a good one, for there are texts and interpretative problems for which more traditional methods seem equally doctrinaire and inappropriate, and where structuralist insights yield intuitively satisfying results. And it so happens that the Old Testament text is particularly rich in such problems: in texts that have no authors, texts that have been endlessly reworked, texts that seem chaotic. That is why some biblical scholars have found structuralism so attractive, though they have (I believe) been mistaken in thinking that they needed to swallow it whole.

In the last chapter I argued, following Hirsch, that it is quite possible to deal with a text which has been extensively rewritten, transcribed and reappropriated in fresh contexts without moving outside a traditional, author-centred method of interpretation. Where a text has been 'creatively transcribed', we simply have two authors: the original one and the later (as we may say) plagiarist. Where an old text has taken on a new significance in a later generation, this is either because its original sense has been felt to have a fresh relevance, or because it has been, in effect, misunderstood. Against strident denials of the importance of the author and his intentions, Hirsch's proposals seem to me eminently sane. But the fact remains that anyone used to the idiom of modern literary criticism is likely to become a little impatient of this constant harping on the author. As we have seen, there is a consensus nowadays, extending well beyond the ranks of doctrinaire critical theorists, that criticism should concentrate on the text rather than on the author. If one is committed neither to New Criticism nor to structuralism, one will have no particular axe to grind on this matter, no wish to outlaw talk of the author's intentions; nevertheless, this will just not seem the natural place to begin. We can concede that, in strict theory, meanings must be traced back to an author's intentions and yet, for the purposes of practical criticism, hardly ever find it necessary to invoke them. And this is particularly likely to be the case when the text being studied derives from a multiplicity of authors: a text whose very unity is in question, and which has been transcribed, reappropriated and misread in all possible ways over a lengthy period. Such a text is the Old Testament; and a critic can surely be forgiven if he defers worrying about who is responsible for the meanings he perceives in it, until he has begun to see more clearly, through a careful analysis of the text itself, just what those meanings are. A structuralist approach, whatever its theoretical shortcomings, at least directs our attention to the shape, genre and conventions of the text. It makes us see what were the limits within which these books were written and read; it alerts us to patterns and structural implications within them. Through it we see that the meaning of Old Testament writings is not simply a matter of 'what they say' – in the sense of the information they overtly communicate – but inheres also in the way they are constructed, and in their relation to other works within the conventional system which is literature. Above all structuralism helps us to recognize that no text, even though it may seem to be a straightforward chronicle, is free from artifice, or exempt from the constraints of conforming to some genre or type, with all the expectations that that genre inevitably arouses in the reader.

One way of putting this may be to say that structuralists have tried to abolish the author, but in fact have succeeded in showing what being an author involves. They have not succeeded in talking impartial critics out of the belief that literary meaning is produced by authors with intentions; but they have succeeded in laying bare some of the *mechanisms* by which meaning is produced, often without the conscious awareness of the author. After reading Barthes on Genesis 32, we may well feel that it matters little how far the 'author' (if any) knew what literary effect he was achieving; the main thing is that Barthes has shown us what that effect is, and how it comes about. Rather than beginning with a decision in theory about what is to count as a 'meaning' in a text, and then asking whether Barthes' suggestions qualify, it seems better to acknowledge that we come away from reading Barthes with a clear impression that we understand the text better, and to let the critical theory take care of itself. Sometimes, in fact, we could easily suspect that an intuition arrived at by no particular method is being forced into a theoretical strait-jacket.[12] Structuralists themselves would regard this as an accusation. But to me it seems merely what one would expect, and tends rather to vindicate the structuralists' claim to be serious critics than to undermine it. If it is true, however, it is desirable that it should be recognized; for it may encourage scholars who are drawn to the text-centred approach to dispense with the pseudo-scientific methodological impedimenta of structuralist writing.

At several points I have taken issue with the more extreme formulations of structuralism as a 'theory of reading', in which meaning becomes entirely a function of literature as a social institution, and communication is rendered impossible. But here, too, there is gold mixed with the dross. As we saw in examining the New Criticism, one of its weaknesses was precisely a tendency to speak as though texts had meaning outside any context whatever. This idea produces some absurdities, of which Borges' 'Pierre Menard' is the refutation. Structuralism, for all its commitment to the text *itself* rather than what lies behind it, is intensely aware of the importance of context in determining meaning:[13] indeed, its fault is the equal and opposite one of making context, in the sense of the institution of reading and writing, a *total* constraint on meaning. Against New Criticism it must be said that the senses we perceive in a text do depend, to a very high degree, on the expectations which the literary system sets up. This is why we cannot read any text until we can assign it to a genre; though, indeed, as we saw in chapter 1, genre-recognition and intelligent reading are usually simultaneous, and we are perfectly well able to admit new genres, provided they bear some resemblance to existing ones.[14]

This can, of course, be taken too far. Structuralists sometimes argue that our expectations are so conditioned by our own culture that we can *never* read with understanding texts written in another culture. But, without going that far, it is quite reasonable to emphasize that expectations are at least *partly* constitutive of meaning. The sorts of expectation I have in mind are these: that a narrative has a beginning, a middle and an end, and is not wholly aimless;[15] that any text recognized as 'one book' is to be read as having some sort of unity or coherence; that verse is not to be seen as communicating information in the same way as prose; that aphorisms point beyond themselves. To write a narrative is to produce a text which is bound to be read as meaningful by reference to expectations about narrative shape; to write a book of proverbs is to produce a text that must be taken as expounding truths of wide and general application. Even if the authors of such works are not *wholly* constrained, it is foolish to deny that they are constrained to some extent, and it is these constraints that structuralists can rightly claim to have explicated better than most other critics. In Old Testament studies the theoretical problems we have been discussing would force themselves on our attention, if we had good reason to think that the ancient Israelites' expectations about narrative coherence (for example) were *radically* different from ours; for then we should be faced with a choice between reading an Old Testament narrative within our own literary conventions (asking what it *means*) and reading it within theirs (asking what it *meant*). With some types of text this problem may indeed arise. In chapter 3, Deuteronomy was cited as a book which is almost 'unreadable' because there are no modern conventions for reading such a work, and the ancient ones are almost unrecoverable because it is such an odd mixture of genres. But in very many cases the lines between asking what an Old Testament text was intended to mean, trying to discover what it can now mean, and reconstructing what the reading conventions of the day permitted it to mean are blurred; and the practical critic is well advised not to induce paralysis in his critical faculties by endlessly worrying about them. It is better to attend to the text, produce an interpretation of what it means, and only then go back to analyse the precise level at which the interpretation operates. We cannot be for ever trying to watch our own eyes moving.

'Poetry Without a Poet'

The particular value a broadly structuralist approach can have for the study of the anonymous, repeatedly reworked texts that make up so much of the Old Testament can be illustrated from a most surprising source: an essay by C. S. Lewis. In the collection *The Personal Heresy* Lewis debated with E. M. W. Tillyard many of the questions about 'affective' versus 'objective' criticism which concerned us in the last two chapters. Lewis sees clearly that 'Romantic' criticism seemed universally applicable largely because it was usually practised on Romantic poets – this is a familiar point by now. To show how little it can be applied to other types of text, he discusses at length Isaiah 13:19–22a, in the Authorized Version, which constitutes, as he says, one of 'a whole class of poetical experiences in which the consciousness that we share cannot possibly be attributed to any single human individual'.[16] He goes on to show that the pleasure we get from such a passage, and the meaning we find in it, have nothing whatever to do with either the personality (the precise point at issue in the debate with Tillyard) nor, indeed, the *intentions* of 'the author'.

In fact, the passage as it stands has no 'author'. Isaiah, or whoever wrote the original Hebrew text, was not trying to convey the sense of melancholy desolation, reaching us across the centuries from the mysterious East, that the modern reader (at least, the modern reader of 1934) perceives this text as conveying. 'The mood to which we are introduced by these lines was not only not normal in the Hebrew writer; it did not and could not exist in him at all.' Indeed, some of it derives from simple mistranslations ('doleful creatures', 'wild beasts of the islands') and much from the intervening literary tradition: 'for us Babylon is far away and long ago; it comes to us through the medium of centuries of poetry about the East and about antiquity', whereas 'Babylon, to the writer, was neither long ago nor far away'.[17] But nor can we say that the sense of the passage derives from the translator; for King James's translators were certainly not aiming at literary effect, but 'worked in fear and trembling to transmit without loss what [they] believed to be the literal record of the word of God'.[18] In fact, the sense of the passage derives from no one; yet that it *has* a sense, and a sense such as we have just described, it is pointless to deny. Lewis continues:

> Every work of art that lasts long in the world is continually taking on these new colours which the artist neither foresaw nor intended. We may, as scholars, detect, and endeavour to exclude them. We may, as critics, decide that such adventitious beauties are in a given case meretricious and trivial compared with those which the artist deliberately wrought. But all that is beside the purpose. Great or small, fortunate or unfortunate, they have been poetically enjoyed . . . *There can be poetry without a poet* [my italics]

. . . To be encrusted with such poetless poetry is the reward, or the penalty, of every poem that endures.[19]

Now this has obvious affinities with New Criticism (of which Lewis shows, surprisingly, no awareness);[20] but it seems to me also to reach forward to some of the underlying assumptions of many modern critics in the structuralist camp. Lewis is saying, in effect, that the meaning (or at any rate *a* valid meaning) of the text is constituted by our conventions for reading it, by the expectations we bring to it. And if this is true for a piece of biblical translation, there is no reason why it should not be true (though I fancy Lewis might have resisted this suggestion) for biblical texts even in the 'original', since, as we have seen, there is often a whole history of re-use and interpretation behind the finished form of biblical books.

An example of how this idea may be fruitful for practical interpretation is provided by Frank Kermode's *The Genesis of Secrecy*, already referred to in the notes on a number of occasions. This is a study of biblical narrative (chiefly Mark's Gospel) from a standpoint which Kermode describes as that of a 'secular critic'. Many parts of his analysis use structuralist methods, but with no ideological commitment; others are more akin to what we may call advanced redaction criticism.[21] Throughout there is no great concern either to deny or to affirm that the 'author' of the second Gospel was responsible for the meanings divined in it; but there is a clear awareness that our perception of such meanings depends on notions about how narrative works, and about the types of coherence that are to be expected in it, which we can feel moderately – but only moderately – sure that we share with the original readers. Kermode eschews claims to scientific certainty, but does not see this as a reason for refraining from all conjectures about meaning that cannot be related to a strict theory. To use structuralist approaches to literary analysis without commitment to the ideology may risk being intellectually flabby; yet it is a pity to deny ourselves the freshness of approach they can bring, for fear of being thought simply eclectic. We may close by quoting some words from Kermode's book that seem to me to get the balance about right.

'Can we find ourselves,' I ask with Paul Ricoeur, 'a position between, on the one hand, a methodological fanaticism which would forbid us to understand anything besides the method we practice, and, on the other, a feeble eclecticism which would exhaust itself in inglorious compromise?' Ricoeur wants to believe that when the structural analysts have done their work, interpretation may take over. When structural analysis becomes structural*ist*, he argues, it turns ideological and begins, quite improperly, to issue bans and censures. I think he is right in this matter, at any rate up to this point, and allow myself some use of neo-Formalist [what we have been calling structuralist] terminology to say things that its inventors and proponents would certainly disapprove of.[22]

Further Reading

J. Culler, *Structuralist Poetics*. London 1975
— *The Pursuit of Signs*. London 1981
J. Barr, *The Bible in the Modern World* (London 1973), pp. 89–111 and 168–81
R. Alter, *The Art of Biblical Narrative*. London and Sydney 1981

13

THE READER IN THE TEXT[1]

My own words take me by surprise and teach me what I think.

Edmund Husserl, quoted in J. Derrida, *Writing and Difference* (London 1978), p. 11

Preliminary Reading

Terry Eagleton, *Literary Theory: an Introduction* (Oxford 1983), pp. 54–90
Robert Alter, *The Art of Biblical Narrative* (London 1981), pp. 3–22

Writers and Readers

Structuralism might be called a 'mechanics' of literature. It shows how texts are enabled to convey meaning by the way they are constructed; and not only enabled, but constrained. For structuralists neither texts nor readers are free agents. The text can only mean what its structures cause it to mean, and the reader can only appropriate this meaning, not find some completely different meaning in it. I referred to this as a 'theory of reading', because it seeks to explain how we come to think that certain texts have certain meanings, and how it is that many readers will often agree on what those meanings are. But, although structuralists were uninterested in the meanings intended by the author, as we have seen, a structuralist theory of reading is not necessarily hostile to authorial intention. A skilful writer, it might be said, is one who can so manipulate the conventions and structures of literature that it conveys the meaning he wants it to convey. One *could* be an intentionalist and a structuralist at the same time, though it might be rather a *tour de force*.

'Post-structuralism', which we shall consider in the next chapter, moves decisively away from the author and removes the last vestiges of connection between the author, the work, and the reader: each goes his/her/its own way. Before we embark on that, however, it will be worth looking at three recent movements which, to some extent independently of structuralist theory, have been interested in how texts come to mean what they do, but for which the mind of the author is not altogether rejected as one element, at least, in the process. The first, rhetorical criticism, is primarily a movement within biblical studies – though its proponents are not unfamiliar with literary theory; the other two, the 'poetics' of biblical texts and reader-response criticism, have a more overt debt to the wider world of literary studies. All are intellectually interesting, and deserve to be taken seriously by students of the Old Testament.

Rhetoric in the Bible

There are not many movements in biblical study whose beginning can be exactly dated, but such is the case with the movement known as 'rhetorical criticism'. The expression was coined by James Muilenberg in his presidential address to the Society of Biblical Literature, in December 1968, which was called 'Form Criticism and Beyond'.[2] Muilenberg took it as a given that form criticism was the dominant mode of study then adopted by American scholars. He argued that form criticism was perfectly valid and satisfactory, but that it might be time to move on from its competence in studying individual pericopes and return to the project of trying to understand texts in their entirety (there are some resemblances here to early canon criticism). What was needed, Muilenberg suggested, was a close attention to the articulation of biblical texts, so that one might see how the *argument* of chapters and books is constructed and thus how it is that chapters and books have persuasive ('rhetorical') force with their readers.

Classical texts have always been studied in this way. Indeed, in ancient times rhetoric was a major branch of study which subsumed much that we might now call literary criticism. The aim of all writers was (and is) to persuade the reader, to talk the reader over to their side of an argument – more obviously in discursive prose than in verse, but there too, if we allow 'persuade' to have quite a broad meaning. In biblical studies questions of rhetoric, Muilenberg argued with good reason, had tended to be neglected, especially since the essentially fragmenting methods of form criticism had deflected attention from the finished work which a redactor had produced from the fragments. In a sense, rhetorical criticism is just redaction criticism by another name. But if so it is a distinctive way of looking at the possibilities of redaction criticism, which concentrates on the way the reader is pulled along through the text rather than on the text in its own right. Rhetorical criticism is interested in how writers or redactors do things to readers. Often this happens through 'structures'; but where structuralists are concerned with archetypal structures of myth or narrative, rhetorical criticism is interested in the structure and shapes of arguments. A recent work on biblical criticism defines rhetorical criticism as seeking to make clear 'the overall argumentative and persuasive strategy that is designed to move the audience or reader to agree with the speaker or writer.'[3]

One of the best illustrations of how rhetorical criticism can work is Muilenberg's own commentary on Isaiah 40–66 ('Deutero– and Trito–Isaiah') in the *Interpreter's Bible*,[4] written before he had formulated a theoretical statement of his position. The commentary is obviously form-critical, in that it begins by dividing the book of Isaiah into pericopes, and is concerned with the possible oral existence of these pericopes in the prophet's (or prophets') own preaching. But Muilenberg sees the pericopes as also arranged in a deliberate way, so as to persuade the prophet's audience to accept certain conclusions – primarily, the belief that Israel is about to return in triumph to the Promised Land from the barrenness of exile. Even if Deutero–Isaiah originally delivered his oracles piecemeal on various occasions, in the finished prophetic book they have been arranged so as to convince the audience of the truth of his whole message. A single example will make the point. In Isa. 40, a lengthy passage about Yahweh as creator of the world (vv. 12–26) is followed by a challenge to the people to accept the prophet's proclamation of salvation, and not raise the objection that God pays them no attention (vv. 27–31: 'Why do you say, O Jacob, and speak, O Israel, "My way is hid from the LORD, and my right is disregarded by my

God"?'). These may once have been two separate oracles; but as they stand, they are mutually illuminating, and to such an extent that the ordering looks deliberate (even though this is a word we have learned to distrust). The praise of God as the almighty creator serves to justify the prophet in rejecting the people's complaint that he takes no notice of them: if God is the creator of everything, sovereign over all mankind, then the idea that he could simply be ignoring Israel, or even be unable to do anything for them, must be mistaken. Thus the juxtaposition of two independent oracles produces what can only be called an *argument*, which has the logical form 'If A is true, B cannot be true; but A is true; therefore B is false'.

Many scholars since Muilenberg have undertaken rhetorical criticism, and there is an excellent survey in Phyllis Trible's *Rhetorical Criticism*.[5] Some, including me, have practised it without realizing it![6] It should be said that it can be a sophisticated way of evading some of the challenges of historical criticism: first, because it enables the question of authorial intention to be elided – when it suits them, rhetorical critics will argue that the rhetorical arrangement of the text is what the author meant, and when it doesn't, that this is just how the text now is, and we have no right to try to get behind it; and second, because they can nearly always 'demonstrate' a rhetorical structure in any given text and so invalidate historical–critical arguments based on its apparent (or evident) formlessness. Thus when rhetorical criticism comes in at the door, critical probing into the text's unity or disunity tends to go out of the window, the demonstration of its unity being taken as an absolute imperative. (These are some reasons why it is not adequate to see rhetorical criticism as merely a branch of redaction criticism.) The job of the exegete, for most rhetorical critics, is not to ask whether the text hangs together rhetorically, but to show that it does. This can make rhetorical criticism an ally of conservative interpretation.

What kind of evidence do rhetorical critics point to in arguing for the persuasive unity of biblical texts? There is widespread agreement about this. Apart from rather loose and intuitive interpretations such as that of Isaiah 40 just described, rhetorical critics appeal in particular to two features shared between Old Testament writings and the literature of the classical world: *inclusio* and *chiasmus*.

Inclusio *and* chiasmus

Inclusio is a fairly self-explanatory term which refers to the tendency to repeat the opening idea of a passage towards its end, in order to signal that an argument is complete and forms a satisfactory whole. Since biblical books as we now have them are seldom divided neatly into sections, it may not be immediately obvious that *inclusio* is at work, but once it is spotted, it often leads the critic to feel that he now has a much better grasp of how the text is structured, and a fresh division into sections may result. The first line or section of an utterance, as we all know, may well have an important role, and if it is repeated at the end it is powerfully reinforced. In between there will be a lot of material that may be ordered in a variety of ways: short lines; lengthy and complicated sentences which include subordinate clauses, often with further clauses attached to (or embedded within) them, which serve to develop the main idea of the passage; medium-length sentences and descriptions. But there may be no ordered progression of thought in this middle section. Finally, however, the last line or section of the utterance, which as we all know often has an important role, recalls or repeats the last line and thus powerfully reinforces it. (Psalm 8 is one of the most obvious examples of *inclusio* in the Old Testament.)

Chiasmus amounts to an ordered set of *inclusio*s, and is a more complicated affair. Its name comes from the Greek letter *chi*, which looks like our X, and at its simplest it describes an ABB'A' arrangement:

For example: 'Tomorrow the weather will be cool and breezy; wind and cold will be the order of the day.' Or, to take a slightly more complex example, the following offensive postcard message generated from a well-known cliché:

> Wish you were here
> Weather is lovely
> Weather is here
> Wish you were lovely

– where an ABA'B' pattern exists alongside a chiastic ABB'A'. But *chiasmus* can be far more complicated than this, and a chiastic passage can be much more tightly organized than with mere *inclusio*: in fact, it often involves a series of *inclusio*s arranged one inside the other like Chinese boxes. The second section or sentence is recalled in the last-but-one section, and this makes it easy to spot what is going on. The theme or imagery of the third section similarly recurs in the last-but-two, and so on, though there is often a central line which is not repeated and which, paradoxically, is thrown into relief by standing alone and unpartnered. Thus the last section but two renews the theme or imagery of the third, and in the last section but one there is a reprise of the second, which makes the technique easy to spot. The Chinese box pattern is completed by the last section, which makes the whole passage a complete *chiasmus* – like an *inclusio*, but in a much tighter way.

Analysing chiastic structures can be an intricate task, as can be seen from any rhetorical-critical work. Critics usually begin by detecting chiastic structures which are not obvious to the unenlightened reader, and then go on to show that an awareness of these structures undercuts other hypotheses, especially the theory that the text in question is composite or incoherent. Here there is a lot of common ground with structuralists: one might think back to Beauchamp's analysis of Gen. 1–2, which argues: since Genesis 1–2 can be shown to exhibit a perfectly symmetrical structure if we take as the unit of analysis 1:1–2:1, it follows that any theory which tries to analyse 1:1–2:3 or 1:1–2:4a is out of order. Hence literary-critical hypotheses about the origin of the text are ruled out on the grounds that they are unnecessary: structural analysis shows the text to cohere well anyway. Similar emphases can be found in the work of Trible, Gitay, and Magonet.[7] The work of J. A. Loader on Ecclesiastes, discussed above as an example of 'biblical structuralism', could also be analysed as rhetorical criticism.

Rhetorical criticism offers a rather surprising compromise between the structuralist concern with 'the text itself', and a more conventional interest in the author for whose intentions, however, only the text itself is allowed to count as evidence (a good New-Critical idea). We might say that it is a kind of redaction criticism in which the disappearance of the redactor is welcomed, since its claimed demonstration that the text is always a perfectly formed whole, rich in persuasive skill because of its structuring, is incompatible with the hypothesis that implies the need for a redactor, that is, the hypothesis that the text is broken and lacking in cohesion. There is little doubt in my own mind that the drive behind rhetorical criticism is often an apologetic one: to show that the text makes better sense than historical critics think. This can of course harden into a conservative dogma, in which we have a positive duty to look for rhetorical coherence in order to vindicate the traditional authorship or divine inspiration of Scripture. But it need not do so. Investigating the possibility that there are rhetorical structures in a text raises fresh possibilities of interpretation, and can increase our respect for he biblical writers, who knew much more about how to present a cogent argument than modern critics sometimes credit them with.

Biblical Poetics

Rhetorical critics are interested in one particular kind of literary technique or convention: the persuasive structuring of arguments. But there are many other types of convention in literature. The reader who is 'competent' in Western literature can recognize, for example, the conventions for writing novels – characterization, plot-structure, 'closure' – or dramatic conventions, rather loose in England, but in French literature traditionally very rigid, involving the 'unities' of place and time. The structuralist idea that we can recognize an 'ill-formed' play or novel is generally convincing.

In the last twenty years or so a number of 'secular' literary critics have come to claim an expertise in the conventions of biblical literature, and have worked towards producing a 'poetics' of the Bible. Such a concern is closer to the work-centred interests of New Critics and structuralists than to a traditional literary-critical interest in the author. It sees itself as standing in the mainstream of modern literary studies, and tends to express a rather low view of specialist biblical critics: occasionally one can detect an idea well described by Michael Payne:

There's an attitude that runs from Moulton to perhaps Helen Gardner, that if a literary critic has a weekend free, he or she can perhaps straighten out problems in biblical studies that fusty scholars have not been able to work through.[8]

What is a 'poetics'? Jonathan Culler describes it as 'a study of the conditions of meaning and thus a study of meaning'.[9] A poetics is an attempt to specify how literature 'works', how it enables us to perceive the meanings we do perceive in it. Like rhetorical criticism, a poetics of the biblical text – or of any text – is interested in how the text is articulated, in how it comes to convey the meanings it does. Meir Sternberg writes, 'contrary to what some recent attempts at "literary" analysis seem to assume, form has no value or meaning apart from communicative (historical, ideological, aesthetic) function.'[10] Sternberg's work is a major attempt to produce a biblical poetics, and it is important to heed his warning that he is interested in how the biblical text conveys ideas, not in a 'literary' study in the sense of a merely formal analysis. Nevertheless, this does not mean that he concentrates on biblical authors and their intentions. He is firmly in the camp of those who, like structuralists, are concerned with the *discourse* of the biblical text rather than with its *genesis*: in our terms, with 'the text itself'.

Sternberg is impatient with some literary theory, and Robert Alter, who must also be placed in this section despite marked differences from Sternberg, generally seems to think that theory obscures more than it illuminates.[11] Both of them are what may be called 'practical' literary critics who are interested in explicating actual literary works, not theorizing about literature as an institution. However, both think that this task requires a sensitivity to recurring patterns in the biblical text.

Type-scenes and Doublets

One of the features that first strikes the reader of the Old Testament is the presence of duplications and repetitions. These are broadly of two kinds, and have been the concern respectively of Alter and Sternberg. First, what appear to be different stories are sometimes told in a similar way, with narrative features in common. For example, when Abraham's servant is seeking a wife for Isaac, he encounters Rebekah at a well, and her readiness to give water to his camels acts as a good omen that she will in due course consent to be Isaac's wife (Gen. 24). But a very similar story is told of Jacob (Gen. 29:1–14) and of Moses (Exod. 2:15–22). These are not really candidates for explanation in terms of different *sources*, since they are about different characters; yet it seems impossible that such similarities could be merely coincidence. Alter dubs such parallels 'type-scenes',[12] and proposes that there were conventions in Israelite story-telling which made use of 'stock' events and characters. The hero who shows his prowess by single-handedly moving a heavy stone from a well-mouth, and is rewarded by finding a wife, is an Israelite stereotype, found in various contexts without regard to historical probability. Competence in reading biblical literature requires us to be aware of this, and not to make the category-mistake of trying to identify any of the wells in question: they are part of the conventions of biblical taletelling, not historical 'facts' about Jacob or Moses.

Much the same is true of the choice of the true king, where the stories of Saul (1 Sam. 10:17–24) and David (1 Sam. 16:1–13) have striking similarities – for example, the 'Cinderella' theme of the true 'hero' who is not thought fit by his family to be presented for divine choice but is then fetched and revealed as the chosen one. Alter's type-scenes in fact bear a certain resemblance to some of Propp's standard types of folktale, and in both cases there is a clear tendency to 'anonymize' the literature in question – if it is composed of so many setpiece components, the room for authorial invention is obviously much reduced. The traditional historical critic would want to ask 'genetic' questions about type-scenes: did the author of Exodus copy Genesis, or vice versa? For Alter such questions are unanswerable, indeed almost unaskable. All we can say is that there are internal relations among the various texts that make up the Old Testament, that the Bible is marked by a certain 'intertextuality'. We can observe the parallels, and we can deduce from them some of the conventions with which Israelite literature operated; origins, historical development and dependence, and underlying events are all beside the point.

Sternberg is interested in something closer to the traditional 'doublets' of the source critics. Frequently in the Old Testament there are two accounts of what must logically be the same event: two stories of how David came to Saul's court, for example (1 Sam. 16:14–23 and 17:31–58). Obviously, from a historical point of view both cannot be true (at least, they cannot both be a true version of David's *first* encounter with Saul). Traditional literary criticism regards such phenomena as evidence for the presence of parallel, incompatible sources underlying the present text and preventing it from enjoying any narrative coherence. Sternberg, on the other hand, sees the use of parallels as one of the particular techniques of the biblical text, one of the things that makes it what it is, and certainly not as an accident of the text's history. There are cross-references among the various doublets, so that, for example, the third 'wife-sister' story (Gen. 26:6–16) 'corrects' the earlier ones (Gen. 13:10–20 and 20:1–18). So far from the presence of doublets showing carelessness or randomness in the composition of the final text, their careful arrangement and ordering demonstrates literary skill of a high order. They are not mistakes, but signs of developed narrative technique.

How much the newer poetic or literary criticism of the Bible is committed to the text in its present form can be seen from Alter's discussion of Gen. 38.[13] Almost all older critics were agreed that this chapter represents an interpolation into the story of Joseph, breaking the narrative thread and spoiling the otherwise particularly smooth progression of Gen. 37–50. Alter argues, on the contrary, that it is an integral part of these chapters (which, after all, the Bible does not itself call 'the Joseph Story') and that it employs various conventions that bring it far closer to the rest of the section than has usually been thought. It is reasonable to see it as an 'excursus', but it is far from being an interpolation. Judah, in v. 1, 'went down from' his brothers; Joseph in 39:1 'was brought down' (same verb) to Egypt. The incident with Potiphar's wife and Tamar's success in becoming pregnant by Judah are told in remarkably similar terms; even more striking are the parallels between Tamar's triumphant vindication of herself against Judah, and the sale of Joseph into slavery. Both involve a kid: in the one case as Judah's payment to Tamar, who poses as a prostitute, in the other as the means of making it seem that Joseph has been killed. Similarly, in both cases the verb 'recognize' is central, in the sense 'take legal cognizance of'. Jacob 'recognizes' Joseph's coat, thus perforce accepting the brothers' explanation that Joseph has been killed by a wild animal; Judah 'recognizes' the signet, the cord, and the staff which he gave to Tamar as pledges, and thus acknowledges his own guilt. Alter points out that these echoes were already seen by the authors of the Midrash on Genesis, who comment:

> The Holy One, blessed be he, said to Judah, 'You deceived your father with a kid. By your life, Tamar will deceive you with a kid . . . You said to your father, *haker-na* ('recognize'). By your life, Tamar will say to you, *haker-na*.[14]

Alter continues:

> This instance may suggest that in many cases a literary student of the Bible has more to learn from the traditional commentaries than from modern scholarship. The difference between the two is ultimately the difference between assuming that the text is an intricately interconnected unity, as the midrashic exegetes did, and assuming it is a patchwork of frequently disparate documents, as most modern scholars have supposed. With their assumption of interconnectedness, the makers of the Midrash were often as exquisitely attuned to small verbal signals of continuity and to significant lexical nuances as any 'close reader' of our own age.[15]

It seems clear that an interest in 'how the Bible works' is here to stay in Old Testament studies, and so long as it is in the hands of such critics as Sternberg and Alter[16] it will probably eschew much engagement with literary theory and concentrate on interpretation of the text in the light of certain broad principles about convention and custom. 'Poetic' critics tend to be impatient with 'genetic' approaches, but that is nothing new – the tendency of each kind of criticism to excommunicate its predecessors has been a recurring theme in this book. But if we do not accept that Alter or Sternberg has shown older criticism to be mistaken in what it asserts – the fragmentary character of the text – we can still agree with them in rejecting what it denies: we can reject the idea that no sense can be made of the text as it stands. These scholars have shown that, on the contrary, *much* sense can be made of the biblical narrative, once we look for the right thing – narrative conventions – rather than the wrong one – historical coherence or the intentions of a single author. They have definitely advanced the quest for 'literary competence' in reading the Old Testament.

The Reader in the Text

So far we have been considering theories or methods that are concerned with why we extract the meanings we do from the texts we read: that is, *what it is about the texts* that generates meaning and enables us to appropriate it. Poetics is interested in the internal mechanisms of literature, which are often hidden from our conscious mind but at a deep level are the reason why we think texts mean what (we think) they do mean. Rhetorical criticism tries to analyse how the text is constructed: not just its verbal patterns or its use of imagery, but how it is articulated, how the argument carries the reader along. Rhetorical critics and proponents of poetics, like early structuralists, are engaged in a process of discovery, finding out what texts mean by establishing how they mean.

But it is possible to be sceptical about the alleged givenness of textual meaning, and to believe that in the dialogue between text and reader the reader contributes more, and the text less, than we naively assume. 'Reader-response criticism' reverses the procedures we have been looking at so far in this chapter by asking *what it is about us* that generates the meaning we find in texts. With this question we approach a 'theory of reading' in a much more unambiguous way than in structuralism, where there was always a belief that the text itself had structures that were not simply contributed gratuitously by its readers. Reader–response criticism moves a stage further, and gives the reader the lion's share in the production of meaning. We will begin by illustrating the kind of theory it implies, then go on to mention the leading figures within the movement, and finally discuss its implications for the study of the Bible.

It is possible to approach reader–response theories by returning for a moment to the work of Sternberg. Sternberg maintains that (as part of its religious style) the Old Testament avoids didacticism, seldom telling us overtly what conclusions we ought to draw from the text. One aspect of this is that the text contains puzzles, such as the 'multiple versions' or doublets which traditional historical critics explain by the hypothesis of 'sources' but which Sternberg himself sees as a characteristic feature of biblical poetics (see above). Another aspect is the presence of gaps or holes in the text: 'non sequiturs, discontinuities, indeterminacies'.[17] This presents something of a paradox. By leaving gaps, a text tells us that it is not prescribing its own meaning, but leaving us to discover – or create? – it for ourselves. Thus the reader becomes not a recipient of meaning but an agent of it.

The importance of the reader can be seen by thinking about the meaning of conversations.[18] Here, to begin with, is a conversation most people would regard as transparent in meaning:

A. Nice weather again today.
B. Really beautiful.
A. I hope the rain stays away tomorrow too.
B. So do I.

And here is one where we probably assume that one or both of the speakers is deaf, because it makes no sense at all:

A. Can I have a football, please?
B. Oh dear, it's Wednesday.
A. This government is doomed.
B. Apples are all very well in their way.

But consider carefully the following:

A. I'll go to London tomorrow.
B. The lawn's in a terrible state.
A. Tom seems to be at a loose end.
B. If a job's worth doing, it's worth doing properly.

This too may initially strike us as lacking coherence. But a moment's thought will suggest that it can be given a plausible interpretation, once we accept H. P. Grice's principle of 'conversational implicature'. According to this we 'read' conversations by assuming (unless and until we are convinced otherwise, as in the second example) that the speakers engage with each other, and hence that each 'speech' is logically connected to the preceding one.[19] We need only to imagine a middle-aged married couple, with a teenaged son called Tom, who tend to bicker about the gardening. B's first remark, 'The lawn's in a terrible state', is then an objection to A's decision to go to London, implying that there is no time for such diversions while the lawn remains uncut. A replies that Tom has nothing to do, has in fact plenty of time to mow the lawn; B ripostes that Tom will make a poor job of it, and A ought not to leave it in his hands but should show a proper concern for horticultural excellence. Thus the speeches interconnect perfectly, but only for someone who knows certain of the conventions of English middle-class conversation, where much is conveyed by indirection rather than by obvious confrontation.

We may say that this conversation has holes or gaps; the line of argument runs underground for much of the time, and the reader or listener has to reconstruct the many logical stages that are not stated. Applying this to literature, one's first reaction will be to distinguish between literature which is similarly indirect and requires the reader to 'read between the lines' (Henry James, for example) and literature which wears its heart on its sleeve (Ernest Hemingway, perhaps?). But in practice the distinction proves very difficult to sustain. For one thing, very 'transparent' literature is often so only within a narrow circle which shares its conventions: notoriously, 'realistic' novels can be shown to appear realistic only because author and readers share the same social conventions, and so do not notice that the story has logical gaps. We notice this where customs have changed. A nineteenth-century novelist could write that Major X was disgraced and shot himself, and imply a certain logical inevitability in the 'and', where a modern reader sees a gaping hole. For another thing, 'nonsensical' literature can sometimes be 'naturalized' by invoking unusual but possible conventions.[20] Our absurd second 'conversation' would not be an infringement of Gricean principles if, for example, the participants were involved in the panel-game that regularly appears on Radio 4's *I'm Sorry, I Haven't A Clue*, where the aim is to say something that has no connection whatever with what the previous speaker has said – a very difficult task, since we are all Griceans at heart. It might even be possible to construct a story which could contain that conversation and make sense of it. The government, let us say, has forbidden the sale of any goods except apples on Wednesdays because it is important that people should use up the European Union apple-mountain. Thus the reader's contribution to making sense of what he is reading is on a sliding scale, but there are probably no pure cases where the text either has no 'gaps' at all, or consists of nothing but gaps. All the interesting cases lie in between. To put it in more technical terms, 'the swerve to the reader assumes that our relationship to reality is not a positive knowledge but a hermeneutic construct, that all perception is already an act of interpretation, that the notion of a "text-in-itself" is empty, that a poem cannot be understood in isolation from its effects, and that subject and object are indivisibly bound.'[21]

Reader–response Criticism and Reception–aesthetics

These intuitions about how we read texts have been developed with great theoretical rigour especially by two scholars at the University of Constance, Hans Robert Jauss and Wolfgang Iser. Jauss's work has the more 'historical' appearance of the two, and is concerned with what he calls 'reception aesthetics' (*Rezeptionsästhetik*), in which much effort is devoted to discovering how certain texts have been 'received' or understood in the past. 'Reception' is a major concern of twentieth-century critics, has been important to all disciples of Hans-Georg Gadamer, and has an obvious importance in biblical studies where there is such a wealth of past commentaries on biblical texts that merit examination both in their own right and for what we might learn from them about the texts they comment on. However, Jauss is far from being interested only in the historical facts about old texts. He regards the process of reception in the past as highlighting how texts are necessarily received in any age – and hence also in our own.[22] It is Iser who uses the term 'reader–response criticism' to focus attention on this contemporary task of textual reception.[23]

Iser's theory centres on the existence of *Leerstellen*, 'empty places', in the text – what we have been calling 'gaps'. These are all the places where the reader has to supply the links between episodes, passages, paragraphs, or other units of text, and to invent in his own mind webs of assumption and convention that will justify one episode in following another – as in our very simple suggestion about the EU apple-mountain. And in supplying these links, the reader is not at the mercy of the text. He is not, as still in structuralism, trying to establish 'scientifically' how the text 'really works', so as to become essentially the text's servant. The boot is on the other foot. The reader–response critic is to a great extent the text's master, *deciding* within what context of expectations he will read the text and so make sense of it. In this system of thought, there are no correct interpretations of texts, only 'readings' which are more or less interesting, illuminating, novel, or valuable; the question what the text 'actually means' is seen as unbelievably naive.

There is a rather more extreme form of reader–response criticism associated with the name of the American critic Stanley Fish, in which the text almost ceases to have any 'rights' altogether, and the reader takes over the role of the writer entirely. A text, in fact, can be made to mean anything, though this is prevented from lapsing into sheer anarchy by a stress on what Fish calls 'interpretive communities', groups of readers who share certain aims and styles of interpretation. There is in fact a good deal in common between the idea of an interpretive community for a secular text and the 'canonical community' which reads the Bible by Childs's canonical method. So long as one remains within that community, one will be constrained to read the text in certain ways. The constraints do not flow, as on a structuralist theory, from the text itself, but from the Church, with its conventions about what certain texts are to be taken to mean. I repeat my usual caution: there is no evidence at all that Childs has been influenced by Fish, but the parallel is still an interesting one.[24]

A style of criticism closer to that of Iser, for whom the relation between texts and readers remains a dialogue, however much the role of the reader is accentuated, is probably the preferred model for most biblical scholars who have found reader–response approaches attractive. The study of the New Testament parables has been particularly influenced by Iser, and it should be obvious why this is so: a parable's meaning is inherently bound up with the reaction of an audience, and it seems to be a form which required a reader–response approach from the very beginning. Of course this can be a false understanding of what reader–response criticism is, if we use the term to refer to reconstructions of the *original* audience and its responses. To respond to a parable may be an exercise in reader–response theory, but to reconstruct someone else's response is pure historical criticism. But not all New Testament critics who use reader–response language have fallen into this elementary trap; most have used their reconstruction of original reactions to the parables to suggest ways in which *we* might respond to them, what we might 'make of' them. This is authentic reader–response criticism.[25] (Old Testament specialists seem as yet to have taken rather less interest in reader–response theory than their New Testament counterparts, but there are examples.[26])

Responding to Ecclesiastes

What might a reader–response critic say about our sample text, Ecclesiastes? Such a critic might point to the wide variety of interpretations, most of them plausible, which are on offer, and argue that this in itself shows how little criticism is a matter of discovering an 'objective' meaning that inheres in the text itself. The oscillations between optimism and pessimism, between the quest for meaning in life and the insistence that life has no meaning, and between hedonism and piety – these are not a *problem* in interpreting the text, but the very datum that invites interpretation – and interpretation of a 'creative', reader–response type: they are the *Leerstellen*, the 'gaps' in the text that the reader needs to fill in.

For example, Eccles. 8:10–13 speaks of God's coming destruction of the wicked and his reward for the righteous: 'though a sinner does evil a hundred times and prolongs his life, yet I know that it will be well with those who fear God . . . but it will not be well with the wicked'. Verses 14–15, on the other hand, note that 'there are righteous men to whom it happens according to the deeds of the wicked, and there are wicked men to whom it happens according to the deeds of the righteous'; and accordingly the author commends enjoyment, 'for man has no good thing under the sun but to eat, and drink, and enjoy himself'. Finally, verses 16–17 argue that it is impossible to find out the work of God 'that is done under the sun'.

Now in our earlier discussion of Ecclesiastes (see chapter 5 above) we took it that this kind of contradiction was a problem. The question was what to do about it. Source critics would use it to argue that the book was originally composite; form critics would examine the oral history of each of the (mutually incompatible) units; redaction critics would ask what can have been in the redactor's mind if he combined all these sentiments to make a single book. From there we moved on to consider readings that were not interested in the intentions of authors or redactors, but only in the book's meaning given that it is part of Scripture (canon criticism) or part of the ordered whole which is 'literature' (structuralism). A reader–response critic would have something in common with many of these approaches, especially perhaps redaction and canon criticism, but would differ from them all in not seeing the book's inconsistencies as a problem in any case. The critic's task is to produce a maximally powerful interpretation, that is, one which takes account of as many features of the book, and in particular as many of its 'gaps', as possible – in full awareness that this interpretation will not necessarily be the author's intended meaning, nor indeed *the* meaning, which does not exist. The text is a kind of exercise for the reader, who has to interpret it (in a rather Gricean way) as coherent in spite of its 'gaps'.

In Eccles. 8 we might attempt a reader–response interpretation as follows. There appear to be gaps between the three pericopes analysed above, which make mutually incompatible points about human life and destiny. As competent readers, however, we can extract from this confusion (whether we call it apparent or real does not much matter) a coherent 'message', by looking for a larger context of our own in which all three sections would make sense. We live as people with a commitment to doing 'good', whatever exactly that means, and we need to do good *as though* God, the universe, or whatever we choose to call it favours well-doing over ill-doing. We cannot think of the difference between good and evil as a matter of mere indifference. At the same time, we may well be sceptical about the real ultimate destiny of mankind, for we know that 'all go to the same place', and we do *not* know whether there is more to be said, or whether death is absolutely the end. And for living our life, the best recipe is to live as though morality made a difference, while acknowledging that we do not know whether this is really so or not, and to accept the mysteriousness of the moral and metaphysical order, for 'even though a wise man claims to know, he cannot find it out'.

This reading of Eccles. 8 more or less supports the 'existentialist' style of living commended by Albert Camus and enshrined most definitively in his novel *The Plague*.[27] *'L'essentiel était de bien faire son métier'* ('The essential thing was to do one's appointed task') writes the narrator, the doctor who supervises medical relief during the plague in Algeria which gives the book its title; and again, when another character warns him that all his victories against the plague will be temporary, he replies, *'Ce n'est pas une raison pour cesser de*

215

lutter' ('That's no reason for giving up the struggle'). What Camus commends is a very austere lifestyle, in which moral duty is everything and is completely altruistic, since there is no assurance at all that morality will end anywhere but in the grave. In suggesting that such is the message of Ecclesiastes, I am not saying that Qoheleth was an existentialist before his time, because I am not attributing any part of my interpretation to Qoheleth anyway: I am saying that the text Qoheleth wrote can become the vehicle for an existentialist meditation on life, and that his words can be read in that way whether or not he would own such a reading. I hope it will be clear that this is a 'reading' of Qoheleth (rather as we speak of a conductor's 'reading' of Beethoven), not an attempt to say what Qoheleth meant. If it is a successful reading, that is not because it reconstructs what was in Qoheleth's mind, but because it allows us to find greater coherence in the text than some alternative readings, and in particular provides a creative account of what at first sight are mere inconsistencies or gaps in the text's progression. The logical spaces between 8:13 and 8:14, and between 8:15 and 8:16, are filled in by this reading so that they are no longer a problem.

Not only is the above not an interpretation of what Qoheleth meant (by now the reader would hardly expect that!); it is not proposed as the 'correct' interpretation of his book either. It is 'a reading' of Ecclesiastes; we might even say (continuing the musical analogy) a 'performance' of the book, which acknowledges freely that other performances or readings are possible and even desirable. In this respect reader–response criticism exhibits the freedom of interpretation which is characteristic of literary study since structuralism, and which does not think in terms of definitive 'answers' to questions about the meaning of texts. Reader–response critics would argue, however, just as practitioners of most of the other new styles of criticism in the last thirty years would also argue, that this does not make their interpretations inferior to those which claim to be 'correct'. On the contrary, it is critics who aim at correctness who are mistaken about what criticism can and cannot do. *All* interpretations of texts are 'readings', not the final word on the subject. Reader–response critics at least acknowledge this, whereas traditional interpreters have deluded themselves into thinking that correct answers exist, if we could only find them. Thus reader–

response interpretation provides the only sorts of readings that are really possible anyway, whereas critics seeking 'objective' interpretations have failed to grasp what criticism is capable of, let alone what specific interpretations it can deliver. In a world where everything is subjective, at least there is some merit in knowing that this is so.

Criticism and Theory

In conclusion, it is worth making a point similar to that made above in discussing structuralism. I have spoken freely of reader–response *criticism*, and have tried to show that it can generate interesting readings of texts, including biblical texts. But although a reader–response approach can indeed be used in the work of practical criticism, it (like structuralism) is ultimately a *theory* about textual meaning rather than a set of techniques which interpreters of particular texts can make use of to extract fresh meanings. I have been writing as though reader–response criticism were particularly useful in reading texts which superficially (or really) have gaps in the argument or failures in connection between sections, because it is the nature of such criticism to concentrate on *Leerstellen* in the text; and so far as it goes, this is perfectly reasonable. But it makes reader–response criticism sound like a technique for handling difficult texts. An ability to make sense of 'gaps' in the text sounds as though it would be invaluable for reading *Finnegans Wake*, but rather superfluous in the case of *The Tale of the Flopsy Bunnies*. My initial examples taken from conversations seemed to confirm this, since they included one text so obvious that it seemed not to need a reader–response interpretation, one so obscure as to resist it (though we subsequently saw that it could in fact be made sense of), and one where there were sufficient 'gaps' for a reader–response method to be both necessary and sufficient in looking for a coherent meaning.

But this was misleading, though it was a useful way into the subject. The reader–response approach is not a special technique for dealing with difficult texts; it is a theory about all texts. *All* texts have 'gaps'. It is simply that we do not notice this in texts we are very familiar with. Reader–response theory shows us, not what meanings we ought to find in obscure texts, but how we find meaning in any texts. In this, as the reader will have seen, it is formally like structuralism, a theory about textual meaning as such. Biblical critics tend always to embrace new theories because of their possible 'pay-off' in terms of throwing light on dark texts. This is not necessarily wrong, but it does tend to 'domesticate' new approaches and draw their teeth; and in the process it also deflects attention from the (more important) question of whether such approaches are satisfactory at a theoretical level. We have seen that biblical interpreters sometimes buy into an approach like structuralism because it offers an attractive way of elucidating obscurities, or the possibility of defending the unity of biblical texts threatened by historical criticism, without realizing that it sometimes rests on a foundation of Marxist atheism which they would never contemplate accepting in other circumstances. Similarly, reader–response theory tells us in effect that all texts are obscure, and tries to lay bare how we go about finding meaning in them – or attributing meaning to them, for on this theory there is little difference. In the dialogue between reader and text, reader–response theorists tend to see the reader as the senior partner, and the one who calls the shots.

A text, from this point of view, is a web of holes joined together with snippets of writing. Our sense that one sentence leads logically or comprehensibly to the next is not something given in the text, but is something that derives from our own cultural background. It has often been noted that a narrative (as opposed to a mere chronicle or listing of events) implies some progression from one event to another according to our sense of what is 'natural' or comprehensible. Take the following narrative: 'They fell in love, so they got married. But then they died'. We read this as coherent and interesting only because we know that falling in love is often followed by marriage, so that the sequence requires no special explanation; and because we know that many people marry at a young age, that people in our society seldom die young, and therefore that 'but then they died' may well indicate a tragic outcome. There is no difficulty in imagining a culture where the sequence of events would seem to contain 'gaps', because (for example) all marriages were arranged and therefore never had anything to do with falling in love, and people in fact never married till they were very old. In such a culture our little narrative would be very puzzling, and 'so' and 'but' would represent points of bewilderment, 'gaps', for the average reader, rather than taken-for-granted connectives as they are for us. Thus the degree to which 'places' in a text are *leer*, 'empty', and so constitute *Leerstellen* in Iser's sense, is culturally determined. It is only the reader, not the writer, who can determine how they are to be filled in.

Reader–response theory shows us how we read, and removes our naive assumption that our reading is dictated by the text we read. A reader–response theory of biblical reading is far more disorientating than critics who see it merely as a handy way of understanding the parables realize. It presents all reading as a matter of what we do with texts, and the texts themselves turn into merely the raw material for our adventures in reading, having no shape or meaning or coherence of their own. Reader–response theory thus belongs to the world beyond structuralism, in which the reader invades the text, and the difference between reading and writing ceases to be real. A little further, and the writer and even the text will disappear altogether. But we will seize the moment before this happens, and attempt to say something about the few short steps that are left along the road, through the kingdom of poststructuralism, deconstruction, and postmodernism. As we shall see, once the reader has got into the text, it seems impossible to get him out again.

Further Reading

Robert Alter, *The Art of Biblical Narrative* (London 1981), pp. 23–62
Phyllis Trible, *Rhetorical Criticism: Context, Method, and the Book of Jonah*. Minneapolis 1994
Anthony C. Thiselton, *New Horizons in Hermeneutics: The Theory and Practice of Transforming Biblical Reading* (London 1992), pp. 516–55
Paul R. House, *Beyond Form Criticism: Essays in Old Testament Literary Criticism* (Sources for Biblical and Theological Study 2). Winona Lake, Indiana 1992

14

THEORY AND TEXTUALITY

I made my debut in literature by writing books in order to say that I could write nothing at all. My thoughts, when I had something to say or write, were that which was furthest from me. I never had any ideas, and two short books, each seventy pages long, are about this profound, inveterate, endemic absence of any idea.

Antonin Arnaud, quoted in J. Derrida, *Writing and Difference* (London 1978), p. 11

And I proceeded to where things were chaotic.

1 Enoch 21:1[1]

Preliminary Reading

Terry Eagleton, *Literary Theory: An Introduction* (Oxford 1983), pp. 127–50

Jonathan Culler, *The Pursuit of Signs: Structuralism, Deconstruction, Semiotics* (London 1981)

Anthony C. Thiselton, *New Horizons in Hermeneutics* (London 1992), pp. 80–141

After Structuralism

Jacques Derrida, the leading figure in post-structuralism, coined the expression *'il n'y a pas de hors-texte'* – there is nothing outside the text. This has (at least) two possible meanings. First, it can be taken to sum up much that we discussed in the previous chapter and indeed in chapters 8, 9, and especially 11. The object of criticism is the text, not something outside the text, such as what the text 'refers' to. Biblical interpreters today tend to agree with structuralist critics that the job of the exegete is to explicate 'the text itself', not the reality to which the text is supposed to refer, nor the ideas in the mind of its author.

But Derrida's dictum does not stop there. Its second meaning (the meaning intended by Derrida, if we can imagine him to have committed the solecism of 'intending' something) is far more radical. 'There is nothing outside the text' not merely in the sense that this or that given text is self-referential and makes no contribution to the outside world, but in the much stronger and more alarming sense that there *is* no 'world' outside the text at all. We could translate Derrida's dictum 'there is nothing but text': everything there is, is characterized by 'textuality'. So far from texts' being one specific and delimited aspect of the world of human culture, all other aspects of human culture are directly or indirectly 'texts'. 'Every signified is also a signifier', or, in other words, texts refer to objects but the objects the texts refer to themselves refer to further objects, and so on ad infinitum. It makes as much sense to say that a text reads me as that I read a text; we are both caught up in the play of signification that is human life/textuality. We can never come to the end of the process of signification, for the final meaning of any text (or any cultural system, or any life) is infinitely 'deferred'[2]: it awaits the final equilibrium of signified and signifier, which never arrives.

All this seems quite a lot to swallow, to put it mildly. We could see it, however, as in a way the logical conclusion of the reader–response approaches just discussed. From a theory in which meaning inheres wholly in texts and we have simply to recognize it, we move to one in which the reader co-operates with the text, as it were, in producing meaning, and then to the rather bolder position that meaning is the reader's contribution to the text – as in the dictum that 'books are like a picnic to which the author brings the words and the reader the meaning'.[3] Only one more small step is needed, and the difference between text and reader dissolves, to be replaced by the institution of textuality, in which the difference between reading and writing no longer exists, but the social reality of the interplay between writers and readers becomes 'yet more shimmering webs of undecidability stretching to the horizon'.[4] The post-structuralist vision of literature reduces the determinacy of meaning to the point where there is no longer really even a division of labour between reader and writer, but both read and both write and neither knows which he is doing at any given moment. The best image I can offer is M. C. Escher's drawing of two hands, each of which is drawing the other.

It sounds as if much fun can be had with post-structuralism. Is there any reason whatever to think it might be correct? The post-structuralist will smile a sweet smile if you ask this, shake his head, and say, 'You really haven't got the point, have you?' Post-structuralism is not a theory which can be tested against the evidence (as structuralism, at least fitfully, thought it was); it is a visionary leap into a whole way of looking at everything. By not claiming to be 'true' – a delightfully old-fashioned concept! – it can never be accused of being false. Readers will probably divide into those who find this attitude immensely attractive, and those who find it extremely infuriating. Perhaps all it really claims to be is an entertaining way of seeing literature. Roland Barthes' post-structuralist study *Le plaisir du texte* (*The Pleasure of the Text*[5]) could perhaps be translated *Fun with Texts* or even *How to Enjoy Yourself with Texts*. Barthes speaks of *jouissance* in connection with texts, and this word, as all commentators point out, usually has a sexual meaning. Post-structuralism is not making truth claims about its methods of inquiry or its conclusions, but simply messing around with texts in an enjoyable way.

But my impression is that post-structuralists usually want to have their cake and eat it. When they are on home ground, they emphasize the playful ('ludic') quality of their interpretations. But as soon as anyone attacks them, they begin to claim some sort of political or moral high ground, and to accuse their opponents of having a repressive view of literature and culture in general – and so of being, in effect, mistaken, even wicked and corrupt, not words that one would expect to belong to the post-structuralist vocabulary. Terry Eagleton's *Literary Theory* is a good illustration of this, written with a passionate antipathy and even hatred towards anyone who does not subscribe to theories which, when playing 'at home', stress chiefly the relativity of all cultural values and the impossibility of ever being 'right'.[6]

Roland Barthes' Second Encounter with the Angel

Post-structuralist concern for the 'undecidability' of textual meaning can be illustrated by looking at Roland Barthes' second attempt to interpret the story about Jacob and the angel in Gen. 32. It will be remembered that his paper of 1971 applied Proppian analysis, filtered through the theories of A. J. Greimas, in order to show how the narrative structures of this text generate an atmosphere of the uncanny. God, Jacob's defender, turns out in the wrestling match at the Jabbok to be also his opponent and attacker. This explains the peculiar *frisson* which the reader experiences; it is in turn explained by the monotheistic theology with which Genesis operates.

In 1988 Barthes returned to the Jabbok to provide no longer a structuralist but a post-structuralist analysis of this incident.[7] This time he concentrated on places where the story is unclear. For example, which side of the river is Jacob on? If he is about to cross the river on his way home, then the contest is a mythical conflict which lends itself to the kind of Propp-like analysis of Barthes' earlier article. But if he has already crossed the river, then the mysterious being who assails him is not trying to prevent him from doing so, and analysis in folkloristic terms is far less appealing. There are similar uncertainties, according to Barthes, about some of the pronouns in the story, as in 'he touched his thigh', which can be seen as ambiguous (though previous commentators have never seen this as a problem), adding to the air of obscurity.

But Barthes' aim is not to point to these previously unnoticed riddles and then to solve them, in traditional exegetical fashion. It is to show that they cannot be solved. The story has an inherent 'undecidability'. It reads, superficially, like a story which ends in 'closure', but more detailed observation shows that all attempts to close it fail. And in this it is not a special case, being studied because it is so unusual. On the contrary, it is the norm. Gen. 32 only shows us in one particular case a general truth about narrative texts, that they resist our attempts to read them as coherent. Here we see a particularly important difference between structuralism and post-structuralism. The former pursues a 'scientific', 'objective' goal, detaching the text from all vague notions of the author's intention and treating it as a solid artefact with an independent existence;

the latter, on the other hand, revels in indeterminacy, and tries to show that all texts contain irreconcilable ambiguities. Though Barthes illustrates this from a particular text, he should not be understood as seeing the biblical story as unusual. On the contrary, for him it is typical of all narrative, without exception. It may be worth recalling our discussion of Iser's reader–response theory, where the idea that the text contains *Leerstellen* that need to be filled in by the reader is not an observation about some texts as opposed to others ('difficult' texts), but a theory about all texts as such.

Writing: A Deconstruction Site

The theme of undecidability can usefully move us on to another great theme in the post-structuralist programme: deconstruction. This term is more often used than understood, especially in biblical studies. Students of the Bible are, as we have often noted, apt to take biblical texts apart to see how they work; and more traditionalist readers of the Scriptures sometimes describe this task – which is most often an exercise in source or form criticism – as 'deconstruction', taking this to be a modish new word for what they see as an attack on the integrity of the text. Sometimes one hears people say that biblical critics deserve to be 'deconstructed' themselves, meaning by this, to have their own arguments dissected in an unsympathetic way. Like many technical terms, 'deconstruction' has to some extent taken on a life of its own, and an uninformed use of the word to signal one's disapproval of the modern world is not surprising. In such popular usage, 'deconstruction' is taken to be more or less equivalent to 'destruction'.

None of this has much connection with the meaning of 'deconstruction' in literary studies. For one thing, in literary theory critics do not deconstruct texts: texts deconstruct themselves. If we do speak of a critic deconstructing a text, we mean by that that the critic shows us the text's own (self-)deconstruction. Deconstruction is a theory about the character of all texts, which claims that every text always and necessarily undermines or contradicts the philosophy on which its own plausibility relies. As usual, it is possible to think of texts where this is obvious. For example, if one sought to argue at length and in very sober prose that all philosophy needed to be conducted in rhyming verse if it was to be valid, then

224

the form adopted would undermine the message being expressed. Similarly, the belief that all important ideas can be expressed in three or four pages will deconstruct itself if it is argued for in a 200,000-word dissertation. On a lighter note, here is a deconstructive limerick:

> There was a young man of Peru;
> This limerick ends with line two.

(The second line is an impossible one within the world of limericks.)

On a more subtle level, works of fiction can be deconstructed if we can show that they rest on assumptions that are at odds with their overt 'message'. A nineteenth-century novel requires the reader to agree (collude) with the author in assenting to a wide range of social attitudes to do with wealth and power, and a novel of this period which operates with these conventions while at the same time undermining them could be said to deconstruct itself, or we could be said to deconstruct it if we pointed out the tensions. A good example might be Trollope's *The Way We Live Now*, where conventions about success and failure are accepted by the protagonists of the novel and apparently by the author (and hence implicitly by the reader), but where the plot demonstrates the bankruptcy of all such ideas. Jonathan Culler sums up the essence of deconstruction as follows; 'to deconstruct a discourse is to show how it undermines the philosophy on which it relies, by identifying in the text the rhetorical operations that produce the supposed ground of argument, the key concept or premise'.[8]

The next move will by now be predictable. Deconstruction is not a theory about how *some* texts undermine themselves, but about how *all* texts do so. Strikingly clear examples of self-undermining can be found, but in principle every text undermines itself. This is so because of the very nature of writing itself. The aim of writing, as Derrida expresses it, is to put an end to writing: we write because we want to make something clear to other people, and when this has been achieved, the writing has fulfilled its purpose. A doctor's prescription does not exist to survive, but to be eliminated: once it has been dispensed, it can be dispensed with. And literature too exists in order to cease to exist, to convey its message and then perish. *But*, says Derrida, this is a delusion. What actually happens is that writing simply engenders more writing. Literature creates criticism, which creates metacriticism, and so on to infinity. The goal writing sets out to achieve never is achieved, but is always 'deferred'. Thus everything written carries within itself a self-contradictory goal. It exists in order to stop existing, and yet this very goal means that it not only continues to be itself, but that it generates infinitely more writing which in turn exhibits a similar self-contradiction. The endless replication of 'final' texts which in fact lead to other texts can be best illustrated from a favourite deconstructionist image, the *mise en abîme*, of which the best example is the effect you get if you place two mirrors facing each other and then peer into one of them: an infinity of mirrors, none showing anything but other mirrors.

The reader may be feeling quite depressed by all this, and may think that deconstructionists really are just destructionists, in the end. Whatever may be the philosophical implications – and I think they will indeed be quite dire, if deconstructionism can ever be shown to be true, which I doubt – the psychological effect of being a deconstructionist is not at all cheerless. Derrida, like Barthes, is having a lot of fun with texts, and wants us to do so, too. Deconstruction is not meant as a reason for giving up literature or philosophy, for 'an opposition that is deconstructed is not destroyed or abandoned but reinscribed'.[9] The fact that we can deconstruct a text, or show that it deconstructs itself, does not imply hostility to that text, for it is not just bad texts that can be deconstructed, but all texts. Learning systematically to distrust texts is a necessary part of reading, just as learning to distrust our own motives is a necessary part of adult life. We are talking about a reading of texts which is self-critical as well as critical of the texts, and which is not naive. Deconstruction, despite its strange jargon and dubious philosophy, is a challenge to the way we read. And if the text we are working with has a high prestige, as the biblical text undoubtedly has, a dose of deconstructive scepticism may be salutary.

Ecclesiastes Deconstructed

There exists at least one deconstructive reading of Ecclesiastes, by J. D. Crossan.[10] Crossan's basic insight – which does not require the full weight of deconstructionist theory, but is compatible with it – is that Ecclesiastes is a *parody* of the wisdom genre. 'Solomon' adopts the posture of a wise man in order to assert that wisdom is foolishness, that 'the wise man dies like the fool' (Eccles. 2:16). The message and the medium are at odds, producing a wisdom book which demolishes wisdom. (There are similar ideas about Job as a sceptical parody in the work of Katharine Dell.[11]) This is deconstruction in a mild form, however, taking a book which is overtly paradoxical and analysing the paradoxes; it bears some resemblance to the redaction-critical possibilities discussed in chapter 5 above. A more wholehearted deconstructionist analysis might treat Ecclesiastes' patent paradoxes as merely very visible examples of the paradoxical character of writing as such.

Rather than begin with the assumption that Ecclesiastes as a wisdom book would be expected to distinguish the wise from the fool, and then showing how this is subverted – quite an easy critical task – we might instead begin with the book's scepticism (agreed on by all) and ask whether this is deconstructed as the work proceeds. From this perspective we could stand the critical tradition on its head and treat the 'conventional' expressions of wisdom not as orthodox interpolations designed to 'save' Qoheleth's sceptical work for posterity, but as part of the text's own strategy to prevent there being any kind of 'last word' in the book. The sceptical and non-sceptical sayings circle around, like the wind in 1:6, and there is no resolution. The juxtaposition of the two categories of saying refuses to allow any moment when the text comes to rest: a resolution of the contradictions is endlessly 'deferred', and at the end of the book we are no wiser (in any sense) than we were at the beginning. It is only when we reach chapter 12 that we can hope to understand chapter 1, but when we do reach it, there is nothing for it but to return to chapter 1 and try again, for exactly the same ambiguous message of scepticism and certainty is uttered at the end as at the beginning. By chapter 12, nothing the text could say would help us to know what we are meant to think, for if sayings declaring ultimate knowledge impossible are simply juxtaposed with those declaring it possible, then knowledge is in practice impossible: there is no way that a positive statement about knowledge could stand outside the book's frame and tell us what to think in a metaliterary way. Even if the text at some points declares that wisdom is better than folly, we cannot tell that this is a frame-breaking assertion and not simply another stage in the alternation of knowl-

227

edge and scepticism which is part of the book's 'plot', so to speak. Reading Ecclesiastes may be like the kind of dream in which you dream you have woken up, but are still in fact firmly in bed (a very deconstructionist dream).

Thus Ecclesiastes does not tell us whether we can have knowledge of ultimate reality or not. But of course in not doing so, it tells us we cannot have knowledge of ultimate reality! If we do not know whether we know something or whether we know nothing, then in practice we know nothing, because any knowledge we think we have is 'under erasure'. Even at an old-fashioned exegetical level, I think this is quite an interesting conclusion. I hope anyway that it illustrates some of the questions deconstruction has to offer.

Grafts

Source critics are open to the possibility that some passages in the Bible result from the *accidental* linking together of units that originally had nothing to do with each other. Source criticism notices 'obvious' inconsistencies in the text, and often explains them through literary accident. As we have seen, most of the methods of Old Testament study that followed in the wake of source criticism disliked explanations in terms of accident or mistake, and looked instead for deliberate purposes that would provide a more 'fitting' explanation of (what they would see as) *apparent* dislocations or errors in the text. Rhetorical criticism has taken this tendency about as far as it can go, and is always ready with a complicated hypothesis, usually involving *chiasmus*, that will 'vindicate' the integrity of the text and its authors.

But deconstruction offers the possibility in such cases of recognizing the dislocations as real and yet at the same time allowing for the meaning that rhetorical critics and others claim to have found in the text as a whole. The term sometimes used to identify the phenomenon to be explained here is *grafting* – the joining of one text to another to produce a third text. Whereas traditional critics (certainly traditional biblical critics) would primarily be interested in the genesis of such a text, or in the intentions of those who produced it by splicing the two smaller texts together, a deconstructionist is concerned with the possibilities of meaning inherent in the finished product without regard to its origin, or (if that sounds too much like a structuralist concern) with the meaning a reader can generate by reading such a text just as it stands. Then – and this is the characteristically deconstructionist move – he can go on to reflect that texts that do not seem to be composite in this way are really just as much a graft: all texts are ultimately grafts.

At a simple level, consider the following piece of text. The first part consists of a speech from *Hamlet*, the second of an excerpt from the Bible:

> O that this too too solid flesh would melt,
> Thaw, and resolve itself into a dew,
> Or that the Everlasting had not fixed
> His canon 'gainst self-slaughter! O God, O God,
> How weary, stale, flat, and unprofitable
> Seem to me all the uses of this world!
> Fie on't, ah fie, fie! 'Tis an unweeded garden
> That grows to seed; things rank and gross in nature
> Possess it merely.

> So he turned and went away in a rage. But his servants came near and said to him, 'My father, if the prophet had commanded you to do some great thing, would you not have done it? How much rather, then, when he says to you, "Wash, and be clean"?' So he went down and dipped himself seven times in the Jordan, according to the word of the man of God; and his flesh was restored like the flesh of a little child, and he was clean.[12]

To satisfy a 'genetic' interest in this passage, I should perhaps say that it was selected *almost* at random. I chose Hamlet's first soliloquy (Act 1, Scene 2), and I then opened the Old Testament as though to practise bibliomancy. However, the first passage this produced was a list of names in 1 Chron. 6, and I did not see why I should give myself such a difficult time; so I tried again, lighting on the passage above (2 Kings 5:13–14), 'and there came out this calf', as Aaron put it. For our present purposes, however, it is strictly a matter of supreme indifference whether the selection took hours of planning or was generated by computer. We are simply confronted with a text, consisting of one subtext grafted on to another (and there is no saying which 'came first'). What could a reader make of this?

From a source-critical point of view, these two texts are purely accidental in their combination. But it is easy to see that there are likely to be coincidences in the juxtapositions of these texts that yield strange flashes of apparent meaning. Any reader is likely to notice that both halves of the text seem to be about *flesh*. A conventional source critic will point out that the juxtaposition is accidental, since the first (verse) section is talking about flesh as a metaphor for burdensome physical existence, the second (prose) one as ʾ literal physical characteristic which has become diseased and needs 'cleansing'. A reader–response critic, on the other hand, such as Stanley Fish, would feel an imperative to see cross-references between the two pieces of text. The difference in meaning between the two uses of 'flesh' would probably matter less than the fact that this word patterns the entire text. The flesh which is a burden can none the less be cleansed if it is washed in the Jordan. Furthermore, this washing restores the character in the text from thoughts of suicide (in the first section) and his obstinate refusal to be free of his illness (in the second). Openness to the suggestions of others is the crucial way of moving from brooding despair to light and peace. Thus the text, taken as a whole, is an excellent piece of encouragement to anyone in despair – almost psychotherapeutic, really.

If we now look at our text from a deconstructionist point of view, we will probably begin by affirming the 'correctness' of this reader–response interpretation. To 'make sense' of the passage, some such concentration on 'flesh' is more or less essential. But the deconstructionist critic will not, like the reader–response critic, pretend not to notice that the passage is composite. On the contrary, he will be delighted about this, because it is then ideally suited for the point he always wants to make: that texts make sense only accidentally. We simply happen to put together two fragments of text that are really quite unconnected, and suddenly we have a coherent passage telling us much that we want to know about human life – sickness, health, hope, despair. This has a fine debunking effect on 'literature' that is carefully planned and laboured over. The deep meaningfulness of our random text deconstructs texts that are not random and shows them up as a tissue of self-deception.

Thus deconstruction challenges all our claims to think profound thoughts, by showing us the role of the trivial and accidental in what we write and read. It suggests that an accidental assemblage

230

of words can be just as good as a planned composition in suggesting ideas we may want to reflect on. Thereby it abolishes the distinction between writing that counts as literature and writing that does not, and leaves us with simply writing – and reading, which is merely the other side of the coin from writing. The passage just analysed hardly depends on a writer – I took two already existing bits of text and stuck them together – but crucially on the reader, who is prepared to make connections and draw conclusions. Such writing (and reading) shows us how texts subvert the literary culture on which they draw by calling in question its claim to sublimity, but then also deconstruct themselves by being unable to sustain the profundity readers think they find in them.

I find all this very overdone, thinking that there remains a difference between intentional and accidental texts, and that critics can give themselves too easy a time by choosing their texts carefully. For example, my example above is (almost) randomly chosen, but its constituent parts come from 'quality' sources – Shakespeare and the Bible. I am sceptical about claims that two randomly combined shopping-lists could plausibly be given an interpretation profound enough to demonstrate that (textual) beauty is in the eye of the beholder.

Reading the Bible through the year

It will be apparent by now that I enjoy deconstruction but do not take it very seriously. However, there is one area of biblical study where the idea of a graft has considerable explanatory value: the study of lectionaries. Many Christian churches follow a set plan for reading scripture in their weekly or daily services. Most of the many systems that exist for organizing this involve more than one lection at a time. Classically, the lectionary at the Eucharist in both the (Eastern) Orthodox and the (Western) Catholic Church has included at least a Gospel reading plus one other biblical reading, usually from the Epistles; recent revisions in the West have restored what is probably the oldest scheme, with lessons read successively from Old Testament, Epistles (including Acts) and Gospels.

There are two main models for selecting readings in the Christian churches: *lectio continua*, in which a book is worked through in order, week by week or day by day, and *lectio electa*, in which lessons are

231

chosen to illustrate a theme. The two systems can be combined, as they are in the Revised Common Lectionary now followed by many churches in the West, by reading the Gospels and Epistles on a more or less continuous basis, but sometimes choosing the Old Testament reading to illustrate what is perceived as the theme of one of the other readings. Whatever system is followed, however, from the point of view of the ordinary worshipper three readings are heard, and inevitably the question arises: Why are we reading these particular passages today? And commonly the worshipper will try to find threads of connection between the readings, which will exceed the message he would extract from any one of them taken alone. This is a classic case of a graft.

This may sound like an issue in modern liturgical or pastoral studies, but it has important ramifications for Old Testament studies. In modern Judaism there is a system for reading the Bible closely similar to that in Christianity (of which it is probably the source). The Pentateuch is read by strict *lectio continua*, right through and with no omissions every year, but there is also a second reading, called the *haftarah*, which is taken from the Prophets (in the Jewish sense: Joshua, Judges, Samuel, Kings, Isaiah, Jeremiah, Ezekiel, the Twelve). This is chosen thematically to match the Torah reading for the day. There have probably been many selections over the centuries, but the one in use today concentrates heavily on certain books, especially Isaiah. Once again, therefore, we have grafts.

It is not known how far back the Jewish system of reading goes; it is usually assumed to have been in place in New Testament times, but this cannot be said to have been proved. Nevertheless, there are many theories about its origins, and one at least proposes that the system actually played a role in the formation of the Old Testament itself. This theory is the work of M. D. Goulder,[13] and has not been given as much attention in Old Testament studies as it deserves, partly because Goulder is seen (correctly) as primarily a New Testament scholar. Goulder thinks that there was a time when the *haftaroth* were also read serially from various books in turn, the present thematic approach having been devised later. He suggests that the 'Deuteronomistic History' and the work of the Chronicler came into being as commentary on the Pentateuchal readings for each sabbath, so that even as the story of each period was being recorded it was also coloured by an awareness of the

Pentateuchal passage it would accompany in the liturgy. Thus when we read Josh. 1 or 1 Chron. 1 we should remember Gen. 1 as the primary text they were meant to accompany, and our reading should involve seeing each through the lens of the others.

This seems to me to be a clear case of grafts, on a larger scale. Even if there is an element of intention in it, with texts planned to correspond to other texts, on the whole worshippers would simply have encountered juxtaposed texts and have been left to work out possible connections themselves. The texts would all have acquired meanings over and above what they meant as isolated units, meanings formed out of the interplay of text with text in a riot of intertextuality. Probably most Old Testament scholars have not been convinced that Goulder is right, but I believe his theory deserves very serious consideration – the more so as it is not invented to serve a particular literary theory; Goulder is most certainly not a deconstructionist. His theory raises the possibility that what the Old Testament texts 'mean' is not related merely to their form and content, but to expectations of meaning created by the context in which they were read, and it reminds us how important are such contexts in the reading and reception of all writing. Anyone interested in deconstruction ought to consider Goulder's ideas, since they offer a rare case of empirical evidence for the kind of developments of which deconstruction claims to give a theoretical analysis.

Postmodernism

Most of the developments surveyed in this chapter can be brought under the general heading of 'postmodernism'. This term seems to provoke much irritation, probably because most people use 'modern' to mean 'of the present' and therefore cannot see how anything that already exists can be described as 'postmodern' – it sounds like describing the present in the future tense. In fact the word has a quite precise meaning. 'Modern', in this way of thinking, is a technical term – sometimes 'modernist' could be used interchangeably with it. It refers to a set of attitudes towards human culture common since the European Enlightenment of the seventeenth and eighteenth centuries, continued in many areas of European life into the post-War period. In modernism (sometimes 'modernity') it was thought that problems could be stated rationally and have solutions on which right-minded people would agree. People worked with a model of steady progress towards an improvement in knowledge and quality of life. The *term* 'postmodern' seems to have been used first in architecture, to refer to architectural styles that did not respect these ideals. Postmodern architecture is all around us now, and can be identified by its tendency to mix styles from different periods. Instead of believing that architecture can make progress and improve on its predecessors, a postmodern approach rejects any notion of a single, linear development towards 'better' design, and simply lives with the whole gamut of the styles that have ever existed, feeling free to draw on any as it likes. The result is always visually arresting, but tends to make the customer worried in case medieval drainage systems or timber framing built to pre-Great Fire of London standards have been included as part of the period flavour.

Applied to literary and cultural theory, postmodernism is to be understood as a hypothesis about epistemology – the philosophy of knowledge. It maintains that knowledge does not form a unified body of data, held together by girders of a shared scientific or humanistic vocabulary and a framework of striving for universal truth. Postmodernists express this by saying that there are no true meta-narratives (sometimes master narratives), only piecemeal information, bits and pieces of temporarily valid ideas. 'Totalities' – such as Christianity, Marxism, the scientific world-view, or a poetics of all literature – are imperialistic attempts to capture and tame a world which is really far wilder than Enlightenment optimism about human progress in knowledge ever realized.

It is not hard to see that post-structuralism and deconstruction are 'postmodern' movements in the sense just defined. Both work with a theory according to which there are no true theories, both are self-undermining and glory in the fact; both refuse even to describe themselves as true. If structuralism was a complete theory about human culture, postmodernism is a deliberately incomplete theory about all theories about human culture, declaring them to be as empty or fragmentary as it is itself. For a postmodernist, there are *no* overarching theories of anything; all theories are 'valid' only for a time and in a given context, and all are 'under erasure'. 'Except for postmodernist theory itself,' the reader may be thinking, thereby uncovering, as he thinks, a fatal flaw in the postmodernist case: for surely to declare all theories false is self-refuting, unless you say 'except the theory that all theories are false'. But postmodernists are entirely unconcerned by the suggestion that their own theory undermines itself unless it is given diplomatic immunity. 'How clever of you to notice,' they reply. 'Now even you can join in our happy word games. For words, in the end, are everything, and in the beginning was the word – definitely with a small "w". Self-refutation is nothing to worry about; we can do twenty tricks of that kind before breakfast. Relax, play with some words, join the party.'

What should one say to someone who has just undermined his own theory, and who knows he has, but who regards it as a matter for self-congratulation? Why should one bother to say anything? If someone claims to be completely committed to a theory he at the same time believes to be false, there seems little point in continuing any dialogue. And here I must come clean ('as if you ever could,' a postmodernist would reply). Some people are not at all *attracted* by postmodernist relativism and self-refutation, but are *convinced* by it, painful as they find it. But I am in exactly the opposite position. As 'a theory' (sometimes, with staggering imperialism, just 'theory', with no article!) claiming to explain or expose culture, art, meaning, and truth, I find postmodernism absurd, rather despicable in its delight in debunking all serious beliefs, decadent and corrupt in its indifference to questions of truth; I do not believe in it for a moment. But as a game, a set of *jeux d'esprit*, a way of having fun with words, I find it diverting and entertaining: I enjoy the absurd and the surreal, and postmodernism supplies this in ample measure. Postmodernist theory is much like postmodernist knitting. You begin to make a sock, but having turned the heel you continue with a neckband; then you add two (or three) arms of unequal length, and finish not by casting off but simply by removing the needles, so that the whole garment slowly unravels. Provided you don't want to *wear* a postmodern garment, nothing could be more entertaining. But when the knitter tells us that garments don't really exist anyway, we should probably suspend our belief in postmodernist theory, and get back to our socks.

Further Reading

Catherine Belsey, *Critical Practice*. London 1980
The Bible and Culture Collective, *The Postmodern Bible*. Cambridge,
    Mass. 1995

CONCLUSION

Interpretation is the revenge of the intellect upon art.

Susan Sontag, *Against Interpretation and Other Essays*
(London 1967), p. 7

This book has three aims: to survey the methods currently used in the study of the Old Testament in such a way that it becomes clear how they are interrelated, and what goals they are meant to achieve; to set Old Testament study against a wider background of literary criticism; and to argue a case against the pursuit of 'correct' methods. In this concluding chapter I must try to make more explicit how the complex arguments of the earlier pages bear on these three objectives.

A Comparison of Methods

Most students of the Old Testament would like, I believe, to be able to see all the methods in common use on a single map, so as to be able to make a real comparison between them. Textbooks that give instruction in actually practising each of the methods are of course essential, but for purposes of comparison they are seldom helpful, since they usually have a partly apologetic aim and so exaggerate the distinctiveness of the particular method concerned. Another problem is that biblical scholars sometimes commend their own favourite method as a better way of achieving some goal that earlier methods also had in view, but were less successful in reaching, and sometimes as a way of answering quite new questions previously unnoticed by scholarship. Terrible confusion comes of this. A good deal of the criticism of structuralism current in British

Old Testament scholarship is merely muddled, attacking structuralism as a failed attempt to achieve traditional historical-critical results. Such attacks wholly fail to engage with its real intentions. Conversely, both structuralists and canon critics often talk as though it were a flaw in (say) redaction criticism not to have allowed for the 'canonical' or 'structural' dimension, or (worse) as though redaction critics had been dimly and feebly groping after the insights now at last revealed. Not surprisingly students sometimes come to feel that each of the methods is in reality a completely separate enterprise, and that no common objective unites them at all. Hence, perhaps, the common experience of Old Testament teachers that their students cannot remember which method is which: no logical progression is perceived from each method to the next, no common themes are noticed.

I have tried to provide the sort of common map we need by borrowing from structuralist vocabulary the term 'literary competence' and adapting it to serve our purpose. The advantage of this model for discussing such widely divergent approaches to criticism is that it does not involve any tacit implication that all the methods are at some deep level really means to the same end. Such an idea is manifestly false and would be repudiated by *all* the parties involved. What we do have in the term 'literary competence', however, is a very broad description of the goal of any criticism of literary texts, which at least makes it clear that Old Testament critics of whatever persuasion inhabit the same universe. They differ on the very question of what it is to be competent at reading the Old Testament, but they would all agree that the methods they pursue are meant to produce competence. Although the term is a structuralist one, I use it without any ideological intention, and I certainly do not mean to imply that all Old Testament critics are crypto-structuralists. Above all the term brings in its wake notions of genre-recognition, and what I have called 'reading as'. These ideas are not themselves methods: they are models for understanding what methods are for. My suggestion is that we can begin to understand all the methods Old Testament scholarship has used, and to see how they are related to each other, if we ask in each case what their proponents are reading the Old Testament and its component books *as*. This is what we may call a meta-critical question, asking not about the meaning of texts, but about the style of various critics' proposals about the meaning of texts. My whole discussion could, indeed, be called meta-criticism, and it is my belief that Old Testament study could benefit from rather more interest in these matters. The *history* of biblical criticism is becoming a large research-field; the *analysis* or mapping of biblical criticism is still rather neglected.

As the discussion has developed it has become clear that 'literary competence' is by no means the only tool with which to draw the map we need. I can best spell out another way of looking at the interrelationships of critical methods by introducing an invaluable scheme for classifying critical theories of literature in general, which was first set out by the American literary critic M. H. Abrams in *The Mirror and the Lamp*, published in 1953.[1] Abrams suggested that all critical theories could be understood with the aid of this diagram:

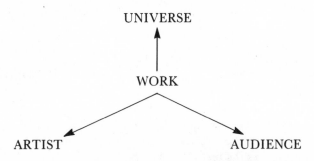

While nearly all theories about literature take some account of all three 'co-ordinates' to which a given work is related, most take one or other as crucial and derive the categories and criteria of their criticism principally from that. Thus some critical theories are concerned with the relation of the literary work to the 'world' ('universe') that it is seen as mirroring: this would be true of any critical approach that valued 'objectivity' and 'realism', just as it would be of theories in the visual arts that favour 'representation' and treat the accuracy with which nature is imitated in art as the major criterion of criticism. Such representationalism is rare today, but it was the dominant view for many centuries. Again, a critical theory may see the important question for the critic as being what the work tells us about its author ('artist'); this would be specially noticeable in Romantic criticism.

239

It would be possible to work with the same diagram, or a slightly modified version of it, in classifying the critical methods used in biblical scholarship. A brief sketch of this should help to schematize and so make more easily memorable the relationships between the various methods we have looked at. We may keep the shape of Abrams's diagram and simply adjust the terms to fit the specific concerns of biblical critics as against those of aesthetic philosophers:

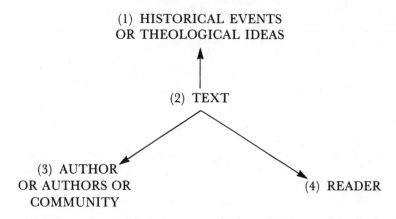

(1) HISTORICAL EVENTS
OR THEOLOGICAL IDEAS

(2) TEXT

(3) AUTHOR
OR AUTHORS OR
COMMUNITY

(4) READER

Biblical criticism as we know it begins (in the work of source critics) when attention moves from the ideas that lie behind or are communicated by the text (1) – the 'theological truth' it conveys – on to the author (3). Biblical scholars cease to ask about the divine meaning of Scripture and begin to ask, 'What did the author of this text mean?' An ahistorical approach to the Old Testament, corresponding to a 'mimetic' or representational view of art in general, comes to an end with the arrival of the 'author' in a human sense, and historical criticism begins. It is important to see that the two subsequent refinements, form and redaction criticism, still belong firmly within the same family of critical approaches as source criticism. This is a point I emphasized in describing them, and which we can now register schematically by saying that for both methods the central concern is to find the meaning of a biblical text by locating its *author*. For form criticism, the author is a group rather than an individual; for redaction criticism, he is a clever compiler of pre-existing fragments, rather than a free creator. But in all three historical-critical methods, the original author in some sense is the place where the method comes to rest. Once we have found the meaning or intention of whoever first wrote the text, we have achieved our goal.

The radical newness of more recent types of Old Testament criticism, which I have stressed from many points of view, finds its visual expression in a move from the author (3) to the work itself (2) and finally to the audience (4). Canon criticism is, as we saw, superficially like redaction criticism, and sometimes B. S. Childs himself speaks as though he is interested in the intentions of the community that 'canonized' the Old Testament. That would put it firmly in the same camp as all the earlier critical methods, with the author (3). But in reality most canon-critical suggestions do not depend on historical investigation at all, but are statements of what the biblical text means taken in itself, and of what individual parts of it mean, once given their relation to other parts. Here for the first time in Old Testament criticism we have a concentration on *the text itself* (2), rather than on its relation to other things. Abrams notes that similar theories (which he calls 'objective theories') about art and literature have appeared only rarely in the history of critical writing, but one of these flowerings is to be found in the 'New Criticism' in English and American criticism of the twentieth century. Our diagram shows Childs in exactly the same position for biblical criticism (at the centre, with the work itself) that the New Criticism occupies in Abrams's diagram, and that may serve as both a reminder and a justification of our long comparison of the two approaches. The move from redaction criticism to canon criticism is thus seen in its true light. It is a move of the magnitude of that from pre-critical biblical study to historical-critical methods; as Childs correctly perceives, this is a far greater move than from source to form criticism.

Structuralist analysis also begins from the text itself (2), without concerning itself with the text's relation to the other three co-ordinates, and this is why some structuralist criticism seems to have close affinities with the work of Childs and his followers. It is hardly surprising to find that similar affinities can be found between the New Criticism and at least early structuralist works, in the wider literary world. Most biblical scholars who practise structuralist analysis seem to believe that the text itself (2) is where they belong, and they often argue that it is only by remaining in this central position that they can practise a truly 'literary' criticism of the Old Testament. As we have seen, it is sometimes argued by such scholars that biblical criticism has never before been properly 'literary', because it has been concerned with questions of theological truth or historicity (1), or with the intentions of historical persons, the biblical 'authors' (3), whereas true literary criticism is not concerned with such matters. Our discussion has suggested that this is a mistaken view of the matter, and that it is only rather recently that *secular* criticism has been concerned exclusively with the work or text itself (2). Not to move to this position may well be a sign that biblical scholarship is getting out of date, as measured against current literary fashions, but it certainly does not mean that it is 'unliterary'; that is to take a very short view of what is to count as a 'literary' approach. Literary criticism as now taught in schools is certainly to be located as position (2), but that is not the whole story. After all, much biblical study as taught in schools is still precritical (position 1)!

Structuralism as it has developed in recent years, however, has itself moved away from 'the text itself' and towards an interest in the relation between text and reader (4); and unless biblical structuralism follows suit, it finds itself left high and dry. For structuralism (or 'post-structuralism') of a more recent kind 'the text' exists only as a function of the institutionalized habit of reading, and the character of the relationship between reader and text is all-important. As I have repeatedly argued, structuralism is ultimately a theory of reading. It does not so much interpret or discover new meanings in texts as account for whatever meanings have been perceived there: it seeks to uncover the mechanisms by which texts have meaning, and it sees these as part of the social institution of reading. Rhetorical criticism, reader–response criticism, and deconstruction all concentrate on the interplay between text and reader as determinative for meaning. This interest in text and reader marks structuralism and post-structuralism off decisively from approaches like canon criticism, which can sometimes resemble it superficially, and even from interpretations which use the language of structuralism but in reality still belong to the world of historical criticism (there are examples in chapter 9). Thus the diagram above provides a clear framework within which the argument of this book can be read, and it may help to explain not only what are the main concerns of each method, but also where the really significant contrasts between methods lie.

Old Testament Study and Literary Criticism

In adapting M. H. Abrams's diagram to biblical criticism I have already provided a way of correlating developments in the criticism of the Old Testament with movements in the wider literary world. My argument has been that biblical studies have always mirrored secular criticism to some extent, ever since historical criticism gained the ascendancy: suggestions that it is only with structuralism that the two worlds have come to be on speaking terms are very wide of the mark and reflect a selective approach to what in secular criticism is to count as 'literary'. The developments in biblical and secular criticism have, in fact, been broadly similar, though not always in step. Biblical criticism was still fairly exclusively historical (i.e. interested in the text and the author) until recent times, whereas in literary criticism generally interest has been shifting to 'the text in itself' since the 1920s at least. Canon criticism may be seen as evidence that the shift has at last reached Old Testament study, while those who inherit a continental European tradition of criticism have come at the same idea *via* structuralism, not having had the New Critics to direct their minds in the same direction as Childs's.

But the aspect of structuralism that seems to be enduring in secular study is less its power of generating fresh interpretations of literary works, more its analytical inquiry into how meaning is perceived in literature at all, which has led to the idea of a 'theory of reading'. This too has begun to make an impact on Old Testament studies. Old Testament critics continue to move with the trend, though at their own speed. They continue to be the children of the intellectual milieu in which they are trained.

The Pursuit of Method

In his book on developments in structuralism over the last ten years or so, Jonathan Culler argues that much 'structuralist' criticism in England and America has failed to break out of the traditional preoccupations of pre-structuralist Anglo-Saxon criticism, because it has insisted on seeing structuralism as a *technique* for producing fresh interpretations rather than as a *theory* about the ways in which texts are capable of having meaning.[2] In essence this is precisely the point I have made about biblical structuralists. Culler says that, for the English-speaking critical tradition, 'criticism' is almost synonymous with 'interpretation': the test of a critical theory is whether it enables us to produce novel, and demonstrably more 'correct', interpretations of particular works. Now it seems to me fair to say that the same is true of 'method' in Old Testament studies. A method – source analysis, or form criticism, or redaction criticism, or the new canon criticism – is supposed to be a set of procedures which, when applied to the text, elicit its 'true' meaning; though, as we have seen, what kind of meaning is the true one is variously defined. But there is little doubt in the minds of many scholars, and still less in those of their students, that biblical criticism is about discovering the meaning of texts: indeed, the suggestion probably sounds so obvious as to be trivial.

The main conclusion towards which my argument has been leading is that this understanding of critical method is mistaken. Biblical 'methods' are *theories* rather than methods: theories which result from the formalizing of intelligent intuitions about the meaning of biblical texts. Texts are perceived as having certain sorts of meaning – or, just as interestingly, as failing to convey meaning – by reading them with certain vague expectations about genre, coherence and consistency, which are either confirmed and clarified, or disappointed and frustrated. Then reading begins again, this time with a sharper focus; and at the end of the process there emerges a distinct impression of what the text means, together with an explanatory theory as to how it comes to mean it. But the theory – which, when codified, will become source analysis or redaction criticism or whatever – is logically subsequent to the intuition about meaning. It may lead to useful insights into other texts, when they are approached in a similar frame of mind, and so may greatly shorten the quest to understand them; but it can never be a technique which can always be used with the assurance that it will yield correct results. The reason why biblical scholars have so often become disillusioned with each of the methods they have committed themselves to is that they have asked too much of them, have

become obsessed with correct method and with the desire to produce novel interpretations of the text. They have turned what were
often startlingly original insights (there is real genius in much of
Wellhausen's or Gunkel's work, for instance) into pedestrian
'methods' which are supposed to provide a key to everything in the
Old Testament. And the disappointment of seeing each method in
turn fail to provide a total reading of the Old Testament has led to
disenchantment with it, and the quest for something new and better.
Thus each new method tries to abolish its predecessors – the more
recent, canon criticism and structuralist analysis, more vociferously
than ever before.

What I should like to imagine is a style of Old Testament studies
that would make sense even if all the interpretative decisions had
already been made. At the moment each method has to work harder
and harder to overturn the conclusions of its predecessors; learned
journals are littered with more and more fresh interpretations of
particular texts, showing how badly they have hitherto been misunderstood. At times this makes me want (however irrationally) to
agree with people who ask me how I can go on studying the Old
Testament, when after all this time it surely must be adequately
understood already. The truth is that the meaning of very many
passages, even of very many whole books, is not very seriously
disputed.[3] There is room for exciting new interpretations, but not
endless room. In such a situation (and let us imagine it as it may
be in fifty, a hundred or two hundred years' time), 'methods' which
yield 'results' are of mainly historical interest, for the results have
been yielded. Where will be the place of criticism then?

If Culler is right, it is at this point that the real interest of
criticism begins. The task of criticism, on his understanding of it,
is not to be always producing new interpretations, but to explain
interpretations on which readers can agree. As we saw, some structuralist approaches even within biblical studies have investigated
this possibility, exploring the way we read the Old Testament and
asking what our presuppositions are: not necessarily in a debunking
way, but in order to make us more self-aware as readers. It is
possible that canon criticism, of which I have been very critical,
could be diverted into this channel to good purpose, if once it would
give up its claim to be normative. The work of Childs and others
has a lot to tell us about what it is for a text to be 'canonical', and

how those who accept its canonicity tend to be constrained to read it; it is a pity if they waste their time in trying to show that we *should* read the Old Testament in such a way, for that can never be shown by biblical criticism of any kind, but only by theological argument lying outside the biblical critic's province.

Indeed, if there is one tendency of biblical criticism it has been my aim to call in question, it is this tendency to seek the normative, a tendency that crops up in every kind of criticism we have examined. Over and over again biblical critics seek *correct* methods, *prescriptive* answers to the question how we may read the Old Testament, *successful* procedures and techniques that will process the text and extract from it the answers that we *ought* to be looking for. In so far as biblical criticism belongs to theory, perhaps there must be some concern for norms and rules; and of course secular literary criticism is far from lacking in prescription and legislation! Yet in our discussion it has emerged that problems with methods almost always begin at the point where they cease to be descriptive and tentative and become rigid and doctrinaire: where codified intuition starts to be counter-intuitive in its results. The basic flaw, I have suggested, is the belief that the question 'How should we read the Old Testament?' can be answered. The pursuit of the 'right' method has taken each illuminating insight in turn – source-critical, form-critical, reaction-critical, canon-critical, structuralist and post-structuralist – and hardened it into this one valid way of understanding the text.[4] If we would abandon this fruitless quest, we might turn again to each of the methods which litter the path of biblical criticism, and see in each the key to certain ways in which we do in fact read the Bible. Instead of asking which method is 'right', we might ask what is really going on in the reader when he is using each of them, what kind of reading they belong to. That inquiry seems hardly to have begun yet in the biblical world, though it is already well advanced in secular criticism. I hope that this book has at least shown that there is a place for it and provided occasional, provisional suggestions of the sorts of results it might achieve.

NOTES

CHAPTER 1: 'LITERARY COMPETENCE' AND GENRE-RECOGNITION

1 See R. E. Clements, *A Century of Old Testament Study*; R. Davidson and A. R. C. Leaney, *Biblical Criticism*. The series *Guides to Biblical Scholarship*, published by Fortress Press, Philadelphia, provides a set of brief guides to the various methods, and some volumes in the series will be cited in notes to the appropriate chapters of this book. K. Koch, *The Growth of the Biblical Tradition*, is useful but concentrates chiefly on form and traditio-historical criticism: the German original was called *Was ist Formgeschichte?*

2 See below, pp. 192–3.

3 Saussure's major work (assembled posthumously from his students' lecture notes) is *Cours de linguistique générale* (English translation *Course in General Linguistics*). Other books which give a basic account of 'competence' in language are J. Lyons (ed.), *New Horizons in Linguistics*, and J. Culler, *Structuralist Poetics*, chapter 1. I shall be relying heavily on Culler's ideas, so it is only fair to point out that his work is not an uncontentious textbook, but an original work that has provoked strong disagreement: see the trenchant criticism in F. Lentricchia, *After the New Criticism*, pp. 103–12.

4 Extreme examples of such ambiguity with regard to the relevant conventions occur with some exclamations. For example, 'Fire!' is both linguistically ambiguous (noun or verb?) and ambiguous in a 'literary' way: is it an instruction to a firing squad, or a warning to the other occupants of a burning building?

5 On genre there is an illuminating (non-structuralist) discussion in E. D. Hirsch Jr, *Validity in Interpretation*, pp. 68–126.

6 See F. Kermode, *The Genesis of Secrecy*, p. 18.

7 Some scholars would argue that it is an error to use criteria based on *content* in assigning books to a particular genre. This, they would say, is a formal question, to be settled on grounds of form alone. I do not believe the matter is that simple: see my comments below on the approach of W. Richter (pp. 22–4).

8 Though, of course, the historian may well use it to recover popular ideas about zoology in the period when it was written.

9 For a standard treatment of the conventions of apocalyptic literature see D. S. Russell, *The Method and Message of Jewish Apocalyptic.*

10 See W. McKane, *Proverbs*, pp. 22–33 and especially 660–4, with reference to Prov. 30:24–31 as discussed by W. M. W. Roth, *Numerical Sayings in the Old Testament.*

11 Kermode, *Genesis of Secrecy*, has useful comments on genre: see especially pp. 162–3, where a genre is described as 'a context of expectation. . . . It is the equivalent, for a longer discourse, of the set of expectations which enables us to follow a sentence as it is spoken.'

CHAPTER 2: 'LITERARY CRITICISM'

1 J. Barr, 'Reading the Bible as Literature', which discusses many of the questions dealt with in this book, draws attention to this difference of usage:

> In general literary study we mean by *literary criticism* a study of the structure and the imagery of works, their modes, symbols and myths, their poetic, dramatic and aesthetic effect; but in technical biblical scholarship the same term means the separating out of historically different layers in composite works, the history of the tradition during the period of its development in written form, as distinct from its development in a spoken form before it was written down. (pp. 20–1).

One effect of this basically historical orientation is that much 'literary' criticism of the Bible strikes ordinary literary critics as very 'unliterary', if not philistine. We return to this question in chapter 10. A clear exposition of the techniques used in literary criticism of the Old Testament to be found in N. C. Habel, *Literary Criticism of the Old Testament.*

2 'Lower criticism' is a term, now largely discarded, for what is usually called 'textual criticism'. This is the attempt to reconstruct the original manuscript wording of a text by comparing all the available later copies, which invariably contain mistakes. We shall not be concerned in this book with textual criticism. For a discussion of textual criticism in Old Testament studies see J. Weingreen, *Introduction to the Critical Study of the Text of the Hebrew Bible*, E. Würthwein, *The Text of the Old Testament*; S. Talmon, 'The Old Testament Text'; and B. J. Roberts, 'The Textual Transmission of the Old Testament'.

3 For up-to-date surveys of the history of Pentateuchal criticism see R. E. Clements, 'Pentateuchal Problems', and *A Century of Old Testament Study*, pp. 7–30 also R. N. Whybray, *The Making of the Pentateuch.*

4 See, for example, R. K. Harrison, *Introduction to the Old Testament*, pp. 505–41; J. W. Wenham, 'Moses and the Pentateuch'. This attack is rebutted by J. Barr in *Fundamentalism*, pp. 145–9.

5 The problem which literary criticism was developed to deal with was not, of course, put in these terms by early critics. On the whole the difficulties they found in the text were linguistic (e.g. the two divine

names, *Yahweh* and *'elohim*, in Genesis) or historical (e.g. Ishmael's age when expelled from Abraham's house is inconsistent as between Gen. 16 and Gen. 21; Moses cannot have written the account of his own death in Deut. 34). Nevertheless the question of genre lies at the root of the matter, for these things are only a problem if we take it as evident that authors do not write inconsistent or repetitive texts. This is generally a perfectly sensible assumption, of course. My point here is simply to emphasize that it concerns the *type of literature* the Old Testament is, not just the accuracy or otherwise of the information recorded in it.

6 See his *Exegese als Literaturwissenschaft*. There is a useful summary of Richter's very complex argument in J. W. Rogerson's review of this book in *JSS* 20.

7 Cf. J. Barr, 'Bibelkritik als theologische Aufklärung', especially p. 31: 'Meines Erachtens liegt der Urgrund der Bibelkritik nicht in der Historie, sondern in der erneuten Wahrnehmung des Genres, der literarischen Gattung eines Textes als Wegweiser, der zum rechten Verständnis des Sinnes führen muss.' ('In my opinion the ultimate basis of biblical criticism does not lie in historical concerns, but in the renewed perception of genre, of the literary type of a text, as the necessary pointer to the true understanding of what it means' [my translation]).

8 For the description of biblical criticism as 'scientific' see J. D. Smart, *The Past, Present, and Future of Biblical Theology, passim*.

9 This is easily said, and is sometimes used as a cheap way of disposing of source criticism. Cf. U. Cassuto, *The Documentary Hypothesis and the Composition of the Pentateuch*, p. 13; 'Let us not approach the Scriptural passages with the literary and aesthetic criteria of our time, but let us apply to them the standards obtaining in the ancient East generally and among the people of Israel particularly.' It would be easier to follow Cassuto's advice if the very texts we are trying to read were not our primary source for what those standards were! Frank Kermode, in *Novel and Narrative*, pp. 7–8, cites some interesting cases from medieval literature of works that seem incoherent according to our notions of orderliness but were not so perceived in their day; see also below, ch. 12, note 11.

10 A valiant attempt is made by G. J. Wenham, 'The Coherence of the Flood Narrative'. See also E. F. Kevan in *New Bible Commentary*, pp. 84–5; and M. G. Kline in *New Bible Commentary Revised*, pp. 88–9. U. Cassuto dismisses a theory of multiple authorship for the flood narrative in *A Commentary on the Book of Genesis. Part II: From Noah to Abraham*, pp. 33–43 – though he is prepared to allow that the author may have drawn on earlier material.

11 The problem of how, and how far, we understand past cultures is the subject of a vast literature. 'Cultural relativism', the belief that cultures are incommensurable and that no one can escape from the culture in which he finds himself, has been a keenly debated issue in recent English

theology: see on this my article 'Reflections on Cultural Relativism' and the discussion in N. Lash, 'Understanding the Stranger', in his *Theology on Dover Beach*, pp. 60–76. Detailed discussions of the theoretical issues involved may be found in A. C. Thiselton, *The Two Horizons*, pp. 52–60 and 70–4. In passing it may be noted that the critique just considered, while it warns against overconfidence in using literary criticism, does not give any comfort to a fundamentalist position. If the possibility that ancient Israel had different ideas of consistency in writing from ours slightly damages the case for source criticism, it totally undermines the fundamentalist position, which takes the idea that all biblical texts are bound to be consistent with each other at every possible level, according to *our* canons of consistency, as a fixed dogma.

CHAPTER 3: FORM CRITICISM

1 *Prolegomena to the History of Israel*, chapters 9–11. 'P' (which Wellhausen called 'Q') is the strand in the Pentateuch that contains the ceremonial and dietary laws, regulations about priesthood and ritual purity, and rules for ordering the nation as a theocracy, which provide much of the distinctive flavour of Judaism down to the present day. On the achievement of Wellhausen see Clements, *Century*, pp. 7–12 and J. Barton, 'Wellhausen's *Prolegomena to the History of Israel*: Influences and Effects', D. Smith-Christopher (ed.), *Text and Experience: Towards a Cultural Exegesis of the Bible*, pp. 316–29.

2 Strictly speaking, as Richter has pointed out (*Exegese als Literaturwissenschaft*, pp. 45–6), we ought to distinguish between *Form* and *Gattung*. *Form* should be used much as we use 'form' in English, to refer to the 'formal' characteristics of a given passage – its shape, structure, metre, internal divisions and so on; *Gattung* should then be used for the general type to which a number of texts exhibiting formal similarities are conventionally assigned – in other words, their genre. For example, a particular poem may be said to have the following *Form*: composed of fourteen lines of equal length, divided into three four-line stanzas and a concluding couplet, with the rhyming scheme A-B-A-B C-D-C-D E-F-E-F G-G. On the basis of a broader knowledge of English literature, we may then go on to classify it as belonging to the *Gattung* 'sonnet' – more specifically, the Shakespearian as against other kinds of sonnet. Richter is quite right to argue that, if we ignore this distinction between *describing* the form of a text and *assigning* it to a general class or genre, then we may jump to premature conclusions. For example, we may assume, without examining the idea carefully enough, that a text is a slightly unusual instance of a genre we are already familiar with, without stopping to consider that it may really be an example of another genre whose existence we did not know about. Worse still, we may extrapolate from a single text and infer the existence of a general type to which it belongs, and then go on to make large claims about the

importance and prevalence of this type of text in Israelite life, when all the time we may be working with a text that is really aberrant, even unique. These criticisms of Richter's need to be borne in mind, though they do not upset the main line of argument here.

3 For a more detailed discussion of the technical terms used in form criticism see Koch, *Growth*, especially pp. 3–5, and G. M. Tucker, *Form Criticism of the Old Testament*.

4 Gunkel's work on the Pentateuch is surveyed briefly in Clements, *Century*, p. 15, and there is a full account of all his work in the standard book on the history of biblical interpretation, H.-J. Kraus, *Geschichte der historisch-kritischen Erforschung*, pp. 309–34, and in the study by W. Klatt, *Hermann Gunkel*.

5 Good examples of these may be found scattered throughout Koch, *Growth*.

6 The main exponent of such a view is I. Engnell, in *Gamla Testamentet* and 'The Pentateuch'. See also E. Nielsen, *Oral Tradition*. Similar ideas had been developed in relation to the books of the prophets in H. S. Nyberg, *Studien zum Hoseabuche*, and H. Birkeland, *Zum hebräischen Traditionswesen*.

7 See *A History of Pentateuchal Traditions*.

8 See 'The Form-critical Problem of the Hexateuch'.

9 This expression ('das Gesangbuch der Gemeinde des zweiten Tempels') is Wellhausen's: see his contribution to F. Bleek, *Einleitung*, p. 507. A classic statement in English of the interpretation of the Psalms as religious lyrics can be found in A. F. Kirkpatrick, *The Psalms*, p. x: 'Lyric poetry is defined as "that which directly expresses the individual emotions of the poet"; and religious lyric poetry is the expression of those emotions and feelings as they are stirred by the thought of God and directed God-wards. This is the common characteristic of the Psalms in all their manifold variety.' Kirkpatrick does, however, anticipate much later research in finding a liturgical origin for certain Psalms, notably 24 and 118, and his commentary (1902) is still a classic.

10 See *Ausgewählte Psalmen*; 'Psalmen'; *Die Psalmen*; *Einleitung in die Psalmen*. Gunkel's work was introduced to a wider readership in this country through W. O. E. Oesterley, *The Psalms*. For a survey of these developments see Clements, *Century*, pp. 76–98; J. H. Eaton, 'The Psalms and Israelite Worship' (where there is a detailed bibliography); and E. Gerstenberger, 'Psalms'.

11 For a detailed account of this way of looking at the Psalms see H.-J. Kraus, *Worship in Israel*, pp. 1–25.

12 S. Mowinckel, *Psalmenstudien I–VI*; *The Psalms in Israel's Worship*.

13 These applications of form criticism may be traced in such works as A. Alt, 'The Origins of Israelite Law': H. J. Boecker, *Redeformen des Rechtslebens*; B. Gemser, 'The Rib- or Controversy Pattern in Hebrew Mentality'; K. Nielsen, *Yahweh as Prosecutor and Judge*; L. Köhler, 'Justice in the Gate', in his *Hebrew Man*, pp. 127–50. A general survey of the

achievements of form criticism is provided by *Old Testament Form Criticism*.

14 See Mowinckel, *The Psalms in Israel's Worship*, vol. i, pp. 1–41.

15 A very clear exposition of these developments is provided by E. W. Nicholson, *Deuteronomy and Tradition*. See also R. E. Clements, *Deuteronomy* (Old Testament Guides).

16 Some of these issues are made explicit in A. D. H. Mayes, *Deuteronomy*; see especially pp. 30–41.

17 Mayes, *Deuteronomy*, discusses recent proposals along these lines. The case is argued in M. G. Kline, *Treaty of the Great King*; and R. Frankena, 'The Vassal-Treaties of Esarhaddon and the Dating of Deuteronomy'. A full discussion with bibliography is provided in M. Weinfeld, *Deuteronomy and the Deuteronomic School*.

18 See K. Baltzer, *The Covenant Formulary*; J. l'Hour, 'L'alliance de Sichem'. For general discussions of the implications of these suggestions see D. J. McCarthy, *Old Testament Covenant*; and L. Perlitt, *Bundestheologie im Alten Testament*.

19 See W. M. Clark, 'Law'; G. E. Mendenhall, *Law and Covenant*.

20 See especially W. L. Moran, 'The Ancient Near Eastern Background of the Love of God'; and cf. the use of 'love' in 1 Kings 5:1 (Heb. 5:15).

21 Weinfeld, *Deuteronomy*, presents the case for a didactic purpose in Deuteronomy; see specially pp. 158–78.

CHAPTER 4: REDACTION CRITICISM

1 This earlier disparaging view of redactors is well traced in J. A. Wharton, 'Redaction Criticism, Old Testament', one of the few articles specifically about Old Testament redaction criticism.

2 On Gen. 26:1, see J. Van Seters, *Abraham*, pp. 175–82.

3 The best general guide to redaction criticism is probably N. Perrin, *What is Redaction Criticism?*, which is in the *New* Testament series of *Guides to Biblical Scholarship*.

4 *Genesis*, pp. 40–2. The introduction to this book provides clearer cases of von Rad's own redaction-critical work, for which see also 'The Form-critical Problem', p. 52.

5 See *Genesis*, pp. 160–2, and 'The Beginnings of Historical Writing'. It is worth noting that the suggestion that we should see 'J' as an author rather than a mere compiler was already made in 1902 by R. Kittel in his *Geschichte des Volkes Israel*, against Gunkel: thus on p. 302 of vol. i he speaks of the 'Schriftstellerpersönlichkeit' of the Yahwist. Von Rad stresses that this question is a complex one. J is not a mere compiler, yet on the other hand he is not composing freely, either: he is turning old, traditional material into creative literature.

6 See M. Noth, *The Deuteronomistic History*, for the classic study of this work. See also W. Brueggemann and H. W. Wolff, *The Vitality of Old Testament Traditions*: this contains two articles originally published

elsewhere, viz. H. W. Wolff, 'The Kerygma of the Yahwist' and 'The Kerygma of the Deuteronomic Historical Work'. There is a good brief survey of the theology of the deuteronomic work in P. R. Ackroyd, *Exile and Restoration*, pp. 62–83.

7 See the survey in J. R. Porter, 'Old Testament Historiography'; P. R. Ackroyd, 'History and Theology in the Writings of the Chronicler' and 'The Theology of the Chronicler' J. M. Myers, 'The Kerygma of the Chronicler'. Classic studies are G. von Rad, *Das Geschichtsbild des chronistischen Werkes*, and S. Mowinckel, *Studien zu dem Buche Ezra-Nehemia*.

8 See for example, D. R. Jones, 'The *Traditio* of the Oracles of Isaiah of Jerusalem'; S. Mowinckel, 'Die Komposition des Jesajabuches Kap. 1–39'; J. Vermeylen, *Du prophète Isaïe à l'apocalyptique*; E. W. Nicholson, *Preaching to the Exiles*; R. P. Carroll, *From Chaos to Covenant*; W. H. Schmidt, 'Die deuteronomistische Redaktion des Amosbuches'. On the editing of the prophetic corpus as a whole, see R. E. Wolfe, 'The Editing of the Book of the Twelve'; R. E. Clements, 'Patterns in the Prophetic Canon'; and B. S. Childs, 'The Canonical Shape of the Prophetic Literature' – though see Chapter 6 for a fuller description of Child's distinctive approach.

9 Apart from Perrin, *What is Redaction Criticism?*, useful material on New Testament redactional approaches can be found in W. Marxsen, *Mark the Evangelist*, which seems to have been the first work to use the term 'redaction criticism'; J. Rohde, *Rediscovering the Teaching of the Evangelists*, which notes that redaction-critical methods were first used in work on the Old Testament (see pp. 42–6); and G. Bornkamm, G. Barth and H. J. Held, *Tradition and Interpretation in Matthew*.

10 On the biblical genealogies in general, an exhaustive treatment is provided by M. D. Johnson, *The Purpose of the Biblical Genealogies*; see also R. R. Wilson, *Genealogy and History in the Biblical World*. There are interesting comments on the New Testament use of them in M. D. Goulder, *Midrash and Lection in Matthew*, pp. 228–35. For the discussion of Gen. 10 that follows, see von Rad, *Genesis*, pp. 135–41.

11 In addition to von Rad, see P. Berger, *The Social Reality of Religion*, pp. 119–230, which provides an admirable, brief summary of the alleged distinctiveness of Israel in regard to ancient ideas of reality.

12 See von Rad, *Genesis*, p. 139. The most recent commentator on Genesis, C. Westermann, does not treat the Table of Nations as having had an independent existence: see his *Genesis*, p. 670. See also J. Hughes, *Secrets of the Times; Myth and History in Biblical Chronology*, pp. 5–54.

13 *Introduction to the Old Testament as Scripture*; see pp. 145–50 for what follows.

14 Von Rad, *Genesis*, p. 61, treats 2:4a as a redactional conclusion to P, and this is quite a common view. Useful surveys of opinion are provided by C. Westermann, *Genesis*, and U. Cassuto, *Commentary on Genesis* I, pp. 96–100. See also S. R. Driver, *The Book of Genesis*, p. 19, for a survey of older views.

15 See *Ancient Near Eastern Texts*, pp. 60–1; W. Beyerlin, *Near Eastern Religious Texts*, p. 82.

16 Barr, *Fundamentalism*, pp. 40–2, shows that fundamentalists are now beginning to say this themselves; in this, paradoxically, they are accepting the force of one of the arguments in the critical armoury of which they have the least reason to be afraid. See below, pp. 163–4.

17 Cf. Kermode, *Genesis of Secrecy*, pp. 60–4 and 70–2, who shows how the interpretations of Mark in the work of Austin Farrer (*A Study in St Mark*) constitute something recognizable as 'literary criticism' by the ordinary secular critic used to the criticism of English literature. And Farrer's work has many similarities to redaction criticism, though it antedated the term by more than a decade.

18 A study in which this can be seen particularly clearly is E. M. Good, *Irony in the Old Testament*. Thus on p. 82: 'The final editor [of Gen. 1–3] was far more than a mere compiler, but was in a true sense an "author".' In some ways however Good's work moves away from redaction criticism towards the 'text-immanent' approaches we shall be investigating in subsequent chapters, since at times he suggests certain literary meanings in the text which cannot be ascribed to any compiler or author, but simply inhere in the text as it now stands (see, for example, p. 81).

19 See above, pp. 26–9.

20 See *The Deuteronomistic History*, pp. 31–3.

21 See H. Conzelmann, *The Theology of St Luke*, pp. 18–94.

22 M. D. Goulder has some brief words on this subject which deserve to be weighed, as they could undermine much redaction-critical work. Writing of studies of the 'Chronicler' which treat him as a modern 'author' he asks, 'Who wrote, who read, works of art in the Jerusalem of 350 BC? The suggestion seems foreign to the Jewish mind, impractical and pointless' (*Midrash*, pp. 218–9).

23 See *The Deuteronomistic History*, pp. 42–53.

24 I owe this phrase to the Revd Dr N. T. Wright, who reports it as coined by the Revd Dr Alec Motyer, but the use I make of it here cannot be laid at the door of either of these scholars. The essential materials for my argument here are present in the following quotation from E. J. Young, 'History of the Literary Criticism of the Pentateuch': '. . . there is a unity in the Pentateuch which the documentary hypothesis does not satisfactorily explain. If the first five books of the Bible were put together in the manner which this hypothesis demands, it is difficult, if not impossible, to understand how the result could be the unity which the Pentateuch actually does exhibit' (p. 35). Cf. also the remarks of G. J. Wenham in 'The Coherence of the Flood Narrative', especially on p. 337.

CHAPTER 5: AN EXAMPLE: ECCLESIASTES

1 Surveys of older approaches to Ecclesiastes can be found in F. Delitzsch, *Commentary on the Song of Songs and Ecclesiastes* (1877), which continues to defend the unity of the book but acknowledges that the inconsistencies are a problem. More recent literature is surveyed in K. Galling, 'Stand und Aufgabe'; E. T. Ryder, 'Ecclesiastes'; and A. Barucq, 'Quohéléth'. Some modern scholarly commentaries are A. Lauha, *Kohelet*; N. Lohfink, *Kohelet*; and R. B. Y. Scott, *Proverbs; Ecclesiastes.*

2 The supplementary or 'complementary' hypothesis flourished in the first half of the nineteenth century and is associated especially with the name of H. Ewald. A good short description can be found in O. Kiaser, *Introduction to the Old Testament*, p. 38. There is a fuller account in H.-J. Kraus, *Geschichte der historisch-kritischen Erforschung*, pp. 182–221.

3 *Prediger und Hoheslied* (1898).

4 This serves as a reminder that 'literary' criticism is strictly speaking not synonymous with 'source' criticism: the existence of parallel *sources* for a given text is one of several possible conclusions to which the separation of various *strata* from a text can lead. Richter (*Exegese als Literaturwissenschaft*, pp. 62–6) urges this point very strongly, showing that critics often jump too quickly from the observation that a text is composite to the conclusion that it is composed of pre-existing sources, each of which formed a complete whole before it was used in our present text. Sometimes, as he stresses, texts may be composite because composed of *fragments* that were never part of any earlier literary 'source'. Similarly (p. 73) he points out that there is a logical gap between establishing the *form* of a text, and establishing that there existed many more texts of the same form, i.e. that the text whose form we are analysing belonged to a widely recognized *genre* (cf. ch. 3 n. 2 above). These cautionary remarks are certainly in order, though they need to be read in the light of our earlier discussion of the inherent circularity of much literary work.

5 *An Introduction to Ecclesiastes* (1904).

6 See, for example, M. Hengel, *Judaism and Hellenism*, vol. i, pp. 115–28, especially p. 116. The only 'editors' allowed by Hengel are the authors of the title and of the two little epilogues in 12:9–14.

7 I would not myself accept the argument from the non-consistency of the Semitic mind, but it appears quite often in Old Testament studies. See above, ch. 2 n. 9, for an example of its application to source criticism of the Pentateuch.

8 See K. Galling, 'Kohelet-Studien' (1932); 'Der Prediger' in *Die fünf Megilloth* (1940), pp. 47–90 (73–125 in the second edition).

9 Critics have been rather cautious about this sort of suggestion, though many have gone some way towards it. A good study from this point of view is that of R. Gordis, *Qoheleth*, especially pp. 95–108. He speaks freely of 'quotations' in Ecclesiastes, but notes,

The term "quotations", as used here, refers to *words which do not reflect the present sentiments of the author of the literary composition in which they are found, but have been introduced by the author to convey the standpoint of another person or situation.* These quotations include, but are not limited to, citations of previously existing literature, whether written or oral (p. 96).

R. N. Whybray, 'The Identification and Use of Quotations', goes a little further and suggests criteria by which to identify quotations which come genuinely from some outside source, rather than being composed by Qoheleth himself as a foil for his own teaching. He isolates the following verses as likely to be such quotations: 2:14a, 4:5, 4:6, 7:6a, 9:17, 10:2, 10:12. But both these scholars take as axiomatic that there *is* an 'author', Qoheleth, to whom the bulk of the book is to be ascribed. (There are interesting parallels to this discussion in H. W. Wolff's study of 'quotations' in the books of the prophets: see his 'Das Zitat im Prophetenspruch'.) The book of Proverbs has long been regarded as an anthology, of course, rather than as the work of an 'author', but here the principles of the final arrangement are very obscure, so obscure that even redaction criticism has not been able to gain much of a grip; see G. von Rad, *Wisdom in Israel*, p. 32.

10 Whybray (see previous note) argues in the same way that some passages show Qoheleth's *own* redaction of earlier proverbs, though here of course the redaction had the opposite effect, radicalizing originally orthodox sayings. Thus in 4:5–7, according to Whybray, we have a somewhat pessimistic old aphorism (4:5) still within the bounds of acceptability, which has been made much more pessimistic by the addition of 4:6 and darkened still further through 4:7. (Our own argument, in what follows, is that this process was later reversed by the editor who added 4:9–12.)

11 See below, pp. 171–4.

CHAPTER 6: THE CANONICAL APPROACH

1 All the problems discussed in this had already been pinpointed in his article, 'Interpretation in Faith' (1964).

2 *Exodus* (1974).

3 Published in 1979. The expression 'canonical criticism' is rejected on pp. 82–3, as tending to suggest that Childs's approach is simply a further type of criticism in the succession source – form – redaction criticism, whereas in reality it represents an entirely new departure, *replacing* the entire historical-critical method. I shall argue strongly that Childs is quite correct in perceiving his approach as radically new. However, 'canon criticism' (which I prefer to 'canonical criticism' as more closely analogous to 'form criticism' and 'redaction criticism') is such a convenient phrase that it is hard to resist, and I shall use it occasionally. Other discussions of 'canonical' themes are to be found

in Childs's articles 'The Old Testament as Scripture', 'The Canonical shape of the Prophetic Literature', 'The Sensus Literalis of Scripture', and 'The Exegetical Significance of Canon' and in his books *Old Testament Theology in a Canonical Context*; and *Biblical Theology of the Old and New Testament: Theological Reflections on the Christian Bible*. A somewhat divergent 'canonical' approach has been developed by J. A. Sanders: see his *Torah and Canon*, and 'Adaptable for Life'. See also M. G. Kline, 'Canon and Covenant'. There is a fascinating anticipation of the 'canonical approach' in A. Gelin, 'La question des "relectures" bibliques'. See also below, pp. 173–8.

4 *Introduction*, p. 79. The same point is made in *Biblical Theology in Crisis*, pp. 141–2; in *Exodus*, p. xvi; and in 'Interpretation in Faith', pp. 437–44.

5 Thus for example *Introduction*, p. 83: 'Attention to the canon establishes certain parameters within which the tradition was placed [by the community of faith that canonized it]. The canonical shaping serves not so much to establish a given meaning to a particular passage [*sic*] as to chart the boundaries within which the exegetical task is to be carried out.'

6 Cf. the following comment, from a supporter of Childs: 'With its epilogue Qoheleth has been overtly thematized by a particular theological understanding of wisdom which closely resembles that in Sirach and Bar 3:9–4:4. Therefore, the epilogue provides a rare glimpse into a comprehensive, canon-conscious formulation of what the purpose of biblical wisdom is' (G. T. Sheppard, 'The Epilogue to Qoheleth'; this quotation is from p. 189, where he goes on to compare Psalm 1 and Hosea 14:10). It may be worth remembering that Judaism has found no incongruity in reading Ecclesiastes liturgically at the feast of Tabernacles, a joyful rather than a sombre occasion.

7 See *Biblical Theology in Crisis*, pp. 151–63.

8 Or traditions: Childs is always intensely aware that the Old Testament is Scripture for two different communities, Christianity *and* Judaism. On the problems this causes, see the next chapter.

9 There is an excellent discussion of Childs's work on canon, as well as the contrasting work of Sanders, in F. A. Spina, 'Canonical Criticism: Childs versus Sanders'. I am grateful to Professor James Barr for drawing my attention to this important essay.

CHAPTER 7: CANON AS CONTEXT

1 See above, ch. 6, n. 3.

2 *The Old Testament of the Early Church* (1964). See also Sundberg's articles 'The Protestant Old Testament Canon', 'The "Old Testament" ', and 'The Bible Canon'. Childs is of course well aware of Sundberg's arguments, but has been, I believe, influenced a good deal by S. Z. Leiman, *The Canonization of Hebrew Scripture*, which argues for a much earlier fixing of the Hebrew canon – unconvincingly, in my judgement. (I am

grateful to Professor Barr for pointing out the importance of Leiman's work for understanding Childs.)

3 Childs's assertion that the Hebrew canon is to be preferred to that of the Vulgate for the purposes of 'canonical' exegesis, because it provides the Church with a canon that is *shared* with Judaism, is dismissed with particular emphasis by James Barr in his review of *Introduction to the Old Testament as Scripture*. See J. Barr, 'Childs' Introduction to the Old Testament as Scripture', especially p. 22:

> If we must 'take the canon seriously' as a basis for faith, then it must be *either* the Jewish canon of the Hebrew Bible *or* the Christian canon of Old *and* New Testaments . . . The Old Testament can indeed be taken as a separate subject within Christianity on the basis of some acceptance of the liberal and historical approach to the Bible; but not on the basis of a canonical approach, pushed as far as this one is.

(Childs's discussion of the question 'Which canon?' appears on pp. 72–4 and 659–71 of the *Introduction*.)

4 We could point up the contrast even more sharply by bringing in Ecclesiasticus. Suppose we were to accept Sundberg's argument that the Greek canon is the real Christian canon: we should then be committed to accepting Ecclesiasticus. But its effect on the point being discussed (life after death) would depend on whether we adopted the Greek text (which is the traditionally canonical one) or the rediscovered Hebrew original (as in the NEB translation). For in a number of places where the Greek Ecclesiasticus speaks of immortality, the Hebrew originally spoke only of the common fate of all mankind, death – rather in the manner of Ecclesiastes. Thus, for example, at Ecclus. 7:17, the Greek text runs, 'Humble yourself greatly, for the punishment of the ungodly is fire and worms' – referring to eternal punishment for the wicked; but the Hebrew had 'Humble yourself greatly, for the expectation of man is worms.' This is only a small example, but there are plenty of others like it.

5 See G. Ebeling, 'The Significance of the Critical Historical Method' for the classic statement of this point. For a discussion of it that shows an awareness of many of the problems Childs is wrestling with, but reaches very different conclusions, see P. Stuhlmacher, *Historical Criticism and Theological Interpretation of Scripture*.

6 See the discussion in R. P. C. Hanson, *Allegory and Event*, especially p. 239. The most comprehensive discussion of the uses of allegory in patristic and medieval exegesis can be found in H. de Lubac, *Exégèse médiévale*; du Lubac has a great deal more sympathy for allegory than have most Protestant biblical critics, Childs included, and does not by any means see it as merely a face-saving device, but as a natural consequence of a high ('canonical') view of Scripture. Childs's position would be far more consistent if he were to follow this line of thinking,

but his loyalty to Reformation principles about the 'literal' sense of Scripture holds him back, producing incoherence.

7 The most strongly worded suggestion of this sort comes from James Barr, who – while accepting that Childs is not himself a fundamentalist – argues that nonetheless

> [Childs's] picture of critical study agrees with the conservative one ... he maintains that critical study has not got to grips with the true nature of the material and suggests that its results follow from the 'hermeneutical presuppositions' adopted ... practically nowhere does Childs concede that [critical study] has made a quite *decisive* difference to our understanding of scripture. ... All this will be deeply welcome to conservative opinion, all the more so because a clearly non-conservative scholar has written it; it will be quoted by conservative polemicists for the next hundred years ('Childs' Introduction').

8 See on this point H. W. Frei, *The Eclipse of Biblical Narrative*, pp. 1–5. Frei is discussed in more detail in ch. 11 below.

9 Cf. Barr, *Fundamentalism*, pp. 172–5, and his article 'The Fundamentalist Understanding of Scripture', especially pp. 71–2.

10 On the novelty of Childs's approach see Barr, 'Childs' Introduction', p. 13: 'No one in the history of theology or of biblical interpretation has accorded so much centrality to the canon.'

11 See especially *Introduction*, pp. 661–71.

12 The phrase 'canonical intentionality' (*Introduction*, p. 78), which Barr attacks as a 'mystic phrase' ('Childs' Introduction', p. 13), seems to be used deliberately in order to rule out any understanding of the canonical approach as merely sophisticated redaction criticism. Childs writes,

> It is not clear to what extent the ordering of the oral and written material into a canonical form always involved an intentional decision. At times there is clear evidence for an intentional blurring of the original historical setting. ... At other times the canonical shaping depends largely on what appear to be unintentional factors which subsequently were incorporated within a canonical context. ... But *irrespective of intentionality* the effect of the canonical process was to render the tradition accessible to the future generation by means of a 'canonical intentionality', which is coextensive with the meaning of the biblical text [my italics].

'Canonical intentionality' seems to be used here with a deliberate air of paradox. Childs is saying, in effect: if we cannot conceive of meaning without invoking 'intention', we shall have to speak as though the canon itself did the intending! In fact, for him, meaning is not a matter of intention at all, but is a function of the relationship of a given text to other texts in the canon. It is this idea that marks the decisive break with historical criticism.

The difference between a historical, redaction-critical approach to the final form of the Old Testament text and Childs's essentially ahistorical interest in meanings generated by the inherent shape of the final form can be seen by comparing Clements, 'Patterns in the Prophetic Canon', with Childs's own study, 'The Canonical Shape of the Prophetic Literature'. Clements analyses the prophetic canon in order to establish how prophecy was being understood by the close of the Old Testament period; Childs, to discover what meaning it is bound to have for a reader of any age who takes seriously the canonicity of its present organization. There are superficial resemblances, but at a deeper level the articles inhabit two different critical universes.

13 Childs makes this contrast explicitly (*Introduction*, p. 73): 'A corpus of religious writings which has been transmitted within a community for over a thousand years cannot properly be compared to inert shreds [*sic*; but perhaps *sherds*?] which have lain in the ground for centuries.'

14 A useful collection of articles on 'canon criticism' is provided by *JSOT* 16 (1980), May number, which was devoted to reviews of Childs's *Introduction*. Barr's 'Childs' Introduction', pp. 12–23, has already been cited: Childs replies sharply to it in 'Response to Reviewers of *Introduction to the OT as Scripture*', pp. 52–60. The other articles are B. Kittel, 'Brevard Childs' Development of the Canonical Approach', pp. 2–11; J. Blenkinsopp, 'A New Kind of Introduction', pp. 24–7; H. Cazelles, 'The Canonical Approach to Torah and Prophets', pp. 28–31; G. M. Landes, 'The Canonical Approach to Introducing the Old Testament', pp. 32–9; R. E. Murphy, 'The Old Testament as Scripture', pp. 40–4; and R. Smend, 'Questions about the Importance of the Canon', pp. 45–51.

CHAPTER 8: STRUCTURALIST CRITICISM

1 Their resemblance is noted by Barr, 'Reading the Bible as Literature', with reference to P. Beauchamp, 'L'analyse structurale et l'exégèse biblique' (particularly p. 123). Barr points out (p. 23) that both structuralism and canon criticism depend on the idea of a fixed corpus of material – either a text or a collection of texts that exhibit (in Beauchamp's phrase) 'clôture' or 'fermeture' – closedness or 'closure'. A classic study in English of this idea is F. Kermode, *The Sense of an Ending*. See also below, n. 22.

2 There is now an enormous literature on biblical structuralism, a small selection of which is listed at the end of ch. 9.

3 *Structuralist Poetics*, p. 50.

4 'Recent Literary Structuralist Approaches to Biblical Interpretation', p. 173. Rogerson's point that we *do* know how to read wisdom and apocalyptic has already been developed in ch. 1. Rogerson's article is the best introduction to biblical structuralism known to me, and I have drawn on it extensively in this chapter and the next.

5 See, for example, R. M. Frye, 'A Literary Perspective', and the com-

ments of Barr, *The Bible in the Modern World*, p. 64. A higher view is expressed by Kermode, *Genesis of Secrecy*, pp. vii–ix; cf. also his comments, comparing biblical critics favourably with some literary critics, in his lecture *How We Read Novels*, pp. 10–11.

6 See J. W. Rogerson, *Myth in Old Testament Interpretation*, pp. 101–27, and *Anthropology and the Old Testament*, pp. 102–14. A general, brief introduction to structural anthropology is provided by E. Leach, 'Structuralism in Social Anthropology' in the very useful collection *Structuralism: an Introduction*, pp. 37–56.

7 See J. Culler, *The Pursuit of Signs*. 'Semiotics' means, etymologically, simply 'theory of signs': its precise use is still a matter for personal choice, so far as I can see.

8 The basic works in this field are R. Barthes, *Système de la mode* – a study of the 'code' of fashion–and U. Eco, *A Theory of Semiotics*. But see also Eco's essay 'Social Life as a Sign System' and J. Culler, 'The Linguistic Basis of Structuralism'. Semiotics sometimes makes grandiose claims to be a new science; it has a learned journal, *Semiotica*, and an *International Association for Semiotic Studies*. Those scholars who know about semiotics seem to divide into fervent enthusiasts and violent opponents, some of the latter seeing the whole discipline as an enormous bubble that deserves to be pricked (in Italy some refer to Eco's work as 'simiotics' – money-tricks). I hold no particular brief either for or against it: indeed, I do not know enough to judge. But it is a useful way of finding one's bearings in the structuralist world.

9 'Misleading advice for foreigners' used to be a recurring item in the *New Statesman*'s regular weekend literary competition.

10 Cf. J. Barr, *The Semantics of Biblical Language*, pp. 107–9 and 114–18; also his *Comparative Philology*, pp. 289–91; J. Lyons, *Introduction to Theoretical Linguistics*, ch. 9.

11 See J. Lyons, 'Structuralism and Linguistics', pp. 9–10, and at more length in an expanded version of this chapter in his *Semantics*, vol. i, pp. 230–69. See also Culler, *Structuralist Poetics*, pp. 10–16.

12 For an application of the same principles to art, cf. J. Wolff, *The Social Production of Art*. Such approaches are attacked with some force in R. Scruton, *The Aesthetics of Architecture*: see especially pp. 158–78 and n. 1 on p. 283.

13 *Structural Exegesis: From Theory to Practice*, p. 10.

14 See Kermode, *Genesis of Secrecy*, p. 53. I shall argue in the next chapter that many 'biblical structuralists' have failed to see this point and have treated structuralism as just one further technique for generating new interpretations of tired texts. This is no wonder, however: Culler argues that just the same thing has happened in the wider literary world, as English and American critics have turned the alien (French) system of structuralism into the kind of literary 'method' they are more at home with, domesticating it into the Anglo-Saxon environment. (Critics to the left of Culler accuse him, in turn, of having done exactly the same

himself.) See Culler, *Pursuit of Signs*, pp. 3–17, and compare pp. 128–9 and 206–7 below.

15 *What is Structural Exegesis?*, pp. 12–14. For a fairly robust attitude to the author, we may turn to D. M. Gunn, who has strong sympathies with modern literary approaches to the Bible: '[It is not] necessary to stick with the author. It is the work that confronts us, not the author. The critic is in business to read words, not minds' (*The Story of King David*).

16 On Russian Formalism in general see the very clear account of V. Erlich, *Russian Formalism*; see also L. Nyirö, 'The Russian Formalist School'. The movement has affinities with Anglo-American 'New Criticism', as well as with French structuralism: see below, ch. 10, n. 20.

17 The reader can test this suggestion by reading the haunting (and horrible) transformations of *Red Riding Hood* in Angela Carter's *The Bloody Chamber*, whose effects, incidentally, bear a strong resemblance to those found by Barthes in Gen. 32: see the next section. Much recent study of folk-tale depends on a work that preceded Propp's by some twenty years: A. Olrik's 'The Epic Laws of Folk Narrative'. Accessible discussions of 'Olrik's Laws' can be found in J. Van Seters, *Abraham*, and in J. A. Wilcoxen, 'Narrative'. On the analysis of narrative sparked off by Propp's work, see Culler, *Pursuit of Signs*, pp. 169–87.

18 See the brief review in Rogerson, 'Recent Literary Structuralist Approaches', and von Rad, *Genesis*, pp. 314–21. A fuller survey of critical opinions, together with a recommendation to study the 'final form' of the text, can be found in F. van Trigt, 'La signification de la lutte de Jacob'.

19 See Barthes, 'La lutte avec lange'. Barthes' approach does not derive directly from Propp, but from the theories of A. J. Greimas, *Sémantique structurale*, which however produce an analysis in many ways similar to that of Propp. Greimas is also a source of much in the terminology and method of Daniel Patte, whose works have already been cited (see n. 13 and 15 above). Barthes' study is discussed in detail by H. C. White, 'French Structuralism and OT Narrative Analysis' see also R. Martin-Achard, 'Un exégète devant Genèse 32:23–33'.

20 See von Rad, *Genesis*, pp. 27–30, 45–50 and 143–50; 'The Beginnings of Historical Writing', pp. 166–76 and 202–4.

21 See the brief discussion in G. Pocock, *Corneille and Racine*, pp.64–5 (with reference to Corneille's *Polyeucte*). In similar vein, George Steiner has argued that Job cannot be read as a tragedy because a *Jewish* tragedy is an impossibility: the distinctive faith of Israel precludes it. See his 'Tragedy: Remorse and Justice' (a broadcast version of the first Hannah Arendt Memorial Lecture, delivered at the University of Southampton in 1979).

22 The classic case of a 'subverted' detective story is Alain Robbe-Grillet's novel *Les Gommes*, which is discussed, along with E. C. Bentley's *Trent's Last Case*, which is more subtly subversive of the reader's expectations, in Kermode, *Novel and Narrative*, pp. 15–17. Barthes, in *Writing Degree*

Zero, pp. 34–5, discusses Agatha Christie's *The Murder of Roger Ackroyd*, in which it is the first-person narrator who proves to be the murderer ('That's cheating', we say as we finish it). An accessible way into French structuralist approaches to narrative is provided for English readers by the novels of John Fowles. Both *The Magus* and *The French Lieutenant's Woman* play cat and mouse with the reader, continually frustrating the expectations that arise from his familiarity with the genre to which they appear to belong; while the short story 'The Enigma' in the collection *The Ebony Tower* begins with all the marks of a detective story, only to turn, in the last few pages, into a love story so absorbing that it leaves the reader, like the detective, no longer interested in solving the original mystery – and therefore, by implication, willing to jettison the bulk of the narrative.

23 See, for example, Mic. 6:1–6 (a lawsuit); Isa. 5:1–7 (a popular song); Amos 4:4–5 (a priestly oracle). There is a discussion of these parodies of secular forms by the prophets in C. Westermann, *Basic Forms of Prophetic Speech*, pp. 199–204.

CHAPTER 9: BIBLICAL STRUCTURALISM

1 Thus Patte, *What is Structural Exegesis?*

2 See R. Barthes, *S/Z* (on Balzac's *Sarrasine*); for similar points see also his *On Racine*; and see Culler, *Structuralist Poetics*, pp. 96–102.

3 For a brief guide to Marxist criticism see Tony Bennett, *Formalism and Marxism*, and for a taste of it in action see T. Eagleton, *Criticism and Ideology*. See too the symposium on 'Modern Literary Theory' referred to in ch. 12, n. 2 below. A classic statement of the view that 'realism' in literature is entirely a matter of the *conventions we have come to accept* as realistic may be found in Barthes, *Writing Degree Zero*, p. 67. Structuralism destroys the innocence of our response to writing and to speech: after reading Barthes, we are likely to be uncomfortable with suggestions that a book, a letter or a person is 'unaffected' in style or speech, or 'artless', or 'straightforward'. We find ourselves saying instead, 'How well he has mastered the conventions for artlessness!' This is not a brand-new idea, of course: everyone knows that it is possible to *decide* to write 'sincerely'. What is new in structuralism is the idea that the author may be as unaware as the reader that he is in the grip of conventions and constraints.

4 See above, pp. 49–51.

5 See, again, Kermode, *Genesis of Secrecy*, pp. 53–5, and Rogerson, 'Recent Literary Structuralist Approaches'.

6 Cf. Culler, *Structuralist Poetics*, pp. 131–60, on 'Convention and Naturalization' (especially p. 138); and G. Genette, *Figures* II. There is an extended discussion of naturalization in Veronica Forrest-Thomson, *Poetic Artifice*. Writers influenced by structuralism enjoy producing works which systematically disorient the reader, making him constantly

readjust his genre-expectations and stretching his capacity for naturalization to its limits: the stock examples are the novels of Alain Robbe-
Grillet. See also above, ch. 8, n. 22.

7 Once again, see Kermode, *Genesis of Secrecy*, p. 65, and Culler, *Pursuit
of Signs*, pp. 3–17; and cf. my remarks above, ch. 8, n. 14.

8 An interesting example of this, too complicated to discuss in detail
here, is D. Jobling's study of Num. 11–12 in his *The Sense of Biblical
Narrative*. Jobling's diagrams are a necessary and integral part of his
argument.

9 An excellent novel would become meaningless (in a very narrow sense
of the word) if bound in a cover reading *London Telephone Directory: A–D*.
Conversely, the reader who complained that the plot of the *Concise
Oxford Dictionary* was spoiled by the author's habit of pausing to define
all his terms had a noble commitment to a reader's duty to find meaning
and order in any text, whatever the odds.

10 See R. M. Polzin, *Biblical Structuralism*. The same seems to me to be
true of R. C. Culley, *Studies in the Structure of Hebrew Narrative*, and of a
great many of the articles cited in the bibliography of biblical structuralist works at the end of this chapter.

CHAPTER 10: THE 'NEW CRITICISM'

1 Cf. Barr, *Fundamentalism*, pp. 90–1 and 98–9.

2 *Introduction*, p. 74.

3 As with most 'movements' there is no agreement who should be
included among the 'New Critics', but any list would be likely to
include W. K. Wimsatt Jr, M. C. Beardsley, Cleanth Brooks, R. Wellek,
A. Warren and Allen Tate.

4 See F. Lentricchia, *After the New Criticism*.

5 Cf. Barr's comments on 'Biblical Theology' as a justifiable *corrective* to
the liberal theologies it replaced, but as less successful in trying to
become a complete alternative system: 'Story and History in Biblical
Theology', p. 2.

6 On a very rough count, there are about 120 'Romantic' to forty 'Augustan' and fifty 'metaphysical' poems: compare this with the figures in n.
13 below.

7 The classic guide to these lines of thought is M. H. Abrams, *The Mirror
and the Lamp* – introductory chapter 'Orientation of Critical Theories'.
From about 1800, he writes, 'expressive' theories came to dominate
critical study: in such a theory

> A work of art is essentially the internal made external, resulting
> from a creative process operating under the impulse of feeling, and
> embodying the combined product of the poet's perceptions, thoughts,
> and feelings. The primary source and subject-matter of a poem,
> therefore, are the attributes and actions of the poet's own mind.

The 'affective' aspect of 'Romantic' criticism is firmly rejected in the New Critical essay by W. K. Wimsatt and M. C. Beardsley, 'The Affective Fallacy'.

8 P. 657. On texts as 'artefacts' bearing their meanings in themselves, see also R. M. Frye, *Perspective on Man*, p. 43, and the comments in Barr, 'Reading the Bible as Literature', p. 22.

9 See T. S. Eliot, *On Poetry and Poets*, pp. 113–14.

10 There is a classic statement of the view of poetry discussed here in Sir Arthur Quiller-Couch's preface to his *Oxford Book of English Verse*, p. ix: 'The numbers chosen are either lyrical or epigrammatic. Indeed I am mistaken if a single epigram included fails to preserve at least some faint thrill of the emotion through which it had to pass before the Muse's lips let it fall, with however exquisite deliberation.'

11 This idea is stated most clearly by T. E. Hulme, *Speculations*, pp. 132–7.

12 It is hard to formulate any theory of what literature essentially is that does not quickly turn into a statement of literary preference. We see it again in structuralism, where the principle that meaning in all literature whatsoever is a function of structure has almost at once turned into a preference for writing that exploits structural complexity and makes the reader aware of how its meaning is generated.

13 For comparison with the figures cited in n. 6 above, this contains about seventy-five 'Romantic' poems to fifty 'Augustan' and eighty-five 'Metaphysical', neatly reversing the balance of 'Romantic' to 'pre-Romantic'.

14 See R. Wellek and A. Warren, *Theory of Literature*, pp. 34–5 and 139.

15 This is why Childs's 'canonical' approach causes such anger, especially to those coping with fundamentalism: it seems to be designed to take the Christian, so recently liberated from the bonds of 'the tradition', 'the canon', 'the *ecclesia docens*', straight back to the Egypt from which he has come. To such critics Childs seems to be undoing both the Reformation and the Enlightenment; small wonder that they treat him harshly!

16 P. 129, quoted from Spender's own contribution to *T. S. Eliot: the Man and his Work*, ed. Allen Tate, p. 46. There is an interesting parallel in a story told of Schumann, as reported in G. Steiner, *Heidegger*, p. 47: 'Asked ... this question [*sc.* 'What does it mean?''] of one of his compositions, Schumann played it again.'

17 The main lines of their thought are already clear in their earlier article 'Intention'. Two important subsequent works are the same authors' *The Verbal Icon* and Beardsley's *Aesthetics*, pp. 17–21 and 26–9. The latter is probably the clearest discussion of the issue available: see especially p. 18: 'We must distinguish between the aesthetic object and the intention in the mind of its creator.'

18 'Intention and Interpretation in Criticism', reprinted in *On Literary Intention*: the present point is on p. 57.

19 See 'Genesis: A Fallacy Revisited'; also in *On Literary Intention*,

pp. 116–38. See especially on p. 136: 'The statement in our essay of 1946 should certainly have read: "The design or intention of the author is neither available nor desirable as a standard for judging *either the meaning or the value* of a work of literary art" ' (my italics).

20 Eliot, commenting on a set of interpretations of *The Love-Song of J. Alfred Prufrock* by critics of a 'New Critical' stamp, wrote: '. . . the analysis of "Prufrock" was not an attempt to find origins, either in literature or in the darker recesses of my private life; it was an attempt to find out what the poem really meant – whether that was what I had meant it to mean or not ('Interpretations', in *On Poetry and Poets*). This exactly captures the mood of New Criticism. According to Erlich (see ch. 8, n. 16), Russian Formalism began from very similar presuppositions about literary meaning: 'They started from the premise – which to-day is widely accepted – that the literary scholar ought to address himself to the actual works of imaginative literature rather than, to quote Sir Sydney Lee, to the "external circumstances in which literature is produced" ' (*Russian Formalism*, p. 172).

21 P. 15; cited in Spender, *Eliot*, p. 74. The existence of a 'canon' of English or world literature has been hotly contested in literary circles in recent years. See esp. H. Bloom, *The Western Canon: The Books and School of the Ages*.

22 Cf. n. 2 above.

23 Cf. Barr, 'Reading the Bible as Literature', p. 24.

24 A rather misleading account of biblical criticism in this respect is provided by N. R. Petersen, *Literary Criticism for New Testament Critics*, which tends to speak as though there had been no contact at all between biblical criticism and 'literary' studies until the new methods of the last twenty years or so. The author achieves this conclusion by so defining 'literary criticism' that it excludes all but the most modern approaches, and on this basis it would be just as easy to show that there was no literary criticism *at all* until twenty years ago. Petersen is opposed to all 'historical' criticism in both biblical and secular literary studies, and I believe this results in his doing less than justice to the criticism of the past, in both spheres. Cf. also the rather intemperate rejection of much traditional biblical scholarship in J. F. A. Sawyer, *From Moses to Patmos*, pp. 8–11.

25 This is as true of form criticism, even though it does not think in terms of *individual* authors, as it is of source criticism: cf. the comments on Barr in *The Bible in the Modern World*, pp. 64–7.

CHAPTER 11: 'THE TEXT ITSELF'

1 16–22 February 1980, p. 69, announcing a talk by Laurens van der Post in a series called 'Shakespeare in Perspective'.

2 There is a very clear statement of this point in relation to biblical studies in M. Weiss, 'Die Methode der "Total-Interpretation" ', p. 91.

3 The leading names are Gottfried Menken (1768–1831) and J. C. K. von Hofmann (1810–77).

4 See *Old Testament Theology*.

5 See Cullmann, *Christ and Time*.

6 *Old Testament Theology* I, pp. 110–12; cf. also pp. 175–8.

7 Cf. also the same author with R. H. Fuller, *The Book of the Acts of God*, in which the first chapter is called 'The Biblical Point of View'. There are many telling criticisms of Wright's position in Barr, 'Story and History in Biblical Theology', p. 3, and *Old and New in Interpretation, passim*.

8 As we shall see later, there is some resemblance here to C. S. Lewis's view of literary art: cf. E. M. W. Tillyard and C. S. Lewis, *The Personal Heresy: A Controversy*.

9 Cf. Lewis, ibid., pp. 113–14: 'What the poet "says" must not be identified with the apparent (i.e. the grammatical) propositions in his poem. . . . What a poem "says" is the total, concrete experience it gives to the right reader.' There is a very full discussion of these issues in Kermode, *Genesis of Secrecy*, especially pp. 101–23.

10 There is a clear case of this reduction of Genesis 1 to its 'message' in the *New Bible Dictionary*, pp. 271–2. For a criticism of such interpretations see Barr, *Fundamentalism*, pp. 41–2, and *The Bible in the Modern World*, p. 172; and, already, von Rad, 'The Old Testament World View', p. 145. Cf. also above, p. 51.

11 Cf. above, pp. 91–2.

12 Barr, 'Reading the Bible as LIterature', p. 70, deals with this problem: how, he asks, do we decide which parts of the Bible are correctly classified as 'literature'? See also my article, 'Reading the Bible as Literature: Two Questions for Biblical Critics'.

13 There is an extended discussion of this point in Hirsch, *The Aims of Interpretation*, pp. 124–45.

14 There is a detailed discussion of these points, which here can only be briefly touched on, in F. W. Bateson, ' "Intention" and Blake's *Jerusalem*', Bateson's conclusion – 'The proper question to put is not "What did Blake mean?" but "What meaning did Blake succeed in conveying to the best of his early readers?" ' (p. 109) – undoubtedly raises as many problems as it solves.

15 Lewis falls into the psychologistic trap in *The Personal Heresy*, pp. 13ff. What he is discussing there is really a case of type (b) below – meaning that goes *beyond* intention.

16 Note, again, the extremes to which such propaganda can go in Petersen, *Literary Criticism for New Testament Critics*, where critics who are interested in intention are regarded as not 'literary' at all.

17 *Labyrinths*, p. 69.

18 On this sort of transcription see Hirsch, *Validity in Interpretation*, pp. 94–8, where there is a discussion of an important correspondence in the *Times Literary Supplement* for January and February 1965 concerning the

possibility of 'accidental' poems created by transcribing prose as if it were verse. See also Culler, *Structuralist Poetics*, pp. 161–4, and Barthes, *The Pleasure of the Text*, p. 11, for whom all reading constitutes a kind of creative transcription, an individual 'performance' of the text.

19 The distinction between meaning and significance is modelled on that between 'sense' and 'reference' in Frege's logic, but though this is a vital issue for modern philosophy, we need not go into it here; Hirsch uses the distinction in a transferred sense. See *Validity in Interpretation*, pp. 209–44, a chapter entitled 'Objective Interpretation', reprinted from *PMLA* 1960 and reprinted in turn in *On Literary Intention*, pp. 26–54.

20 *History of King Lear*, 1681; the text can be found in Montague Summers, *Shakespeare Adaptations*, pp. 175–254. Tate's *Lear* was the standard acting version of the play from the end of the seventeenth century until 1838, when the Fool was finally restored to the text, though it underwent various modifications from time to time.

21 Cf. Kermode, *Novel and Narrative*, p. 26: 'Barthes, against his will, has outlined a method for the formal definition of a classic' – which can be formulated as follows: a classic is a text which is always capable of being read in a new way, 'structured anew' in Kermode's terminology. The classic discussion of 'classics' in modern criticism is H. G. Gadamer, *Wahrheit und Methode*, pp. 269–75 (= *Truth and Method*, pp. 253–8).

CHAPTER 12: THE TEXT AND THE READER

1 For structuralists, a decisive breakthrough in Western literature came when writers became conscious of the artificiality of their own work. Barthes sees Flaubert as crucial: 'an art drawing attention to its very artificiality' (*Writing Degree Zero*, pp. 59–65).

2 *Structuralist Poetics*, p. 255, quoting Saussure. There is now a very large literature on structuralism and related theories. A brief guide is provided by the symposium 'Modern Literary Theory: Its Place in Teaching', *TLS* for February 1981, following a much-publicized debate in the English faculty at Cambridge; see also the works of Culler and Robey, already cited; *French Literary Theory: a Reader*, ed. T. Todorov; and *Structuralism: A Reader*, ed. M. Lane. For a particularly strong attack on structuralism see G. Strickland, *Structuralism or Criticism?*

3 Cf. above, ch. 8, n. 15.

4 *The Aims of Interpretation*, p. 157; cf. also p. 147.

5 Barthes, in the passage cited in n. 1 above, provides a particularly clear account of the transition from a 'classical' understanding of writing as *instrumental* to the modern concentration on writing as an activity in its own right.

6 On 'stylistics' as a branch of linguistic study, see S. Ullmann, *Semantics*, pp. 48–53 and 253–4; *Style in the French Novel*, Introduction. A useful introductory guide is G. W. Turner, *Stylistics*.

7 It should be said that this would not apply to 'post-structuralism'

and other movements within what, to the outsider, still looks like the structuralist camp: see Culler, *Pursuit of Signs*, for further details. On this, see ch. 13 below.

8 See Culler, *Structuralist Poetics*, pp. 131–3, with special reference to J. Derrida, *Marges de la philosophie*.

9 This sort of approach has been associated with the journal *Tel Quel*, and with the structuralist or 'post-structuralist' writers Julia Kristeva, Jacques Derrida and Michel Foucault.

10 Kermode, *Genesis of Secrecy*, p. 72, speaks of 'the French utopians . . . condemning the desire for order, for closure, a relic of bourgeois bad faith'. He continues, 'but this is an announcement of revolutionary aims: they intend to change what is the case'.

11 Kermode's lecture *Novel and Narrative* has some fascinating remarks about certain medieval writers who could be seen as forerunners of structuralism in a similar way: for example, the author of the *Chanson de Roland*, and Chrétien de Troyes, who do not seem to feel our need for consistent temporal succession or for closure (the 'sense of an ending'; the title of another of Kermode's books). He draws attention to the discussions in E. Vinaver, *The Rise of Romance*, pp. 5–16. In the *Roland*, Kermode notes, 'Roland dies three times, almost as if in a novel by M. Robbe-Grillet' (*Novel and Narrative*, p. 7).

12 There is a very clear example of this in D. and A. Patte, *Structural Exegesis*, p. 77, where Mark's attitude to political matters is deduced by constructing a highly formalistic 'semiotic square' but is then modified to fit intuitions about the 'themes' of the gospel in general, in a quite traditional, harmonizing way.

13 Cf. pp. 181–2 above.

14 On genre cf. Kermode, *Genesis of Secrecy*, p. 162; Hirsch, *Validity in Interpretation*, pp. 102–11.

15 Kermode's *The Sense of an Ending* is now classic on this point; cf. also his comments in *Genesis of Secrecy*, pp. 53–5 and 60–72.

16 *The Personal Heresy*, pp. 12–15. Closely related points are made in Lewis's essay 'The English Prose *Morte*'.

17 *The Personal Heresy*, p. 14.

18 Ibid., p. 15.

19 Ibid., p. 16. In other moods, Lewis might well have sought to exclude the 'new colours' which the artist neither foresaw nor intended.

20 Tillyard gently rebukes Lewis for this (p. 31). Lewis had cited 'an ambiguous passage from T. S. Eliot' as supporting 'the personal heresy', but (as Tillyard says) Eliot's 'Tradition and the Individual Talent' represents an uncompromising attack on any such psychologistic theory. Tillyard clearly regards Eliot and Lewis *alike* as modernizers, probably doomed to rapid extinction; but he was certainly quite right to see it as extraordinary to cite Eliot, of all people, as an example of a prevalent interest in authors' personalities instead of in their works!

21 Kermode's closest affinities, as he says himself, are with the work of

Austin Farrer. See especially A. M. Farrer, *A Study in St Mark*; *St Matthew and St Mark*; *A Rebirth of Images*; *The Revelation of St John the Divine*. See Kermode's comments, *Genesis of Secrecy*, pp. 62 and 70–2.

22 *Genesis of Secrecy*, p. 80. Much of Kermode's own work is characterized by a non-ideological use of structuralist approaches. Cf. also the work of David Lodge, as exemplified by his collection *Working with Structuralism*, whose atmosphere is summed up in the title of Graham Hough's review in the *TLS*, June 1981: 'Just a *soupçon* of Paris'. A recent study which strikes a balance between establishing the conventions of biblical literature and analysing the conscious art in it is R. Alter, *The Art of Biblical Narrative* (see next chapter).

CHAPTER 13: THE READER IN THE TEXT

1 This title is taken from Susan R. Suleiman and I. Crosman (eds.), *The Reader in the Text: Essays on Audience and Interpretation*.
2 James Muilenburg, 'Form Criticism and Beyond'.
3 See *The Postmodern Bible* by The Bible and Culture Collective, p. 150.
4 J. Muilenberg, 'The Book of Isaiah: Chapters 40–66', *Interpreter's Bible* 5.
5 P. Trible, *Rhetorical Criticism: Context, Method, and the Book of Jonah* (Guides to Biblical Scholarship). See also D. Patrick and A. Scult, *Rhetoric and Biblical Interpretation*.
6 See, for example, J. Barton, *Amos' Oracles against the Nations*; 'History and Rhetoric in the Prophets', in *Bible as Rhetoric: Studies in Biblical Persuasion and Credibility*, ed. Martin Warner, Warwick Studies in Philosophy and Literature, pp. 51–64.
7 See Trible, *Rhetorical Criticism*; J. Magonet, *Form and Meaning: Studies in Literary Technique in the Book of Jonah*; Y. Gitay, *Prophecy and Persuasion: A Study of Isaiah 40–48*.
8 Frank Kermode and Michael Payne, *Poetry, Narrative, History: The Bucknell Lectures in Literary Theory*, pp. 70–1.
9 Quoted in Elizabeth Freund, *The Return of the Reader: Reader–response Criticism* (New Accent series), p. 79.
10 M. Sternberg, *The Poetics of Biblical Narrative: Ideological Literature and the Drama of Reading*, p. xi.
11 See R. Alter and F. Kermode (eds.), *The Literary Guide to the Bible*, p. 111 – earning him the disdain of the authors of *The Postmodern Bible* (a fairly disdainful group of people, it must be said).
12 Alter, *The Art of Biblical Narrative*, pp. 47–62. The term 'type-scene' is borrowed from Homeric studies.
13 Ibid, pp. 3–13.
14 Midrash Genesis Rabba 84:11, 12.
15 Alter, *Art of Biblical Narrative*, p. 11.
16 Cf. also S. Bar-Efrat, *Narrative Art in the Bible*, and H. Fisch, *Poetry with a Purpose*.

17 Sternberg, *Poetics*, p. 42.
18 This discussion depends heavily on the work of H. P. Grice and his theories of 'implicature' in conversations. I am grateful to Anita Matthews for introducing me to Grice's work.
19 See H. P. Grice, 'Logic and Conversation'.
20 See above, p. 127.
21 Freund, *Return of the Reader*, p. 5.
22 See H. R. Jauss, 'Literary History as a Challenge to Literary Theory'.
23 See W. Iser, *The Implied Reader*; *The Act of Reading*. There is a very helpful discussion of Iser, his rivals, and his critics, in A. C. Thiselton, *New Horizons in Hermeneutics: The Theory and Practice of Transforming Biblical Reading*, pp. 515–23.
24 Fish's best-known work is probably *Is there a Text in this Class? The Authority of Interpretive Communities*.
25 See, for example, Susan Wittig, 'A theory of Multiple Meanings'; Jouette Bassler, 'The Parable of the Loaves'.
26 See D. J. A Clines, 'A World Established in Water' and F. O. García-Treto, 'A Reader Response Approach to Prophetic Conflict: The Case of Amos 7:10–17', in J. C. Exum and D. J. A. Clines (eds.), *The New Literary Criticism and the Hebrew Bible*, pp. 79–90 and 114–24 respectively.
27 A. Camus, *The Plague*; tr. of *La Peste*.

CHAPTER 14: THEORY AND TEXTUALITY

1 I have borrowed this use of Enoch's words from James Barr, 'Jewish Apocalyptic in Recent Scholarly Study'.
2 This word represents Derrida's famous pun on the two verbs *différer*, one of which means 'to differ' and gives the noun *différence*, while the other means 'to defer' and yields *différance* (same pronunciation). The importance of *difference* in understanding both language and literature derives from Saussure – see above, pp. 106–9 – and Derrida is playing with this idea to make a quite non-Saussurean point.
3 Quoted on p. 121 above as the epigraph to chapter 9.
4 Terry Eagleton, *Literary Theory: An Introduction*, p. 146.
5 London 1975.
6 Compare the comments of R. Tallis in his splendidly named *Not Saussure: A Critique of Post-Saussurian Literary Theory*.
7 R. Barthes, 'Wrestling with the Angel: Textual Analysis of Genesis 32:23–33', in R. Barthes, *The Semiotic Challenge*. See the discussion in *The Postmodern Bible*, pp. 132–5.
8 Jonathan Culler, *On Deconstruction: Theory and Practice after Structuralism*, p. 86.
9 Culler, ibid., p. 133.
10 J. D. Crossan, *Raid on the Inarticulate: Cosmic Eschatology in Jesus and Borges*.
11 K. J. Dell, *The Book of Job as Sceptical Literature*.

12 *Hamlet, Prince of Denmark*, Act 1, Scene 2; 2 Kings 5:12–14.
13 Goulder, *Midrash and Lection in Matthew*.

CONCLUSION

1 See the Introductory Chapter, 'Orientation of Critical Theories'. I have discussed Abrams' theory in my article, 'Classifying Biblical Criticism'.
2 Culler, *Pursuit of Signs*, pp. 1–17.
3 In this connection it is interesting that Childs (*Introduction*, p. 131), Sanders (*Torah and Canon*, p. 53) and Clines (*Theme of the Pentateuch*) broadly agree on what the 'canonical meaning' or 'theme' of the whole Pentateuch is: the fact that God made promises to the patriarchs, but that they were only *partially* fulfilled by the time of Moses' death. All of these scholars see the fact that the Torah ends with Deuteronomy, not Joshua, as significant: there is some meaning in the 'decision' that there should be a Pentateuch, not a Hexateuch. They differ somewhat in what *kind* of meaning they think this is – intended or simply inherent in the text, a matter of how Israel's history was being understood in various periods or a matter only of how the text can be read, once its boundaries have been established; but they agree on *what* the meaning is.
4 Cf. C. Radford and S. Minogue, *The Nature of Criticism*, for an extended examination of the status of criticism which shows many points of agreement with the argument of the present book. In particular they argue that criticism is not a science, but that this does not mean that it can never arrive at truth. The thesis that criticism is *neither* scientific *nor* merely subjective is always difficult to defend, because it posits a third type of mental activity where much discussion assumes there can be only two. See also the classic essay by Isaiah Berlin, 'The Divorce between the Sciences and the Humanities'.

BIBLIOGRAPHY

Abrams, M. H., *The Mirror and the Lamp: Romantic Theory and the Critical Tradition.* New York 1953.

Ackroyd, P. R., *Exile and Restoration.* London 1968.

—, 'History and Theology in the Writings of the Chronicler', *Concordia Theological Monthly* 28 (1967).

—, 'The Theology of the Chronicler', *Lexington Theological Quarterly* 8 (1973), pp. 101–16.

Alt, A., *Die Ursprünge des israelitischen Rechts.* Leipzig 1934 = 'The Origins of Israelite Law' in *Essays on Old Testament History and Religion* (Oxford 1966), pp. 79–132.

Alter, R., *The Art of Biblical Narrative.* London and Sydney 1981.

Alter, R., and Kermode, F., *The Literary Guide to the Bible,* London 1987.

Analyse structurale et exégèse biblique, ed. R. Barthes, F. Bovon and others. Neuchâtel 1971 = *Structural Analysis and Biblical Exegesis.* Pittsburgh 1974.

Ancient Near Eastern Texts, ed. J. B. Pritchard. Princeton 1969.

Baltzer, K., *Das Bundesformular,* WMANT 4, second edn 1964 = *The Covenant Formulary.* Oxford 1971.

Bar-Efrat, R., *Narrative Art in the Bible,* Sheffield 1989.

Barr, J., 'Bibelkritik als theologische Aufklärung' in *Glaube und Toleranz: Das theologische Erbe der Aufklärung,* ed. T. Rendtorff (Gütersloh 1982), pp. 30–42.

—, *The Bible in the Modern World.* London 1973.

—, 'Childs' Introduction to the Old Testament as Scripture', *JSOT* 16 (1980), pp. 12–23.

—, *Comparative Philology and the Text of the Old Testament.* Oxford 1968.

—, *Fundamentalism.* London 1977, second edn. 1981.

—, 'The Fundamentalist Understanding of Scripture', *Concilium* (1980), pp. 70–4.

—, *Holy Scripture: Canon, Authority, Criticism.* Oxford and Philadelphia 1983.

—, 'Jewish Apocalyptic in Recent Scholarly Study', *BJRL* 58 (1975), pp. 9–35.

Old and New in Interpretation. London 1966.

—, 'Reading the Bible as Literature', *BJRL* 56 (1973), pp. 10–33.

—, 'Revelation Through History in the Old Testament and in Modern Theology', *Interpretation* 17 (1963), pp. 193–205.

—, 'Story and History in Biblical Theology', *JR* 56 (1976), pp. 1–17; reprinted in *The Scope and Authority of the Bible* (*Explorations in Theology* 7), London 1980.

—, *The Semantics of Biblical Language.* Oxford 1961.

Barthes, R., 'La lutte avec l'ange: analyse textuelle de Genèse 32.23–33' in *Analyse structurale et exégèse biblique*, q.v., pp. 27–40.

—, *Le plaisir du texte.* Paris 1975 = *The Pleasure of the Text.* New York and London 1976.

—, *Sur Racine.* Paris 1963 = *On Racine.* New York 1964.

—, *Système de la mode.* Paris 1967.

—, *S/Z.* Paris 1970

—, *Le degré zéro de l'écriture.* Paris 1953 = *Writing Degree Zero.* London 1967.

—, 'Wrestling with the Angel: Textual Analysis of Genesis 32:23–33' in R. Barthes, *The Semiotic Challenge* (New York 1988), pp. 246–60.

Barton, J., *Amos' Oracles against the Nations* (Society for Old Testament Studies monograph series 6), Cambridge 1980.

—, 'Classifying Biblical Criticism'. *JSOT* 29 (1984), pp. 19–35.

—, 'History and Rhetoric in the Prophets', in *The Bible as Rhetoric: Studies in Biblical Persuasion and Credibility* (Warwick Studies in Philosophy and Literature), ed. M. Warner (London and New York 1990), pp. 51–64.

—, 'Reading the Bible as Literature: Two Questions for Biblical Critics', *Journal of Literature and Theology* 1 (1987), pp. 135–53.

—, 'Reflections on Cultural Relativism', *Theology* 82 (1979), pp. 103–9 and 191–9.

—, 'Wellhausen's *Prolegomena to the History of Israel*: Influences and Effects', in *Text and Experience: Towards a Cultural Exegesis of the Bible*, ed. D. Smith-Christopher (Sheffield 1995), pp. 316–29.

Barucq, A. 'Quohéléth' in *Supplément au dictionnaire de la bible* 50B (Paris 1977), pp. 609–74.

Bassler, J., 'The Parable of the Loaves', *JR* 66 (1986), pp. 157–72.

Bateson, F. W., ' "Intention" and Blake's *Jerusalem*', *Essays in Criticism* 2 (1952), pp. 105–14.

Beardsley, M. C., *Aesthetics: Problems in the Philosophy of Criticism*, New York 1958.

Beauchamp, P., 'L'analyse structurale et l'exégèse biblique', VTS 22 (1972), pp. 113–28.

—, *Création et séparation.* Paris 1969.

Bennett, T., *Formalism and Marxism.* London 1979.

Bentley, E. C., *Trent's Last Case.* London 1929.

Berger, P., *The Social Reality of Religion.* London 1964 = *The Sacred Canopy.* New York 1967.

Berlin, I., 'The Divorce Between the Sciences and the Humanities' (Second Tykociner Memorial Lecture). Chicago 1974; reprinted in *Against the Current: Essays in the History of Ideas*, ed. H. Hardy. London 1979.

Beyerlin, W., *Religionsgeschichtliches Textbuch zum Alten Testament.* Göttingen

1975 = *New Eastern Religious Texts Relating to the Old Testament.* London 1978.

Bible and Culture Collective, The, *The Postmodern Bible*, Yale 1995.

Birkeland, H., *Zum hebräischen Traditionswesen.* Oslo 1938.

Bleek, F., *Einleitung in das Alte Testament*, 4th edn. Berlin 1878.

Blenkinsopp, J., 'A New Kind of Introduction: Professor Childs' *Introduction to the Old Testament as Scripture*', *JSOT* 16 (1980), pp. 24–7.

Bloom, H., *The Western Canon: The Books and School of the Ages*, London 1994.

Boecker, H. J., *Redeformen des Rechtslebens im Alten Testament*, 2nd edn. Neukirchen 1970.

Borges, J. L. 'Pierre Menard, Author of the Quixote' in *Labyrinths* (London 1970), pp. 62–71. Originally published in *Sur* 1939, later in *Ficciones* (Buenos Aires 1956) and in English in *Ficciones*, ed. and tr. A. Kerrigan. London 1962.

Bornkamm, G., with Barth, G., and Held, H. J., *Tradition and Interpretation in Matthew.* London and New York 1963.

Brueggemann, W., and Wolff, H. W., *The Vitality of Old Testament Traditions.* Atlanta 1975.

Camus, A., *The Plague*, London 1948; tr, of *La Peste*, Paris 1947.

Canon and Authority, ed. G. W. Coats and B. O. Long. Philadelphia 1977.

Carroll, R. P., *From Chaos to Covenant: Uses of Prophecy in the Book of Jeremiah.* London 1981.

Carter, Angela, *The Bloody Chamber.* London 1979.

Cassuto, U., *A Commentary on the Book of Genesis. Part II: From Noah to Abraham.* Jerusalem 1964 (Hebrew original 1949).

—, *The Documentary Hypothesis and the Composition of the Pentateuch.* Jerusalem 1961 (Hebrew original 1941).

Cazelles, H., 'The Canonical Approach to Torah and Prophets', *JSOT* 16, (1980), pp. 28–31.

Childs, B. S., *Biblical Theory in Crisis.* Philadelphia 1970.

—, *Biblical Theology of the Old and New Testament: Theological Reflections on the Christian Bible*, London 1992.

—, 'The Canonical Shape of the Prophetic Literature', *Interpretation* 32 (1978), pp. 46–68.

—, 'The Exegetical Significance of Canon for the Study of the Old Testament', VTS 29 (1978), pp. 66–80.

—, *Exodus.* Philadelphia and London 1974.

—, 'Interpretation in Faith: the Theological Responsibility of an Old Testament Commentary', *Interpretation* 18 (1964), pp. 432–49.

—, *Introduction to the Old Testament as Scripture.* Philadephia and London 1979.

—, 'The Old Testament as Scripture', *Concordia Theological Monthly* 43 (1972), pp. 709–22.

—, *Old Testament Theology in a Canonical Context*, London 1985.

—, 'Response to Reviewers of *Introduction to the OT as Scripture*', *JSOT* 16 (1980), pp. 52–60.

—, 'The Sensus Literalis of Scripture: an Ancient and Modern Problem' in *Beiträge zur Alttestamentlichen Theologie: Festschrift für Walther Zimmerli zum 70. Geburtstag*, ed. H. Donner, R. Hanhart and R. Smend (Göttingen 1977), pp. 80–93.

Christie, Agatha, *The Murder of Roger Ackroyd*. London 1926.

Cioffi, F., 'Intention and Interpretation in Criticism', *Proceedings of the Aristotelian Society* 64 (1963–4), pp. 85–106; reprinted in *On Literary Intention*, q.v., pp. 55–73.

Clark, W. M., 'Law', in *Old Testament Form Criticism*, q.v., pp. 99–139.

Clements, R. E., *A Century of Old Testament Study*. Guildford and London 1976.

—, *Deuteronomy* (Old Testament Guides), Sheffield 1987.

—, 'Patterns in the Prophetic Canon' in *Canon and Authority*, q.v., pp. 42–55.

Clines, D. J. A., *The Theme of the Pentateuch*, JSOTS 11. Sheffield 1978.

—, 'A World established in Water', in *The New Literary Criticism and the Hebrew Bible*, q.v., pp. 79–90.

Conzelmann, H., *Die Mitte der Zeit: Studien zur Theologie des Lukas*, BHTh 17, Tübingen 1954; second edn 1960 = *The Theology of St Luke*. London 1960.

Crossan, J. D., *Raid on the Inarticulate: Cosmic Eschatology in Jesus and Borges*, New York 1976.

Culler, J., 'The Linguistic Basis of Structuralism', in *Stucturalism: an Introduction*, q.v., pp. 20–36.

—, *On Deconstruction: Theory and Practice after Structuralism*, London 1983.

—, *The Pursuit of Signs: Semiotics, Literature, Deconstruction*. London and Henley 1981.

—, *Structuralist Poetics*. London 1975.

Culley, R. C., *Studies in the Strtucture of Hebrew Narrative*. Philadelphia and Missoula, Mont., 1976.

Cullmann, O., *Christus und die Zeit*. Zurich 1950 = *Christ and Time: The Primitive Christian Conception of Time and History*. London 1951.

Davidson, R., and Leaney, A. R. C., *Biblical Criticism* (Pelican Guide to Modern Theology vol. iii). London 1970.

Delitzsch, F., *Hoheslied und Koheleth* (Biblischer Commentar iv:4) Leipzig 1875 = *Commentary on the Song of Songs and Ecclesiastes*. Edinburgh 1877.

Dell, K. J., *The Book of Job as Sceptical Literature* (BZAW 197), Berlin 1991.

Derrida, J., *Marges de la philosophie*. Paris 1972.

Driver, S. R., *The Book of Genesis*, sixth edn. London 1907.

Eagleton, T., *Criticism and Ideology: A Study in Marxist Literary Theory*. London 1976.

—, *Literary Theory: An Introduction*, Oxford 1983.

Eaton, J. H., 'The Psalms and Israelite Worship' in *Tradition and Interpretation*, q.v., pp. 238–73.

Ebeling, G., 'The Significance of the Critical Historical Method for Church and Theology in Protestantism' in *Word and Faith*. Philadelphia 1963.

Eco, U., 'Social Life as a Sign System' in *Structuralism: an Introduction*, q.v., pp. 57–72.

—, *A Theory of Semiotics*. Bloomington 1976.

Eliot, T. S., *On Poetry and Poets*. London 1957.

—, 'Tradition and the Individual Talent' in *Selected Essays*. London 1932.

—, *The Waste Land*. London 1922; reprinted in *The Complete Poems and Plays of T. S. Eliot*. London 1969.

Engnell, I., *Gamla Testamentet: En traditionshistorisk Inledning*. Stockholm 1945.

—, 'The Pentateuch' in *Critical Essays on the Old Testament* (London 1970), pp. 50–67.

Erlich, V., *Russian Formalism: History – Doctrine*. The Hague 1955, fourth edn 1980.

Farrer, A. M., *A Rebirth of Images*. London 1950.

—, *The Revelation of St John the Divine*. Oxford 1964.

—, *St Matthew and St Mark*. London 1954.

—, *A Study in St Mark*. London 1951.

Fisch, H., *Poetry with a Purpose*, Bloomington 1988.

Fish, S., *Is there a Text in this Class? The Authority of Interpretive Communities*, Cambridge, Mass. 1980.

Forrest-Thomson, V., *Poetic Artifice: A Theory of Twentieth Century Poetry*. Oxford 1974.

Fowles, John, *The Ebony Tower*. London 1974.

—, *The French Lieutenant's Woman*. London 1969.

—, *The Magus*. London 1966, second edn 1977.

Frankena, H., 'The Vassal-Treaties of Esarhaddon and the Dating of Deuteronomy', *OS* 14 (1965), pp. 122–54.

Frei, H. W., *The Eclipse of Biblical Narrative: A Study in Eighteenth and Nineteenth Century Hermeneutics*. New Haven and London 1974.

Freund, E., *The Return of the Reader: Reader-response Criticism* (New Accent series), London and New York 1987.

Frye, R. M., 'A Literary Perspective for the Criticism of the Gospels' in *Jesus and Man's Hope, Pittsburgh Festival on the Gospels* vol ii (Pittsburgh 1971), pp. 194ff.

—, *Perspective on Man: Literature and the Christian Tradition*. Philadelphia 1961

Gadamer, H. G., *Wahrheit und Methode*. Tübingen 1960 = *Truth and Method*. New York 1975.

Galling, K., 'Kohelet-Studien', *ZAW* 50 (1932), pp. 276ff.

—, 'Der Prediger' in *Die fünf Megilloth* (HAT 1:18) (Tübingen 1940, second edn 1969), pp. 73–125.

—, 'Stand und Aufgabe der Kohelet-Forschung', *ThR* NF 9 (1934), pp. 355ff.

García-Treto, F. O., 'A Reader Response Approach to Prophetic Conflict: The Case of Amos 7:10–17', in *The New Literary Criticism and the Hebrew Bible*, q.v., pp. 114–24.

Gardner, H., *The New Oxford Book of English Verse*. Oxford 1972.

Gelin, A., 'La question des "relectures" bibliques à l'intérieur d'une tradition vivante', *Sacra Pagina* 1 (1959) (*Proceedings of the International Catholic Congress of Biblical Studies, Bruxelles-Louvain 1958*), pp. 303–15.

Gemser, B., 'The Rib- or Controversy Pattern in Hebrew Mentality', in *Wisdom in Israel and in the Ancient Near East*, q.v.

Genette, G., *Figures* ii. Paris 1969.

Gerstenberger, B., 'Psalms' in *Old Testament Form Criticism*, pp. 179–223.

Gilkey, L., 'Cosmology, Ontology, and the Travail of Biblical Language', *JR* 41 (1961), pp. 194–205.

Gitay, Y., *Prophecy and Persuasion: A Study of Isaiah 40–48*, Bonn 1981.

Good, E. M. *Irony in the Old Testament*. London 1965.

Gordis, R., *Qoheleth: the Man and his World* (*Texts and Studies of the Jewish Theological Seminary of America* 19). New York 1951.

Goulder, M. D., *Midrash and Lection in Matthew*. London 1974.

Greimas, A. J., *Sémantique structurale*. Paris 1966.

Grice, H. P., 'Logic and Conversation', in *Syntax and Semantics* 3: Speech-Acts, ed. P. Cole and J. L. Morgan (New York 1975), pp. 41–58.

Gunkel, H., *Ausgewählte Psalmen*. Göttingen 1904.

—, *Einleitung in die Psalmen*. Göttingen 1933.

—, *Die Psalmen* (HKAT 14). Göttingen 1929 (fifth edn 1968).

—, 'Psalmen' in *Die Religion in Geschichte und Gegenwart* vol iv (1913), cols. 1927–49, rev. 1927 and tr. as *The Psalms*. Philadelphia 1967.

Gunn, D. M., *The Story of King David: Genre and Interpretation*, JSOTS 6. Sheffield 1978.

Habel, N. C., *Literary Criticism of the Old Testament* (*Guides to Biblical Scholarship* Old Testament Series). Philadelphia 1971.

Hanson, R. P. C., *Allegory and Event: A Study of the Sources and Significance of Origen's Interpretation of Scripture*. London 1959.

Harrison, R. K., *Introduction to the Old Testament*. Grand Rapids, Mich., 1969 and London 1970.

Hengel, M., *Judentum and Hellenismus: Wissenschaftliche Untersuchungen zum Neuen Testament*, second edn. Tübingen 1973 = *Judaism and Hellenism*. London 1974.

Hirsch Jr, E. D. *The Aims of Interpretation*. Chicago and London 1976.

—, *Validity in Interpretation*. New Haven and London 1967.

l'Hour, J., 'L'alliance de Sichem', *RB* 69 (1962), pp. 5–36, 161–84 and 350–68.

Hughes, J., *Secrets of the Times: Myth and History in Biblical Chronology*, Oxford 1990.

Hulme, T. E., *Speculations*, ed. Herbert Read. London 1924.

Iser, W., *The Act of Reading*, London 1978.

—, *The Implied Reader*, Baltimore 1974.

Jauss, H. R., 'Literary History as a Challenge to Literary Theory', in *New Directions in Literary Theory*, ed. R. Cohen, London 1974.

Jobling, D., *The Sense of Biblical Narrative. Three Structural Analyses in the Old Testament*, JSOTS 7. Sheffield 1978.

Johnson, M. D., *The Purpose of the Biblical Genealogies*, Cambridge 1969.

Johnson, Samuel, *The Vanity of Human Wishes* in the *Yale Edition of the Works of Samuel Johnson*, ed. B. L. McAdam Jr. and G. Milne, vol. vi. New Haven and London 1964.

Jones, D. R., 'The *Traditio* of the Oracles of Isaiah of Jerusalem', *ZAW* 67 (1955), pp. 226–46.

Kaiser, O., *Einleitung in das Alte Testament*. Gütersloh 1969, rev. 1973 = *Introduction to the Old Testament*. Oxford 1975.

Kermode, F., *The Genesis of Secrecy*. Cambridge, Mass., and London 1979.

—, *How We Read Novels*. Southampton 1975.

—, *Novel and Narrative*. Glasgow 1972.

—, *The Sense of an Ending*, New York 1966.

Kermode, F., and Payne, M., *Poetry, Narrative, History: The Bucknell Lectures in Literary Theory*, Oxford 1990.

Kirkpatrick, A. F., *The Psalms*. Cambridge 1902.

Kittel, B., 'Brevard Childs' Development of the Canonical Approach', *JSOT* 16 (1980), pp. 2–11.

Kittel, R., *Geschichte des Volkes Israel*. Gotha 1902.

Klatt, W., *Hermann Gunkel, zu seiner Theologie der Religionsgeschichte und zur Entstehung der formgeschichtlichen Methode*. Göttingen 1969.

Kline, M. G., 'Canon and Covenant', *Westminster Theological Journal* 32 (1969).

—, *Treaty of the Great King: The Covenant Structure of Deuteronomy*. Grand Rapids, Mich., 1963.

Koch, K., *Was ist Formgeschichte?* Neukirchen 1964, second edn 1967 = *The Growth of the Biblical Tradition*. London 1969.

Köhler, L., *Der hebräische Mensch*. Tübingen 1953 = *Hebrew Man*. Nashville, Tenn., 1956.

Kraus, H.-J., *Geschichte der historisch-kritischen Erforschung des Alten Testaments von der Reformation bis zur Gegenwart*. Neukirchen, second, rev. edn 1969.

—, *Gottesdienst in Israel*. Munich 1954, second edn 1962 = *Worship in Israel* Oxford 1966.

Landes, G. M., 'The Canonical Approach to Introducing the Old Testament: Prodigy and Problems', *JSOT* 16 (1980), pp. 32–9.

Lash, N., *Theology on Dover Beach*. London 1979.

Lauha, A., *Kohelet* (BK). Neukirchen-Vluyn 1978.

Leach, E., 'Structuralism in Social Anthropology' in *Structuralism: an Introduction*, q.v., pp. 37–56.

Leiman, S. Z., *The Canonization of Hebrew Scripture: The Talmudic and Midrashic Evidence*. Hamden, Conn. 1976.

Lentricchia, F., *After the New Criticism*. London 1980.

Lewis, C. S., 'The English Prose *Morte*' in *Essays on Malory* (Oxford 1963), pp. 7–28.

Loader, J. A., *Polar Structures in the Book of Qohelet*, BZAW 152 (1979).

Lodge, D., *Working with Structuralism*. London 1981.

Lohfink, N., *Kohelet* (Die neue Echter Bibel). Würzburg 1980.

Lubac, H. de, *Exégèse médiévale: les quatre sens de l'écriture*. Paris 1959–64.

279

Lyons, J., *Introduction to Theoretical Linguistics*. Cambridge 1968
—, *Semantics*, vol. i. Cambridge 1977.
—, 'Structuralism and Linguistics' in *Structuralism: an Introduction*, q.v., pp. 5–19.
McCarthy, D. J., *Old Testament Covenant*. Oxford 1972.
McKane, W., *Proverbs* (OTL). London 1970.
McNeile, A. H., *An Introduction to Ecclesiastes*. Cambridge 1904.
Magonet, J., *Form and Meaning: Studies in Literary Technique in the Book of Jonah*, Sheffield 1983.
Martin-Achard, R., 'Un exégète devant Genèse 32:23–33' in *Analyse structurale et exégèse biblique*, q.v., pp. 41–62.
Marxsen, W., *Der Evangelist Markus*. Göttingen 1956 = *Mark the Evangelist*. Nashville, Tenn., and New York 1969.
Mayes, A. D. H., *Deuteronomy* (New Century Bible). London 1979.
Mendenhall, G. E., *Law and Covenant in Israel and the Ancient Near East*. Pittsburgh 1955.
'Modern Literary Theory: Its Place in Teaching', *TLS*, February 1981.
Moran, W. L., 'The Ancient Near Eastern Background of the Love of God in Deuteronomy', *CBQ* 25 (1963), pp. 77–87.
Mowinckel, S., 'Die Komposition des Jesjabuches Kap. 1–39', AcOr(L) 11 (1933), pp. 267ff.
—, *Offersang og Sangoffer*. Oslo 1951 = *The Psalms in Israel's Worship*. Oxford 1962.
—, *Psalmenstudien* i–vi. Oslo 1921–4.
—, *Studien zu dem Buche Ezra-Nehemia*, SNVAO ii, NS 3, 5 and 7. Oslo 1964–5.
Muilenberg, J., 'Form Criticism and Beyond', *JBL* 88 (1969), pp. 1–18.
—, 'The Book of Isaiah: Chapters 40–66', *Interpreter's Bible* 5 (New York 1956), pp. 381–419 and 433–773.
Murphy, R. E., 'The Old Testament as Scripture', *JSOT* 16 (1980), pp. 40–4.
Myers, J. M., 'The Kerygma of the Chronicler', *Interpretation* 20 (1966), pp. 259–73.
New Bible Commentary, second edn. London 1954.
New Bible Commentary Revised, ed. D. Guthrie and J. A. Motyer. London 1970.
New Bible Dictionary. London 1962.
New Horizons in Linguistics, ed. J. Lyons. London 1970.
New Literary Criticism and the Hebrew Bible, The, ed. J. C. Exum and D. J. A. Clines. Sheffield 1993.
Nicholson, E. W., *Deuteronomy and Tradition*. Oxford 1967.
—, *Preaching to the Exiles: A Study of the Prose Tradition in the Book of Jeremiah*. Oxford 1970.
Nielsen, E., *Oral Tradition: a Modern Problem in Old Testament Introduction* (SBTh 1:11). London 1954.
Nielsen, K., *Yahweh as Prosecutor and Judge*, JSOTS 9. Sheffield 1978.

Noth, M., *Überlieferungsgeschichtliche Studien I*, Schriften der Königsberger Gelehrten Gesellschaft 18 (1943), pp. 43–266; second edn (Tübingen 1957), pp.1–110 = *The Deuteronomistic History*, JSOTS 15. Sheffield 1981.

—, *Überlieferungsgeschichte des Pentateuch.* Stuttgart 1948 = *A History of Pentateuchal Traditions.* Englewood Cliffs, N. J., 1972.

Nyberg, H. S., *Studien zum Hoseabuch.* Uppsala 1935.

Nyirö L., 'The Russian Formalist School' in *Literature and its Interpretation*, ed. L. Nyirö (The Hague, Paris and New York 1980), pp. 7–68.

Oesterley, W. O. E., *The Psalms.* London 1939.

Old Testament Form Criticism, ed. J. H. Hayes. San Antonio, Tex., 1974.

Olrik, A., 'Epische Gesetze der Volksdichtung', *Zeitschrift für deutsches Altertum* 51 (1909), pp. 1–12 = 'The Epic Laws of Folk Narrative' in *The Study of Folklore*, ed. A. Dundas (Englewood Cliffs, N. J., 1965), pp. 129–141.

On Literary Intention, ed. D. Newton-de Molina. Edinburgh 1976.

Patrick, D., and Scult, A., *Rhetoric and Biblical Interpretation*, Sheffield 1990.

Patte, D., *What is Structural Exegesis?* Philadelphia 1976.

Patte, D., and Patte, A., *Structural Exegesis: from Theory to Practice.* Philadelphia 1978.

Peake's Commentary on the Bible, ed. M. Black. London 1962.

Perlitt, L., *Bundestheologie im Alten Testament*, WMANT 36, 1969.

Perrin, N., *What is Redaction Criticism?* (*Guides to Biblical Scholarship*, New Testament Series). Philadelphia and London 1970.

Petersen, N. R., *Literary Criticism for New Testament Critics* (*Guides to Biblical Scholarship*, New Testament Series). Philadelphia 1978.

Pocock, G., *Corneille and Racine: Problems of Tragic Form.* Cambridge 1973.

Polzin, R. M., *Biblical Structuralism: Method and Subjectivity in the Study of Ancient Texts.* Philadelphia and Missoula, Mont., 1977.

Porter, J. R., 'Old Testament Historiography' in *Tradition and Interpretation*, q.v., pp. 125–62.

Propp, V., *Morfologija skazki.* Leningrad 1928 = *Morphology of the Folktale*, second edn. Austin, Tex., 1968.

Quiller-Couch, A., *Oxford Book of English Verse.* London 1900.

Rad, G. von, 'The Beginnings of Historical Writing in Ancient Israel' in *The Problem of the Hexateuch*, q.v. = *Archiv für Kulturgeschichte* 32 (Weimar 1944), pp. 1–42.

—, *Das formgeschichtliche Problem des Hexateuch*, BWANT IV: 13. Stuttgart 1934. Also in *Gesammelte Studien zum Alten Testament.* Munich 1958 = 'The Form-critical Problem of the Hexateuch' in *The Problem of the Hexateuch and other essays*, q.v.

—, *Das erste Buch Mose, Genesis.* Göttingen 1956 = *Genesis* (OTL). London 1961, rev. edn. 1963.

—, *Das Geschichtsbild des chronistischen Werkes*, BWANT 55 (1930).

—, *Theologie des Alten Testaments*, 2 vols. Munich 1957 and 1962 = *Old Testament Theology*, 2 vols. Edinburgh and London 1962 and 1965.

—, 'The Old Testament World View' in *The Problem of the Hexateuch*, q.v.

—, *The Problem of the Hexateuch and Other Essays*. Edinburgh and London 1965.

—, *Weisheit in Israel*. Neukirchen-Vluyn 1970 = *Wisdom in Israel*. London 1972.

Radford, C., and Minogue, S.,*The Nature of Criticism*. London 1981.

Richter, W., *Exegese als Literaturwissenschaft*. Göttingen 1971.

Robbe-Grillet, Alain, *Les Gommes*. Paris 1953 = *The Erasers*. London 1966.

Roberts, B. J., 'The Textual Transmission of the Old Testament' in *Tradition and Interpretation*, q.v.

Rogerson, J. W., *Anthropology and the Old Testament*. Oxford 1978.

—, *Myth in Old Testament Interpretation*, BZAW 134 (1974).

—, 'Recent Literary Structuralist Approaches to Biblical Interpretation', *The Churchman* 90 (1976), pp. 165–77.

—, Review of W. Richter, *Exegese als Literaturwissenschaft* (q.v.), *JSS* 20 (1975), pp. 117–22.

Rohde, J., *Die redaktionsgeschichtliche Methode*. Hamburg 1966 = *Rediscovering the Teaching of the Evangelists*. London 1968.

Roth, W. M. W., *Numerical Sayings in the Old Testament*, VTS 13 (1965).

Russell, D. S., *The Method and Message of Jewish Apocalyptic*. London 1964.

Ryder, E. T., 'Ecclesiastes' in *Peake's Commentary on the Bible*, q.v.

Sanders, J. A. 'Adaptable for Life: the Nature and Function of Canon', in *Magnalia Dei: the Mighty Acts of God* (New York 1976), pp. 531–60.

—, *Torah and Canon*. Philadelphia 1972.

Saussure, F. de, *Cours de linguistique générale*. Paris 1916, 3rd edn 1967 = *Course in General Linguistics*. Nw York 1959, second edn New York and London 1974.

Sawyer, J. F. A., *From Moses to Patmos: New Perspectives in Old Testament Study*. London 1977.

Schmidt, W. H., 'Die deuteronomistische Redaktion des Amosbuches', *ZAW* 77 (1965), pp. 168–92.

Scott, R. B. Y., *Proverbs; Ecclesiastes* (Anchor Bible). New York 1965.

Scruton, R., *The Aesthetics of Architecture*. London 1979.

Sheppard, G. T., The Epilogue to Qoheleth as Theological Commentary', *CBQ* 39 (1977), pp. 182–9.

Siegfried, C., *Prediger und Hoheslied* (HAT). Göttingen 1898.

Smart, J. D., *The Past, Present and Future of Biblical Theology*. Philadelphia 1979.

Smend, R., 'Questions about the Importance of Canon in an Old Testament Introduction', *JSOT* 16 (1980), pp. 45–51.

Spender, S., *Eliot*. London 1975.

Spina, F. A., 'Canonical Criticism: Childs versus Sanders' in *Interpreting God's Word for Today: an Inquiry into Hermeneutics from a Biblical Theological Perspective* (Wesleyan Theological Perspectives 2), ed. J. E. Hartley and R. Larry Shelton (Anderson, Ind., 1982), pp. 165–94.

Steiner, G., *Heidegger*. London 1978.

—, 'Tragedy: Remorse and Justice', *The Listener* 102 (1979), pp. 508–11.

Sternberg, M., *The Poetics of Biblical Narrative: Ideological Literature and the Drama of Reading*, Bloomington 1985.

Stoppard, Tom, *Rosencrantz and Guildenstern are Dead*. London 1967.

Strickland, G,. *Stucturalism or Criticism? Thoughts on How We Read*. London 1980.

Structuralism: an Introduction, ed. D. Robey. Oxford 1973.

Structuralism: a Reader, ed. M. Lane, London 1970.

Stuhlmacher, P., 'Historische Kritik und theologische Schriftauslegung' in *Schriftauslegung auf dem Wege zur biblischen Theologie*. Göttingen 1975 = *Historical Criticism and Theological Interpretation of Scripture: Towards a Hermeneutic of Consent*. Philadelphia 1977.

Summers, M., *Shakespeare Adaptations*. London 1922.

Sundberg, A. C., 'The Bible Canon and the Christian Doctrine of Inspiration', *Interpretation* 29 (1975), pp. 352–71.

—, 'The "Old Testament": a Christian Canon,' *CBQ* 30 (1968), pp. 143–55.

—, *The Old Testament of the Early Church*. Cambridge, Mass., and London 1964.

—, 'The Protestant Old Testament Canon: Should It be Re-examined?', *CBQ* 28 (1966), pp. 194–203.

Tallis, R., *Not Saussure: A Critique of Post-Saussurian Literary Theory*, London 1988, second edn. 1995.

Talmon, S., 'The Old Testament Text', in *Cambridge History of the Bible* I (Cambridge 1970), pp. 155–99.

Tate, A., *T. S. Eliot: the Man and His Work*. London 1967.

Theologisches Wörterbuch zum Neuen Testament, ed. G. Kittel. Stuttgart 1933–74 = *Theological Dictionary of the New Testament*. Grand Rapids, Mich., 1964–76.

The Reader in the Text: Essays on Audience and Interpretation, ed. S. R. Suleiman and I. Crosman. Princeton 1980.

Thiselton, A. C., *New Horizons in Hermeneutics: The Theory and Practice of Transforming Biblical Reading*, London 1992.

—, *The Two Horizons*. Exeter and Grand Rapids, Mich., 1980.

Tillyard, E. M. W., and Lewis, C. S., *The Personal Heresy: A Controversy*. London 1939.

Tradition and Interpretation, ed. G. W. Anderson. Oxford 1979.

Trible, P., *Rhetorical Criticism: Context, Method, and the Book of Jonah* (Guides to Biblical Scholarship), Minneapolis 1994.

Trigt, F. van, 'La signification de la lutte de Jacob près du Yabboq, Genèse xxxii 23–33', *OS* 12 (1958), pp. 280–309.

Tucker, G. M., *Form Criticism of the Old Testament* (*Guides to Biblical Scholarship*, Old Testament Series). Philadelphia 1971.

Turner, G. W., *Stylistics*. London 1973.

Ullmann, S., *Semantics: An Introduction to the Science of Meaning*, Oxford 1962.

—, *Style in the French Novel*. Cambridge 1957.

Van Seters, J., *Abraham in History and Tradition*. New Haven and London 1975.

Vermeylen, J., *Du prophète Isaïe à l'apocalyptique: Isaïe I–XXXV, miroir d'un demi-millénaire d'expérience religieuse en Israël*. Vol. i, Paris 1977; vol. ii, Paris 1978.

Vinaver, E., *The Rise of Romance*. Oxford 1971.

Weinfeld, M., *Deuteronomy and the Deuteronomic School*. Oxford 1972.

Weingreen, J., *Introduction to the Critical Study of the Hebrew Bible*, Oxford 1982.

Weiss, M., 'Die Methode der "Total-Interpretation" ', VTS 22 (1972), pp. 88–112.

Wellek, R., and Warren, A., *Theory of Literature*. London 1949.

Wellhausen, J., *Geschichte Israels I*. Marburg 1878; (second edn 1883 as *Prolegomena zur Geschichte Israels*) = *Prolegomena to the History of Israel*. Edinburgh 1885 (reprinted as *Prologmena to the History of Ancient Israel*. New York 1957).

Wenham, G. J., 'The Coherence of the Flood Narrative', *VT* 20 (1978), pp. 336–48.

Wenham, J. W., 'Moses and the Pentateuch' in *New Bible Commentary Revised*, q.v., pp. 41–3.

Westermann, C., *Grundformen prophetischer Rede* (EvThBeih 31). Munich 1964 = *Basic Forms of Prophetic Speech*. London 1967.

—, *Genesis* (BK I/1), vol. i, Neukirchen-Vluyn 1974.

Wharton, J. A., 'Redaction Criticism, Old Testament', in *The Interpreter's Dictionary of the Bible*, supplementary vol. (Nashville, Tenn., 1976), pp. 729–32.

White, H. C., 'French Structuralism and OT Narrative Analysis: Roland Barthes', *Semeia* 3 (1975), pp. 99–127.

Whybray, R. N., 'The Identification and Use of Quotations in Ecclesiastes', *Congress Volume, Vienna 1980*, ed. J. A. Emerton, VTS 32 (1980), pp. 435–51.

—, *The Making of the Pentateuch*, Sheffield 1987.

Wilcoxen, J. A., 'Narrative', in *Old Testament Form Criticism*, q.v.

Wilson, R. R., *Genealogy and History in the Biblical World*. New Haven and London 1977.

Wimsatt, W. K., 'Genesis: A Fallacy Revisited' in *The Disciplines of Criticism: Essays in Literary Theory, Interpretation, and History*, ed. P. Demetz, T. Green and L. Nelson Jr Cambridge, Mass., 1968), pp. 193–225; also in *On Literary Intention*, q.v., pp. 116–138.

Wimsatt, W. K., and Beardsley, M. C., 'The Affective Fallacy' in *The Verbal Icon*, q.v.

—, 'Intention', in *Dictionary of World Literature*, ed. J. T. Shipley (New York 1942), pp. 326–30.

—, 'The Intentional Fallacy', *Sewanee Review* 54 (1946), pp. 468–88; also in *On Literary Intention*, q.v., pp. 1–13.

—, *The Verbal Icon: Studies in the Meaning of Poetry*. Lexington 1954.

Wimsatt, W. K., and Brooks, C., *Literary Criticism: a Short History*. London 1957.

Wisdom in Israel and in the Ancient Near East, ed. M. Noth and D. Winton Thomas, VTS 3 (1955).

Wittig, S., 'A Theory of Multiple Meanings', *Semeia* 9 (1977), pp. 75–105.

Wolfe, R. E., 'The Editing of the Book of the Twelve', *ZAW* 53 (1935), pp. 90–129.

Wolff, H. W., 'The Kerygma of the Deuteronomic Historical Work', in *The Validity of Old Testament Traditions*, q.v., tr. from *ZAW* 73 (1961), pp. 171–86.

—, 'The Kerygma of the Yahwist' in *The Vitality of Old Testament Traditions*, q.v., reprinted from *Interpretation* 20 (1966), pp. 131–58, tr. from *EvTh* 24 (1964), pp. 345–73.

—, 'Das Zitat im Prophetenspruch', EvThBeih 4 (1937), pp. 3–112 = *Gesammelte Studien* (Munich 1964), pp. 36–129.

Wolff, J., *The Social Production of Art*. London 1981.

Wordsworth, W., *The Prelude, or, Growth of a Poet's Mind*, 1805 (second text 1850), ed. E. de Selincourt. Oxford 1959 (2nd edn).

—, *Ode. Intimations of Immortality from Recollections of Early Childhood*.

Wright, G. E., and Fuller, R. H., *The Book of the Acts of God*. New York and London 1960.

Würthwein, E., *Der Text des Alten Testaments*, 1952, fourth edn 1973 = *The Text of the Old Testament*. Oxford 1957, second edn. London 1979.

Young, E. J., 'History of the Literary Criticism of the Pentateuch', in *New Bible Commentary Revised*, q.v., pp. 35–40.

INDEX OF MODERN AUTHORS

INDEX OF SUBJECTS

INDEX OF BIBLICAL REFERENCES